G000096223

Breath of Life

Breath of Life

Ann Armstrong

BRITISH BROADCASTING CORPORATION

Dedicated to all caring people

Published by the British Broadcasting Corporation
35 Marylebone High Street London W1M 1AA

ISBN 0 563 20243 2

First published 1985

© Ann Armstrong 1985

Typeset by Phoenix Photosetting, Chatham
Printed in Great Britain by Mackays of Chatham Ltd

Contents

The BBC *Woman's Hour* serial
based on this book was abridged
and produced by Pat McLoughlin.
It was read by Margaret Tyzack.

Introduction

*by The Right Honourable
Jack Ashley, CH MP*

Of all the tribulations known to mankind, the onset of sudden and permanent paralysis is undoubtedly one of the most traumatic. It demolishes all known boundaries of activity, constricting the individual to the narrowest cage. His or her body is imprisoned without bars, held rigidly as if with bands of steel. People who become gradually severely disabled eventually face similar problems; but they have time to adapt themselves to encroaching disability. They are not flung into a rigid trap overnight.

Ann Armstrong faced precisely this terrifying ordeal. It was even worse because, surviving polio, she was not only trapped but unable to breathe of her own accord. She faced a literal life and death struggle and clinically died but, as the fates dictated, recovered and survived. Her account of facing death, and what seemed to her later a living death in an iron lung, has the ring of truth. She writes from grim, personal experience. The horror is graphically yet coolly conveyed. But having averted a sudden death, she then had to face a daunting life, unable to move any of her limbs. In a major crisis of this kind no one knows how anyone will react. We cannot fathom why one person gives up and another trounces impossible odds. Perhaps victory goes to the brave, but bravery itself is not enough.

Ann Armstrong was sustained not only by her courage but also by her faith. Not every disabled person will share her views. Some will maintain that if God is as omnipotent as he is assumed to be, he should not permit such terrible suffering. Ann Armstrong not only refuses to make this accusation against the Almighty but praises him for allowing free will and loving humanity.

Yet even her courage and faith do not provide the complete answer to the paradox of a gentle person fighting fate like a tiger. Undoubtedly her family play a very large part. The profound emotional attachment to her husband and sons provides a further powerful weapon in what becomes a formidable armoury.

However ultimately, it comes down to the character of the

person herself. Courage, faith and family buttress, rather than provide, the dynamic. Deep inside, Ann Armstrong has an individuality which, however battered and shaken, brooked no argument on the basic issue of survival. Curiously enough, this remarkable battle was fought on two – or probably more – levels. While she was battling for life, robbed of all movement of her limbs, dependent on an iron lung or the physical pressure of nurses on her chest for breath, she was fighting for a transfer to a cuirass, a newer type of respirator.

Her fierce argument with the medical establishment on this subject may seem like a sideshow. But not to Ann Armstrong. She fought it desperately and derived satisfaction from winning the battle, as well as from survival. In truth they were part of the same struggle. Fighting for life, and for the kind of life she wanted to lead, were inextricably intertwined.

Her experience illustrates, in an extreme form, the problems faced by all severely disabled people. The loss of independence, vulnerability to the vagaries of institutions and officialdom, constant frustration, realisation of what might have been – all of these afflict all severely disabled people in one form or another.

Ann Armstrong was quick to realise that when she was paralysed, one life had ended, yet she also knew that another had begun. It is unlikely that many would share her philosophical attitude, or her appreciation of the little things in life. But these infuse her new life with real meaning. They also help to explain why her beloved family, her friends and professional helpers, find living and working with her so rewarding. Not for her the gloomy dwelling on life's cruelties, recognise them though she does. Instead she seeks – and finds – something of value in everyday living even without any control of her body. Ann Armstrong is blessed with a noble husband – a real and genuine hero – a loving family and friends. But, like most of the good things in life, she has earned them.

This indomitable woman will provide inspiration for many people less disabled than herself. In parts of her book she writes of her love of roses. She reflects, without too much hope, that in time she may grow one lovelier than any now grown. She says, 'If ever I do I shall call it Phoenix – and you will know why.'

Yes, we will know why. And not only because she has arisen and built a castle from the ashes. But because the example of her life will inspire and enrich the lives of countless other people.

PART I
LIFELINES

Chapter 1
The End

No one told me that life as I had known it had come to an end. No one told me that my competence had come to an end. No one told me that all those little things that a wife and mother usually does had come to an end. Possibly no one knew.

All I knew was that this strange doctor came into my bedroom, followed by my husband Ken. The doctor looked at me. I watched him lift up my right arm. When he released his grasp and let my arm drop, I felt my own fist fall as though it did not belong to me. It hit me in my right eye.

The doctor took my husband from the room. I watched them go and heard them whispering. 'How long has she been unable to move?' the doctor asked.

'Since she woke up,' Ken answered.

'Has she been sick?'

'Yes – suddenly, last night.' Their voices faded into the distance as they went down the stairs.

Left by myself, I remembered that I had first woken very early. I had known that something was odd about the day. I had felt hot and had terrible pains in my head. The house had been strangely silent. Normally our two small sons – Brian and Andrew – would have been leaping about on the bed or climbing in for a cuddle, trying to wake me up.

I recalled that I must have fallen asleep again and had been woken once more when Ken had given me a shake. I had seen him standing by my bed with a cup of tea. He had held out the cup for me to take, as usual, but incredibly I had not been able to move. It did not dawn on me that I really could not move or that this condition would last for more than a few minutes. I did not seem able to understand why Ken just stood there looking at me in a puzzled sort of way and holding out the cup of tea towards me. I did not ask myself 'Why can't I move?' I merely wondered why he did not put the cup down on the bedside table.

No explanation had come into my head to help me deal with my stillness. I had been too preoccupied in trying to drift out of my strange serenity into action. We had a train to catch. I had to get up. I had to start somewhere . . . I had needed to lean up on my elbow, put out my hand and take my cup but – temporarily it seemed – I had lacked the wherewithal to do it. I must then have registered the fact in my mind that I could not move but this did not alarm me. Unnaturally I did nothing but wait quietly, just as I might do if I had been sitting for too long on my feet and had discovered that they had gone to sleep under me.

Now that the doctor had been, I knew that something was very wrong. A few thoughts surfaced in my mind. The persistent pain in my head might mean polio or meningitis. . . . It looked unlikely that we would be able to go to London today as we had planned.

I should have felt frantic with horror at the prospect of polio but my mind continued its abnormally normal preoccupation with our previous arrangements for the day. I calmly but sadly considered the disappointment of not going to London to meet the rest of the family on the long anticipated Saturday the fifteenth of October – the date on the invitation of Auntie Lottie's silver wedding celebration in Finchley.

My thoughts ran on. The day was not like other days. I should have been up and cooking the breakfast, not lying in bed and waiting for something to happen. I wished that the pain in my head would go away. It amplified every little noise.

I heard the stairs creak. Ken came back into our room. He covered me up and as he tucked the blankets around me he said, 'The doctor says he'll be sending an ambulance soon. You need to go to hospital for observation.'

I accepted this information with as little concern as I had felt while I was considering whether I had polio or meningitis. Unrealistically I suggested, 'You could take Brian and Andrew to Auntie Lottie's and pick me up from the hospital later.'

He replied, 'You'll be in for some time, I should think.'

'I'll be home again soon. I must. Brian and Andrew need looking after. No one else can do that.'

He continued, 'I've taken the boys into next door but one. Mick says she doesn't mind. They were playing with her children when I left. You get some sleep while I ring Mum.'

I objected weakly, 'Don't tell her yet. It'll spoil the party. I shall be better soon.'

Ken put his face next to mine. 'You mustn't stay too near me just in case I have something catching,' I said. He took no notice but continued to open and close his lips on my forehead in firm but gentle kisses, as he did on the rare occasions when I had a headache.

This headache was different from any other that I had known. I seemed to have thrown it off last night but it came back with a vengeance when I had heard Ken's key in the front door. It was a shame to spoil his homecoming. He would have expected to find me fit and welcoming instead of sick and feverish. He deserved better after his week's work away in Morecambe. I said, 'Thank God you are back. I'll be better now that you're here.'

My mind drifted through the rest of the time until Ken came to say that the ambulance had arrived. I was pleased to see the men. The throbbing pain in my head was so intense I was eager to go with them to wherever they were taking me. Best to get it over and done with quickly. I would not have been so pleased to see them had I realised that I was never to sleep in my own bed again and our family life as we had known it had come to an end.

Chapter 2
Admission

There was a problem in getting me from my bed to the ambulance. The narrow landing and stairs determined my being strapped into a kind of mountain-rescue carrying stretcher and manoeuvred in all directions. Eventually they managed to settle me into the ambulance and we were on our way.

Every sound and every movement seemed to be beyond my threshold of tolerance. A feeling of thankfulness flooded through me when the ambulance doors were closed and we drove slowly towards the crossroads. Ken sensed my relief and smiled encouragement but as we bumped and jolted our way down the hill the intermittent thumping pain in my head increased. It seemed as though heavy blows were being struck on my head and neck by a sledgehammer.

As we turned into the main road the ambulance bell shrilled its way through the traffic. My head seemed to swell with the sound as though liquid was being forced into my brain until it must burst. I was in such agony that all I could say was a child-like, 'Are we nearly there?'

We had moved to Newbury – sixty miles west of our beloved London – only a few months before but I knew where the hospital was and thought we were taking an unconscionable time reaching it. I asked in panic, 'Have they passed the hospital? It shouldn't be as far as this.'

'We're going to Reading, to the isolation hospital,' Ken assured me. 'We'll soon be on the main road. It'll be smoother there. Then you won't be jolted so much.'

The journey seemed to last for thousands of years. I wanted to put my hands on my splitting head to hold it still and press on it, but nothing I could do would make them move.

When we arrived at the hospital, the ambulance stopped bumping me and the bell stopped clanging but the sound continued to echo in my head. I was wheeled from the noisy hustling bustle of the bright outside world into the peace and quiet of a white-walled isolation ward.

As we rapidly penetrated the dark coolness inside the hospital, the brilliant after-glow of the sunshine outside remained with us. It was difficult to adjust my eyes to the new surroundings and focus on where I was and what was going on. I did not know anyone at the hospital but looked around confidently for the help that would soon be forthcoming.

A strange doctor walked in out of the gloom.

'Hello, I'm Dr Graham. We would just like to do a few tests.' He examined my head, eyes, ears, neck, arms and legs; ran pins down my limbs which I could feel and then told me to take a big breath. It was most curious. I tried to inhale deeply but nothing seemed to happen. I tried and tried and tried again and then said, with an air of detachment as though I were merely observing and agreeing with him, 'I can't, can I?'

'Don't worry about that,' he said, and continued his examination, tapping my knees with a little hammer.

I should have been very frightened but I was still filled with an unnatural and unassailable calm. It was as though one part of my mind was informed of the fix I was in but another part stopped any normal response or understanding of the implications. It was not a case of mind over matter. I just did not seem able to care whatever was the matter. Maybe the enormity of my situation was too shocking to take in.

The examination over, I was moved from the admission cubicle to the ward. There the sister told me that I was to be put into an iron-lung. It would help me to breathe while I was ill. But first I needed a lumbar puncture so that the pathology lab could determine what was wrong with me. I was turned on to my side. Someone's seemingly iron hand pushed my head forward until I could have screamed in agony and my neck seemed about to snap. I did not complain as I supposed that my back had to be in such a position to separate the vertebrae and allow the passage of the needle through to obtain the required cerebro-spinal fluid. I felt the needle being pushed painlessly and skilfully between my vertebrae but was too busy coping with my existing pain to care what was being done to me. It was soon over.

A team of anonymous helpers gathered and I was slammed home into a tank respirator – popularly known as an iron-lung. This was a kind of long closed box, with an opening at one end for my head to stick out. A sort of hatch door was pulled down and locked around my throat. A thick rubber collar was fitted to protect my neck and to make an airtight seal. This was in order that the lung should maintain the correct intermittent air pressure. Immediately the lung took over my breathing I felt more comfortable and relaxed but my crashing headache continued.

The sound around me made a vivid impact on my mind. The slow, steady, sonorous whoosh-shoosh, whoosh-shoosh of the in and out rush of air through the pipe that connected the lung to its bellows sounded like a giant breathing. I thought to myself, so this is what the wrong side of an iron-lung is like.

I reflected on my last job – in the days when I had worked for King's Fund, helping with a census of iron-lungs during a polio epidemic – contacting hospitals and finding out how many mechanical respirators they possessed, whether they were in good condition and if they could be loaned to another hospital in an emergency. I had never seen one, except in pictures. I had listed their whereabouts and arranged for their transfer to help other people. How strange that I should deal with iron-lungs only in relation to other people! It had never entered my head that I should ever need to be breathed by one. How ironic that six years later I should find myself inside one.

Although the feel of the iron-lung was unfamiliar, the sound was not. It seemed to carry an echo from the past. My past, at sea in the WRNS. The noise of its motor reminded me of the throb of our ship's engine on its way to Egypt and coloured my rapidly approaching delirium. The heat and dryness of my fever stimulated my memory and made me dream of desert sands. As my temperature increased I fell into a deep but troubled sleep in which I travelled back ten years in time to 1945 when Ken and I were swimming together in the Mediterranean. In our real-life swimming-races he had never let me win. He would challenge, 'I'll race you', dive into the water and travel like a torpedo to the buoy that was anchored in the bay, haul himself on to it then stand triumphantly waiting for me to come gasping alongside. In my recurrent delirium I would be swimming hard but could not catch Ken up. I struggled frantically in deep water – fighting for my breath. I would search and not find him. At times I was so puffed and exhausted that I would feel unable to go on, but somehow the treadmill-type need to breathe and survive continued.

In real life, in the ward, Ken knew that I was at sea in my delirium. Although I did not know it, he sat by my head at the neck of the iron-lung for hours on end. Sometimes I would talk strangely to him – not as he was in real life, sitting by the lung, but as he was in my frantic dreams. I would say such things as 'Look Ken, sea horses'. Ken, following my unseeing gaze, would observe the ward clock. He would watch its hands pointing inexorably a time in the tangible world of grief and pain that was ten years out of synchronisation with the world in which I was splashing around, thanks to the defence mechanisms of my mind. Ken, glad of any sign of life from me, would agree and say, 'Yes, sea horses.'

At other times in my delirium, I drifted back to my experiences of ten years earlier still. I was a little girl of nine again, running down the cliff path to the sea at Sandown in the Isle of Wight. Halfway down the cliff, the path turned sharply to the beach and you had to put your hands up to check your pace to scoot yourself round the turn safely. We were not allowed to run, but I kept dreaming over and over again that I was running fast and I must fling my hands up quickly to avoid being smashed face-first into the cliff.

In my fever I kept reliving those scorching days under the torturing sun of the Mediterannean and the sunny summers on the radiant sands of my childhood, some ten and twenty years before.

Life was not all delirium. Gradually, as my temperature fell, my dreams were punctuated with lucid spells. I expected to return to normal but my waking existence was far from normal. Real life had become unreal. How could I really be living day after day in an iron-lung? That could only happen to other people – not to me. I was active while sleeping and helpless when awake. How could that be possible with someone as strong-willed as myself?

As I became more aware of my surroundings, I learned I was in a ward to which several children had been admitted with non-respiratory polio but I could not see or hear them. Flat on my back, my usual vista was the cracked ceiling. I saw only people who came to do things for me. In the real world of unreality, people in white seemed to swim silently into my field of vision. Between me and the hatch door of the lung, white-masked faces appeared. Their mask-emphasised eyes searched my face. I could not turn my head to look at them. My neck was rigid. I never knew where anyone was unless we were eye to eye. They might just as well be a million miles away for all I could see with my limited vision or hear above the noise of the machinery.

In my confusion I blamed the iron-lung for the restrictions on my life and pleaded to be taken out of it. I did not admit to myself that I really could not move. It did not occur to me that my condition was probably permanent. Each time that I woke up to the incredible fact of paralysis, I believed I would be better soon. I seemed unaware that I was living permanently in a body over which for the first time in my life, I had no control. It was so natural on waking to want to stretch, rub my eyes, move around and get up and go about my day. I felt it was inhuman to keep me shut up so long in a narrow box. I thought such treatment, although kindly meant, would debilitate even a strong person such as myself. They must take me out of this trap and let me work my way back to being fit.

Chapter 3
Confusion

Slowly, I returned more and more to a real life that was a nightmare, but unrealistically I persisted in being optimistic and expected to find I was better each time I woke up.

As I recalled the endless swimming and cliff-path dashes of my delirium, I marvelled at the resources of our minds. Had I been capable of deliberately thinking up situations to stimulate my urge to breathe or to move my hands, I could not have chosen better examples from my memory bank or my imagination. My memory was so unreliable it was incredible that my mind had grabbed those two particular instances and used them to help me.

Confusingly, it was difficult to talk. Apart from my general weakness, it was impossible to speak as the lung breathed me in. (It is impossible for anyone to talk while breathing in, as you will discover if you try it.)

Gradually I learnt to speak in little rushes of words on my outgoing breaths. I tried to discipline myself to use very short sentences, making the pauses imposed by the iron-lung seem as natural as possible. I could not now say words such as 'changing', 'singeing', 'Cheshire' or anything with 'sh', 'ch' or the soft 'nge' or 'ge' sounds, because there was some disablement in the muscles of my mouth. I was glad that my name was not Angela, Rachel or Sheila. I accepted the challenge of finding alternative words and constructions, thinking that the mental exercise would be good for me, but could not say the word 'challenge' at all.

The two most frequently used words in my vocabulary were 'thank you' and 'sorry'. It seemed impossible to express often enough or deeply enough my heartfelt gratitude for or my regret about the things that I needed other people to do for me.

When I was able to make myself understood, I claimed I would manage better out of the lung, especially as it was making me have nightmares and robbing me of essential sleep. I was so tired. Confusingly, everyone behaved as if it were perfectly natural for me not to be able to move. People did things for me and to me as though I could not be expected to do things for myself, but I *did* expect to perform my own tasks. I had been vigorously active since before I was born and knew no other way of living.

I insisted that Ken should help me become stronger. I was so mixed up in my mind that I had no idea he was my husband. Ken was always there and seemed completely at ease in hospital surroundings in spite of being dressed up in a white gown and mask. Temporarily, in my mind, Ken became part of the hospital. In his mask and gown he was a different person from the man I remembered in my dreams. I kept asking for him, unaware that he was from my own world outside but instinctively feeling that there was more to him than just medical understanding.

It was easy for this to happen as Sister Allen, the ward sister, welcomed visitors to her ward. She instructed them as she had taught her nurses and in so doing solved several problems. For instance, visitors did not feel that they were in the way, as they did in many hospitals, but in carrying out the tasks that were assigned to them, enjoyed truly therapeutic visits to their loved ones. The staff shortage which some hospital sisters merely grumbled about was eased by this adept use of visitors and, when the time came for the patients to leave hospital, their nearest and dearest knew how best to help with their medical routines in their own homes.

Sister Allen had shown Ken how to put his arm through the porthole of the iron-lung at the precise moment when such an action would not interfere with my breathing and how to rub my limbs to improve my circulation. The big problems of paralysis were there all the time. In addition there was an accumulation of irritations which took on monstrous proportions. Yet I had to master these, to please those around me and to give myself the best possible chance of a quick recovery.

It was a revelation to discover how many times people put their hands up to their faces, even without realising that they have done so. Now that I could not touch my own face, it posed an enormous problem. Its skin itched all over constantly and Ken rubbed it. My eyes smarted and watered and Ken wiped them. My nose was always blocked and Ken cleaned it. My head itched frantically too and Ken spent hours brushing my hair to relieve the irritation. My fever, my medicines and the central heating combined to make me itch intensely in many places at once. Being unable to scratch was a misery. I discovered that the longer an itch remained unscratched, the more urgent it became. I fantasised about having every part of myself marked off in lines of latitude and longitude so that I could say exactly where I itched and obtain immediate relief.

That is, I could get relief if I could summon the courage to ask someone to scratch me. Somehow it did not seem a very socially acceptable request. Eventually, I managed to ask people to scratch the side of my nose or my forehead, but I could never ask someone to scratch my head, especially as my hair had not been washed since the week before my illness.

I was glad I had led a disciplined life and was capable of exerting mind over matter but the unrelenting nature of my condition allowed me neither relief nor time to gather extra strength of mind needed to cope with my extra-tiresome situation. Consciously I thought I managed very well and was even surprised at the amount of frustration and irritation with which I coped constantly, always dry-eyed and usually cheerfully. But I had no ambitions or needs to prove myself to myself or anyone else. I had suffered more than my share of difficulties in my young life, although usually I never gave them a second thought, and longed only to earn the chance to live a normal life again.

All my normal nourishment needs were beyond me and I relied on Ken and the hospital staff to fill the gaps. Ken fed me a whole bottle of Lucozade every day as well as copious glasses of Robinson's barley water. Between my iron-lung-regulated breath, I gulped a drink through a plastic straw then paused for breath as this was the best way to stop liquid going up the back of my nose. Nurses fed me lumps of ice made with orange juice and glucose. I secreted the ice between my cheek and my back teeth and let it trickle into my throat until it became necessary to gulp again. I was so hot, I craved the feel of the ice on my throat. The nurses shivered. They said, 'How can you keep lumps of ice between your teeth and cheek like that? Doesn't the cold make your teeth ache?'

The nurses were all sweet and similar, with names like Jane, Linda and Susan. They talked to me when they were feeding me but I was too busy concentrating on my swallowing to be able to answer them except to say the predictable 'Thank you' every time they did anything for me, or 'Sorry' when drink was spilt on my chin or when I had to ask them for something. I smiled at them a lot and they seemed content to regard a smile as an adequate reply. They talked about books, their families, their homes, their hopes and their looming SRN examinations.

Under the guidance of the doctors, Sister Allen and her lieutenant – Staff Nurse Hull – the nurses took infinite pains with my care. They helped Sister and 'Staff' with my nursing routines. They patiently stuffed cushions into my back and under and around my legs for support. Only one girl made the mistake of running her fingernail down the sole of my foot for a laugh. She was the first person I met – but by no means the last – who mistakenly believed that as I was unable to move I could not feel anything. Sister Allen happened to see her and took her outside for enlightenment. She never did it again.

One day a nurse asked me, 'Have you any children?' 'No,' I replied very primly, 'I am not married.' (Later I thought how extraordinary it was that I had known that in our culture children are supposed to come after marriage, although I could not recall being married or having children). She looked through the left porthole of the iron-lung, as she was sure she seen a wedding ring on my finger, but it was missing.

She waited for the pump to reach the required pressure, pushed her hand through the porthole quickly and felt around until she found what she was searching for.

'Look,' she said, 'here is your wedding ring. It must have slipped from your finger into the iron-lung.' I looked blankly at her and at the ring. It shone brightly from friction where the pressure in the lung had rubbed it constantly up and down against the sheet. I could not find anything in my mind about being married. I could not visualise a husband, let alone children. In fact I could not remember very much about who I was or where I was. In my confusion I asked her, 'Where is this?'

'This is the isolation hospital,' she said.

'Where is that?'

'Prospect Park, near Reading.'

The words Prospect Park etched themselves on my brain and the word prospect kept repeating itself in my mind – prospect, prospect, prospect. I caught an echo from a half-remembered line '. . . such sweet prospect' but could not remember where I had heard it before.

The nurse continued talking: 'Prospect Park is one of the Reading group of hospitals.'

'Which ward am I in?'

'David Ward.'

'Have I been here long?'

'About two weeks, I think. You came straight here from Andrew Ward on admission.'

'How long was I there?'

'About half an hour.'

'Why was I moved?'

'Andrew Ward isn't a ward at all really. It's the isolation cubicles. Don't you remember? You were admitted and examined

there. Staff Nurse Morgan has just come over from the cubicles to
help us out here.'

'I thought she was new to the hospital.'

'No she's only new to this ward.'

'Is this an isolation ward?'

'It is temporarily. It's usually a men's ward. The hospital is
divided into pavilions. We're in the men's pavilion but all the ten
patients have been squeezed into the other half of the pavilion to
make way for the patients in this half.'

'Patients. I'm not alone then?'

'No. There are several children at the end of the ward but in the
cubicles there are three more women with polio.'

'All in iron-lungs?'

'No, they all have non-respiratory polio. You're the only one in
a lung.'

I tried to piece together these bits of information but my
fractured memory failed me. When had polio caught me? How
had it occurred? What would happen next? The more I tried to
remember the things that I needed to know, the more I became
distracted by the flotsam that kept bobbing up in my mind. The
sea seemed to surround me. Useless information was awash in my
head and it seemed as though I caught the drift of what was there
as much by sound as by sight. I could hear the words with an
understanding that they had been very important once but now as
they drifted closer and became part of a new experience, they
would not help me. I did not need them but they challenged me to
listen to each idea in case something fresh revealed itself.

The words that rolled into my consciousness from a great
distance were mainly concerned with the sea. A voice seemed to
be reciting and often misquoting snatches of associated ideas,
such as:

'I must go down to the seas again,
To the lonely sea and the sky.'

'Alone, alone, all, all alone,
Alone on the wide dark sea.'

'The wine dark sea . . .'

'The king sits in Dunfermline town
Drinking the blude-red wine.
"Och, where will I find a skeely skipper

23

To sail this ship of mine?"
Then up and spake an eldern knight
That sat at the king's right knee,
"Sir Patrick Spens is the best sailor
That ever sailed the sea".'

'There is a tide in the affairs of men
Which, taken at the flood, leads on to fortune.'

'Flood of your flood are we
Blood of your blood we be
Beating the eternal measure
To
The pulses
Of the sea.'

'Full fathom five thy father lies.'

'Underneath are the everlasting arms . . .'

'The quality of mercy is not strain'd;
It droppeth as the gentle rain from heaven
Upon the place beneath.'

'From the Cotswolds and the Chilterns,
From your fountains and your springs,
Flow down O London river
To the seagulls' silver wings.
Isis or Ock or Tame
Forget your olden name
And the lilies and the willows
And the weirs from which you came.'

I could not imagine why I remembered so much old stuff that had obviously poured into my head during my childhood but could not remember more recent things.

The trouble with my head was not confined to my memory. It ached all the time. My eyes were now as bad at focusing as my mind. An ophthalmic specialist was called in and he peered into my eyes with his instruments. He assured me there was nothing to worry about and then walked away with Dr Graham to discuss his findings. My lack of perception and perspective confused me deeply and robbed me of my pre-polio certainty that I must 'Take arms against a sea of troubles and, by opposing, end them.'

Chapter 4
Recollection

I cannot recall how long it took me to remember that Ken was my husband. I only know that in the beginning he seemed to be always there, rubbing or scratching me, whenever I woke. At first he stayed at the hospital, living and sleeping in. He spent some of the time at the other end of the ward with the several children who were suffering from non-respiratory polio. He told them stories and read to them, just as he usually did to Brian and Andrew.

When Ken returned to his normal routine, he went to work full-time as usual. His mother had taken Brian to her home near Bedford and my mother had taken Andrew to hers in London. Ken always came straight from work to the hospital, put on his white gown and mask like everyone else and stayed with me until he left to catch the last bus home. When he arrived home it was to a cold, unlit and empty house. The dark silence contrasted sharply with the bright welcome he would normally expect from us. Life was very different now that we were all scattered to various parts of the country.

My lost wedding ring seemed to symbolise my lost marriage. On Ken's next visit I told him that the nurse had said I had lost so much weight that my wedding ring would not stay on my finger any more and she had put it in the locker. I tried not to show how much I cared.

Ken said, 'I'll keep it safely in my pocket for now.'

'Can't I wear it around my neck on a chain?'

'That isn't very wise with only your head outside the tank. The weight of the ring would probably make the chain tight around your throat.'

I had forgotten that I could not put up my hand to adjust things. I agreed with him. He was usually right. He continued, 'I'll bring your handbag the next time I come. You can keep your ring in there. Meanwhile, look what I've brought you.'

He held up my gold locket and showed me the photo of Brian and Andrew in it. He suspended it from the front of the lung so that I could see it, although as my eyes were troubling me, it was not very clear. When Ken went home, my mind was full of the children. The picture in the locket hung straight in front and Brian and Andrew seemed to smile right back at me. As I could not look to the right or the left, I could not avoid remembering them. Once the memories started to flow, they were unstoppable.

I remembered the week I was going down with polio. The last week in which we all spent Sunday together. It was a hot day at the end of a hot summer – perfect polio weather. We had not been swimming in the local baths because of the danger of polio. Not that we had seemed vulnerable as I considered myself far too fastidious in the way that I cared for myself and my family. I remembered how the sun had shone that Sunday. I pictured Ken laughing as five-year-old Brian turned head-over-heels on the back lawn. I was holding Andrew on my hip. He was only three and had grown tired of romping around. Suddenly the autumn sun had lost its power and there was a distinct nip in the air. Andrew had shivered against me and I called out to the other two, 'Time for tea. We'll race you indoors.'

Once inside the kitchen we had felt instantly warmer. Andrew had stomped upstairs to his bedroom while I put the kettle on and filled plates with savoury sandwiches as well as shortbread and an iced sponge which the children had helped me to decorate with chocolate buttons. Ken had then trooped into the kitchen with Brian, carrying logs, coal and kindling between them. As he passed me he said, 'I thought I'd light the fire to try the fireplace out. You might need to use it this week while I'm away.'

As I had pushed the trolley through from the kitchen to our one long living-room, I had met Brian trying to struggle up the stairs past his brother. Andrew was on the bottom stair dragging his big box of road safety toys behind him.

We always kept Sunday tea different from the other meals in the week. We did not set the table but sat around the trolley, helping ourselves and each other to easy-to-hold food. After tea, Ken, Brian and Andrew stretched full-length on the floor, setting up a network of streets that Ken had made of plywood with bridges, traffic lights, Belisha beacons, crossings, farms, garages, animals, people, Dinky and Matchbox cars and lorries, policemen and motorbikes and so on. Brian and Andrew kept up a steady *brmm, brmm, brmm* sound as they pushed their vehicles along the wooden roads by hand.

With Ken and the children happily occupied, I had picked up the *Sunday Times* and read the date. What date must that have been, I now wondered. I counted back. I had been pushed into the lung on Saturday October the fifteenth; the previous Sunday must have been the ninth. What a hallowed day that seemed now! I had held my husband and my children in my arms and done so many other normal, blessed, day-to-day things for the last time and not realised it. As usual on Sundays, I had some letters to write. I had taken my pen and notebooks from my handbag and had made a couple of lists. The first was a list of distant friends to whom I owed letters. The second was a list of topics. For instance, there was Ken's impending week at Morecambe on a Road Safety Conference and our trip to London at the end of it. There were the new green curtains that I had made and hung at the windows so that they could 'drop' before I turned up the hems; there was the super Butterick pattern from which I had been making a fine knobbly-tweed pinafore dress (it had an incredibly long zip so that it fitted like a second skin) and so on.

I suddenly remembered how the logs had blazed when I had run out of things to write about and I looked at the fire for inspiration. I commented, 'Aren't we lucky to be so cosy? I feel too happy for words.'

The sun had suddenly shone with dazzling brightness through the gathering clouds. I had picked up my pen to continue my letters but in doing so had accidentally squeezed a wasp that had crawled on to it. It had stung me and in an instant reaction of pain and surprise I had flicked it straight into the fire. I had poured vinegar on my finger and hopped up and down for a few minutes. I had then said, 'It doesn't do to talk about being too happy, does it? There's always some fly in the ointment or wasp on your fountain pen waiting to spoil things.' Thank God I had not known just how true my words were going to prove. I had been completely unaware of the polio virus that was already insidiously wearing me down. How long ago all that seemed now! It was a different world.

The next time Ken came to the hospital he brought my handbag. As I could not look in it, he asked if he should open it. He searched around for my purse as he wanted to put my ring in it. He could not find it, so he turned my bag upside-down and tipped the contents on to my locker. 'Good Lord,' he said, 'the things women carry about with them.' He began sorting out – a needlecase, my watch, lipstick, compact, wallet, a newspaper clipping which said Ken's paintings were reminiscent of the early Graham Sutherlands, a counterfoil for some photographs which should have been collected and a bunch of keys. There were several different notebooks and lists, including the two that I had been writing the letters from and, somehow most poignant of all, there was my little fountain pen. My French friend Simone had sent it to me from Paris on my twenty-first birthday and I had used it constantly since. Ken hung my watch beside the locket which held the photos of Brian and Andrew. I could watch the time and make better use of it. My purse, I imagined, must still be at home in my coat pocket where I had put it after paying the bus fare home from the shops on that unlucky Thursday the thirteenth of October, the last day on which I had been out and about.

When Ken had gone, I began to recollect the other sorts of days that incredibly we had shared together. Recollection was vital if the power and strength of our real life together was not to be diminished by the unreal incarceration. The sterile hospital existence was proving so overwhelming. It seemed to have gone on almost for ever and there appeared no escape.

The following morning I woke up with my family still on my mind. Sister Allen appeared at the side of my lung.

'Good morning,' she said briskly. Then, seeing me blink, 'Sorry I startled you.'

'I was miles away,' I replied.

'About seventeen miles, I suppose,' she answered, imagining that I would be thinking about my home in Newbury.

'About that,' I answered. 'Seventeen miles and a million days away.'

My mind went right back to the last active Sunday. I recalled how I had been playing about with Ken and the children on the lawn, standing on my head, doing back-bends and splits.

'Can you remember that week now?' she asked.

'Yes,' I said, 'I have gradually worked it out. I can remember the Monday because that was the day that Ken went away and everything began to go wrong.'

'How do you mean, wrong?'

'I had a headache when he left, but I didn't tell him.'

Having said so much, I stopped to recover my breath gradually. I could not take any deep breaths at all but just had to lie there, letting the lung breathe me until I felt better. Sister Allen understood and waited for me to continue each time I paused, busying herself meanwhile with routine duties around the iron-lung.

I remembered thinking to myself that the headache was through standing on my head too long the day before. The ground had been baked hard day after day in the long hot summer. My mind dwelt on that last Monday, when I had stood on the pavement with

Brian and Andrew, watching Ken as he strode down the hill, waving until he was out of sight. We had gone back indoors and rushed about getting Brian ready for school. I usually started the washing early on Mondays but this particular morning I had left it until Ken had gone. I could not remember anything else except that we had gone on a picnic after collecting Brian from school. yes, that was a point.

I said to Sister Allen, 'I've just remembered. We went for a picnic on the Monday. Brian didn't want to go because he had a headache as I had. I coaxed him along, thinking he would benefit from a little walk after being cooped up in school all day.'

Sister remarked, 'That's interesting. How long did he have the headache?'

'Only for that evening.' I answered, 'he was as bright as a button the next morning. He loves school and is always eager to go. There were no more picnics because I had begun to feel poorly. We had tea at home on Tuesday and went to bed early.'

She asked, 'Did you stay in bed from then on?'

'No,' I replied. 'The next evening – Wednesday – we went to tea with Mrs Gauntlett. Ken had stayed at her house when he first came to work in Newbury.'

Sister disappeared from view. My thoughts ran on. As I cast my mind back to Mrs Gauntlett's house, I knew I could never forget that evening. . . or that night. We had just eaten our tea when suddenly such a vicious pain hit me, I could not believe it. I tried to cope with it so that I could get the children home to bed, but I just could not stay upright. I asked Mrs Gauntlett if she would mind if I sat down on the settee for a few minutes and closed my eyes while I gathered myself together to get the children home. She took the boys into another room and I struggled to collect myself. On her return I asked her to telephone for a taxi to take us home, as I could hardly stand.

That pain! It was so intense that it was difficult not to cry. When we arrived home we all went to bed but I had not been in bed long before I found Brian and Andrew sleeping either side of me. I wriggled myself out from between them and climbed into Brian's bed, only to be woken later to find them back in with me again, all squeezed in together. I managed to extricate myself again and returned to my own big bed, but I must have disturbed them and before long I found them cuddled in beside me again. This time I went into Andrew's bed but they still followed me, so I drifted back to my own bed again and stayed there.

I must have been quite idiotic at the time as I did not think to ask them not to follow me around. It was as though I was frightened to upset them because I knew something was terribly wrong and I did not want them to think it was their fault. I remembered having said to them when we climbed out of the taxi that they must be good boys and help me because I did not feel very well. I suppose they were looking after me in their little ways by coming from bed to bed with me.

Sister reappeared and asked, 'Are you still thinking out your week?'

'Yes,' I answered, 'I've arrived at Thursday, when we all woke up surprisingly fresh considering our vagrant night with Brian and Andrew following me from bed to bed. I was so thankful to feel better.'

Sister nodded, 'That's thought to be typical of polio. People are said to feel better and rush around trying to catch up with the work they haven't done while they felt poorly. They can suffer a lot of damage in consequence.'

I reflected on this before answering, 'Yes, I had a lot of catching up to do. I took Brian to school and as it was market day in Newbury, walked into town with Andrew in the pushchair.'

I pictured myself walking all the way to Marks and Spencer, some two miles I supposed. Then that headache had begun again. I stood at the bus-stop with Andrew on one arm and my shopping and pushchair on the other but I tired of waiting. I put the shopping in the pushchair and Andrew held my hand as we walked towards the next bus-stop. I remembered waiting there, clasping my hands across my middle as my arms would not hold together somehow. I felt desperately tired and anxious to be home. My hands would keep coming unclasped and I had to keep joining them together again.

Eventually the bus came and I climbed on thankfully. I will never know how. I could not remember arriving home. I went straight upstairs, put Andrew to bed and then went to bed myself. A hammering on the back door woke me. I did not feel like answering it but Andrew had crept down to see who it was. He came back to tell me it was the gas-man. Somehow I struggled downstairs to let the man in to read the meter.

Mrs Gauntlett then called to see how I felt. She left me a jar of home-made soup and a little book on Christian Science but I was too busy to read it.

That evening, after I had put Brian and Andrew to bed, I tried to finish a dress that I was making for the weekend. I had wanted to herring-bone stitch along the hem but although herring-boning uses a lot of cotton, I had not seemed able to pull the cotton through. I could not have been very bright at the time, because I kept threading the needle with fresh cotton and then finding that I could not complete the stitch but had to keep pulling the cotton through with my fingers, an inch at a time.

It had not occurred to me then but it was obvious now that I had not been able to stretch out my arm. How strange that I had not realised it at the time. My mind must have been slipping badly then, I thought. Had I realised the weakness of my arms I would never have taken a bath that night. I could have drowned, leaving two tiny children asleep in the house. Good job I had not washed my hair but had decided to leave it until Friday when I thought I would feel better.

Friday morning seemed a bit hazy. I remembered that when I woke I just could not get up. I asked Brian to go downstairs and set out a breakfast of cornflakes and bananas for himself and Andrew. He got ready for school and took himself off. Andrew spent the morning in bed beside me. I heard him *brmmm-brmmm-ing*, playing with his cars and hopping in and out of bed. Once I woke to unwonted silence and found him playing with a box of fireworks that he had discovered on top of the wardrobe. Thank God he had not tried to light any.

Sister reappeared, 'That's finished that little job. Have you remembered what happened on Friday yet?'

'Yes,' I said. 'I struggled out of bed about two o'clock and Andrew and I drank some soup. I felt better afterwards and as I was very aware that Ken would be home soon, I rushed about wielding the vacuum-cleaner and duster. I made a bread pudding ready for Brian coming home from school. He brought three or four other little boys with him. They all sat around my kitchen table with a hunk of bread pudding on a saucer and a dish of brown sugar to share among them. Do you think that polio would have infected the bread pudding and any of the children will be incubating it now?'

Sister said, 'I shouldn't think so, and anyway it was cooked.'

'Oh yes, I remember. I had been kneeling beside the cooker cleaning it while it was warm and suddenly I knew I was going to be sick. I stood up, took two steps to the empty sink and was swiftly sick. I knew I wasn't going to vomit any more. I disinfected the sink and turned round to the table full of children to say I was sorry, but they were so busy laughing and talking among themselves, they hadn't noticed what was happening.'

Sister asked, 'What time did Ken get in?'

'I don't remember now, but perhaps it will occur to me later.'

31

I went back to thinking my own thoughts. The time of Ken's return did not seem to matter, but I remembered that when he did arrive I had felt desperately inadequate. I had realised that I was not my usual self and had said, 'I think I've had flu or something, but I feel better now you're here.'

I had managed to pack everything for the weekend and to get most of the jobs done, but I had felt so rotten I had had to ask him to put the children to bed and to sleep in Brian's room. I had gone straight upstairs so that I could have an early night and wake up ready to go to Auntie Lottie's the next morning.

That night I had slept the sleep of the just. I knew nothing until I saw Ken standing beside me trying to wake me up and being faced with the shocking realisation that I could not move.

The last I had seen of my children was when they had run to Ken when he came home from the conference. He had put them to bed, slept in the same room as one or the other of them, kept them quiet the next morning and taken them to my neighbour Mick, so that I would not be disturbed. On that occasion I had not realised that I would not see them again, not even to say goodbye, before I was put into the ambulance. I wondered whether they had seen me go or whether Mick had kept them away from her window. It was impossible to see them now in this isolation hospital, so full of infection. As much as I longed to see and hear them, I could not disagree with the ruling that they were not allowed to come to the hospital because of the risk of infection.

The more I thought about my children, the more desperately I longed to be with them. In the days that followed I made Ken's life very miserable by insisting that I should return home.

Ken said, 'You must be patient. You will be home soon.'

'Not soon enough. I want to go home now.'

'I must make many arrangements first.' Ken replied, 'I need time to organise things. You must see what progress you make. You can't come home in an iron-lung, can you?'

'I don't see why not.'

'Where would we put it?' Ken asked. 'That is, supposing we can get it through the front door?'

I insisted, 'You would find a way if you wanted me home as badly as I want to come home.'

'Of course I want you home, but we have to be sensible and get you well again first. Don't fret. Try to sleep and I'll see you again tomorrow.'

Yet nothing Ken said could assuage my longing for my home and children.

Chapter 5
Isolation

An unwelcome change occurred in my experiences when Ken went back to work. While he was living at the hospital he seemed to be there every time I woke up but when he was away all day and came to the hospital only during the evenings I missed him very much. He was allowed back into the outside world because I was spending more hours awake but these very hours of being conscious meant that I registered my immobility and isolation deeply.

For much of this time I felt relatively happy as I had plenty to think about. My whole life had to be rethought in terms of what I believed to be my temporary disablement. I had to decide what to do about Ken, Brian and Andrew and how to get them all back together again while I worked my way towards recovery. I had been brought up to ignore illness and had found that most ailments could be worked off if I got up as usual and flung myself into the activities of the day. Unfortunately this philosophy did not work with polio.

As I could not get up, I would think my own thoughts for a while but eventually I would feel an intense longing to talk to or to listen to some other person. There was always a nurse in the ward but she was usually busy with the children. Various other people were constantly in and out, some of them to keep routine watch on me and my machinery. The noise of the iron-lung motor drowned the sound of their approach and unless they were within range of my eyes – and I had them open – I was not aware of anybody, not even if they were sitting quietly by my iron-lung thinking I was asleep. As my neck was still rigid, all I could see was the ceiling above me and the hatch door of the iron-lung in front of me. People could be looking at me through the plastic windows of the iron-lung, watching my breathing, and I would not know that they were there.

I learnt that these coffin-type respirators had been made in America about 1929 by a man named Drinker. Later, in this country, the firm of Siebe-Gorman had made a few in very heavy boiler plate – hence the name iron-lung. Just before the war, an Australian engineer named Both, who was working in England, designed a cheap cabinet respirator. Subsequently, Lord Nuffield mass-produced about a thousand light-weight iron-lungs on his production line at Oxford. I was now in one of these iron-lungs and wondered how many other people had been in it before me. The sensation of being repeatedly put back into the iron-lung after treatment was as though I was returning to the womb. I had less breathing power or breathing potential than an unborn baby. My umbilical cord was the air-feed pipe from the respirator motor.

Sometimes, when I was being taken out of the lung, I felt like a butterfly escaping from the chrysalis. I had the strange impression that one day I would emerge and discover that all necessary movement had developed while I was lying inert in the chrysalis lung. This feeling was heightened by my need to hear above the noise of the machinery what was happening beyond my immediate surroundings. I seemed to grow antennae as my hearing sharpened.

When people spoke of the breathing-machine, meaning the iron-lung, I thought of human-breathing machinery – heart, lungs, ribs and controlling muscles and nerves – which makes human beings who can breathe adequately seem enviably efficient compact breathing-machines in their own right. I was often reminded of the natural mechanics of our bodies and horrified that a whole beautiful coordinated human body was so vulnerable to damage. We needed to be more like clocks with replaceable man-made parts and winders to start us up again when we run down.

As the winter complications set in in the outside world and more and more people were admitted to the hospital, the staff were working flat out in their attempts to cope with the extra patients. Although I longed to be able to ask someone to talk to me, I realised that hospital staff are always busy and must not be delayed in their errands of mercy. Paradoxically, it seemed, a seriously ill person is removed from his normal surroundings where there is always someone familiar to talk to or listen to and is left in the company of the hospital staff who by definition have no time to fill the gaps that a wrench from everyday human relationships must bring.

I caught a glimpse of what it must be like to be Almighty God, the God who was all-powerful but who, being spirit, has no hands but ours to perform even the most urgent tasks and who can work only through people. I would have changed my paralysis, had I had the choice, for the satisfaction of doing everything for myself and my family. Not because I was ungrateful for the things that were being done but because life is so simple when your own abilities are available to you, as I knew well as I had tasted both kinds of lives.

In trying to contain my own frustration with good grace and being determined to cope without the use of my hands, I received a tiny intimation of the graciousness of God.

It seemed to me that God was in effect handicapped by giving us free will. We could do with impunity whatever we wished to this beautiful world and one another. God has relinquished power to stop us, unless by the dreadful and wonderful power of love our eyes are opened.

It takes a great deal of love for a parent to watch a child spoil things in order that he may learn to care for them. Is it this kind of love that God gives us? God must love us very much to trust us to care for the world and one another. A love so great that I could never fathom it. Only through being desperately deprived have I had this small insight into the tremendous strength of God's affection for us. What loneliness do we inflict when God has to wait until a God-given pair of hands is free, able and disposed to help and comfort.

I tried to imagine this as I began to experience a loneliness and longing not only for my own family but also for any member of the human race. Within this loneliness I experienced a deeper long-ing. It was a dreadful unappeasable hunger for the company of my own body. Now that I lacked control over my physical self, I found that I could not even flex the muscles around the especially painful parts such as my fingers and wrists, elbows, bottom, shoulders and the back of my neck. No matter how great the hurt, it was impossible to stimulate the familiar response and expected movements.

I realised what a comfort I had been to myself when I could move about, automatically arranging and rearranging my body according to what I was trying to do. I thought how marvellously we were made, and how my old boss Mr Bright – a planning engineer – would have defined the engineering principles and properties of the human body for me. He was a shrewd, dry Mancunian with a beautiful economy of words and a store of memorable technical terms such as 'metal fatigue', 'planishing hammer' and 'rat-tail file'. I wondered how he would describe the condition of my sore spots, how he would analyse the stress and plan a schedule of processes to alleviate it and maintain the living machinery of my body.

I was deep in thought about Mr Bright when I was suddenly made acutely aware of life in the ward again. All at once I needed to move quickly. A wasp zoomed across my mouth, no doubt attracted by the orange juice with which I had just been fed. The memory of being stung recently flashed vividly on my mind. Now I could not shake my head nor fend off the wasp with my hands. I dared not open my mouth. I was terrified it would sting my tongue and throat and I had enough breathing troubles already. In any case I could not muster enough breath to shout for help. The nurse would never hear my soft voice. She was busy at the end of the ward. What could I do?

My dilemma was resolved by Mr Rackham, the head porter. He was a life-saver in the true sense of the words. His constant care of all breathing machinery ensured its smooth running. He was the kind of calm, capable man you felt you could trust with your life, as indeed we did.

Luckily for me he was just changing my sucker jar – part of the vacuum equipment I needed for my throat to be sucked clean to remove my saliva when I could not swallow it.

Mr Rackham drove the wasp away with his hand. He said, 'Beastly things. They're very late dying off this year. Don't expect them to be buzzing around at the end of October.'

I agreed with him and thought to myself that wasps must have an affinity with the polio virus, for that too was supposed to be active in warm weather but had attacked me in October. I realised I needed some means of attracting attention in emergencies. I could press my feet on the foot-board in the lung and locate them. I longed to be able to send them off on their own to fetch me things, or at least to use them in some compensatory way. Surely I could operate a pedal or bush-button of some kind.

I asked Mr Rackham, 'Do you think I could have an alarm bell by my foot? Then if another wasp comes I could press the button.'

He said, 'Yes, of course. I think I have one somewhere and Ben, our engineer, will soon fix it up so that you can work it. I'll just go and find him.'

I was going to be able to use my feet. I thought what marvellous progress. The words '*I have found my feet. I have found my feet*' ran excitedly through my mind.

A strange pair of feet strode up to my iron-lung. A large happy face looked down at me. The grin was infectious. I smiled back.

The happy man said, 'I'm Ben Smith. Frank asked me to find you a bell. I think the one I have here is just the job.'

He had already obtained Sister's permission to experiment with his wires and screws. She knew he was very experienced and could be relied upon not to break the rhythm of the breathing help that my iron-lung provided. Mr Rackham returned.

I said to him: 'No sooner the word than the deed.'

He answered, 'Always happy to be of service.'

I asked, 'Where did you both learn so much about respirators? They're not exactly two a penny, are they?'

He answered, 'I was in the RAF as medical orderly, mostly in Africa. Ben here can turn his hand to anything mechanical – he was in the Navy.'

I exclaimed, 'So was Ken, and I'm an ex-Wren.'

Ben grinned. 'I might have known it. You keep pretty cool about all this.'

I answered, 'I might seem cool now, but I was bit hot under the iron-lung collar a few minutes ago when that wasp flew at me.'

'I should think so too, but from now on there won't be any more problems like that. Can you just try this bell? See if I've put the button in the easiest place for you to press it with your toe.'

I pushed the button. The bell rang shrilly. I said, 'Thank you. Couldn't be better.'

We all beamed at one another. Ben said, 'Any more problems, shipmate, just send us a signal on the bell.'

I answered, 'Shall do.'

They both patted me on the head as they said cheerio and went about their other duties around the hospital.

It was one thing to have a bell at my feet but it was something else again to summon the resolve to use it. The idea of ringing a bell for help seemed autocratic and out of character. I was democratic and self-reliant by nature. I hated bothering other people, although I enjoyed doing good turns myself. Now that I was on the receiving end, I wondered whether I had ever intruded on others with my offers of help. I hoped not but I could not be sure. Other people would have been as polite in accepting my good deeds as I now was in letting people do things for me, really I longed to jump up and do them for myself.

My independence had meant more to me than I had known. I was not going to surrender it easily, even though I was totally reliant on other people for the very basic necessities of life such as being fed, washed, having my hair and teeth brushed and so on.

As Ben and Frank moved away, my mind filled with memories of my WRNS service. I remembered the intense feeling of isolation one night when we were on our way to the Mediterranean.

Our convoy had journeyed a considerable way into the Atlantic before turning to steam towards Gibralter. We were forbidden to show a light of any kind or make a noise, for even a cigarette glow or human voice could give away our presence to lurking U-boats. We had practised our boat drill and memorised our stations. As the smallest Wren in the line, I had been standing next to the tallest RAF pilot in the next squad. He had slipped some chocolate into my hand and as the night was warm the chocolate began to melt. We were all intent on listening and watching and trying to blot out stories of what it was like to be torpedoed. We knew if we were sunk, the land was too far to reach. The ocean had seemed vast – limitless.

As my mind came back to the ward, I was again reminded how like a ship's engine the throb of the iron-lung motor sounded. I felt as lonely as if I were clinging to a buoyant plank for survival in hostile water in pitch darkness.

Sister Allen suddenly appeared at the side of my iron-lung. She said, 'We can hear that bell ringing right down the end of the ward.'

I said, 'Ben has done a good job. My heart nearly stood still when I saw that wasp homing in on me. Can't let that happen to my heart when polio hasn't stopped it beating. Can the polio virus affect the heart muscles?'

'No, it never does directly. The heart is made of a special kind of muscle which is peculiar to itself. It will go on beating when everything else seems to have failed.'

'It's a pity other muscles can't take a lesson from our diligent hearts,' I mused. 'Will the children at the end of the ward recover the use of the muscles in their legs?'

'It's difficult to say. You can never tell in the early stages what's going to happen.'

'Had they been swimming?'

'Some of them had, but some of the others must just have been unlucky and caught it through somebody else's bad hygiene.'

'I can't think how I caught mine. Do you think I could have picked it up in the Mediterranean? There was so much polio there. Could it have lain dormant inside me all these years?'

'I don't think so. It's thought that the incubation period is seven to fourteen days. It's debatable. Some people say it can be as little as four days.'

'Do you think they'll ever develop a vaccine against it?'

'It's got to come in time, but it's such a small virus and so dangerous that the greatest care has to be taken.'

'What does the virus do exactly?'

'It attacks the motor nerves.'

'Can't they be helped to recover quickly?'

'We don't know of anything that can regenerate nervous tissue, but often nerves are not as completely knocked out as they seem to be. It is thought that recovery can take place for up to two years afterwards.'

'Two years,' I gasped, 'I can't stay here two years!'

'I'm not saying you will have to. It's early days yet and any recovery is in the future.'

'Perhaps I didn't have polio.'

'I'm afraid you did.'

'Couldn't it have been something else? For instance, about a month before I was ill, when I was weeding a path under a window, some paratroopers were being dropped over Newbury Race-course. I stood up suddenly when a neighbour called me to watch them coming down and cracked my head hard under the steel window-frame. I saw stars for a while but was all right afterwards. On another day, a B.47 bomber flew low over our house as it was taking off from the Greenham air base. I was a third of the way down the stairs at the time. Brian and Andrew were in the garden. They rushed in, just as I leapt the rest of the stairs. I cuddled them under me, as it sounded for all the world like a bomb coming down.'

She answered, 'Your symptoms would have been different if you had cracked your skull or broken your neck. You would have lost your sense of feeling. You can feel pain.'

While Sister Allen had been talking, her nurses had been fetching the things they needed to start my out-of-the-lung routine.

Dr Graham as usual undid the locks at the end of the iron-lung and fixed the legs of the stretcher trolley on which I was lying inside the iron-lung, so that he could trundle me out. He held a mask over my face with an air supply from a positive pressure machine for, once out of the iron-lung, I had no breathing powers. Mr Rackham monitored the positive pressure machine on a trolley and made sure that my air supply to the mask was properly maintained. He pushed the trolley alongside Dr Graham, keeping in step with him until I was entirely out of the lung. They settled themselves each on a stool and my nursing care began.

The nurses washed me, supporting each floppy limb carefully as they did so. They rubbed my pressure areas but what I had not realised for some time was that all the extra rubbing and wiping around my bottom was not only to prevent pressure sores but also to clean me up because I was incontinent or had a period. Once I had realised this, I felt humiliated. I did not see myself as someone who could not cope with these elementary things.

Usually I found it impossible to talk about incontinence, but at last I overcame my embarrassment. I plucked up my courage and said, 'How can you bear to keep dealing with an old stinker like me?'

Sister said, 'You changed your babies' nappies, didn't you?'

'Of course.'

'You didn't mind that?'

'Of course not.'

'Well, nor do we,' she said happily.

'It isn't the same thing,' I protested.

'Not quite,' she replied, 'and yet it is in a way. You helped your babies because they needed your care. We're helping you in the same spirit.'

She was always so sensible and kind and took the sting out of the hurt to my pride that incontinence meant. She continued, 'We don't mind incontinence. Constipation is far more difficult to cope with.'

'Constipation is more difficult?' I questioned, thinking that laxatives were available even outside hospital.

'Yes, it is', she said, 'and if ever you experience it you will know what I mean.'

I settled for this happier state of incontinence on her advice. Dr Graham seemed oblivious of everything. He was singing softly 'Sospan Bach' and other Welsh morale-boosting songs. The assurance in his voice instilled in me the necessary confidence to remain relaxed and able to cope with being out of the lung.

Everyone was very kind to me. I would be swamped with great waves of gratitude and affection for them. In my isolation from my nearest and dearest, it seemed that I had changed my family for a while. I now belonged to the hospital staff. Thinking along the lines of my new physical dependency as Sister Allen had indicated, I realised that physically I was their baby and must be as good and helpful to them as I expected my own children to be to me. Even when I was being fed, washed and cleaned up, I only minded it because I was old enough to be able to do these things for myself. It was all a matter of time-scale really. Had I been only a few days old, there would have been no problem. It would have been perfectly natural for me to be cared for by someone more skilled and able than myself.

My new family was a big one. It consisted of the members of staff who were immediately concerned with my care. For instance, Dr Graham came several times a day to observe my condition and on two of these visits he breathed me with the mask from the positive pressure machine, when I was taken out of the lung. Sometimes he was joined by Dr Harris, the Medical Consultant at Prospect Park Hospital, who also came twice a day. On other occasions they were accompanied by the Consultant Physician. The night sister seemed to be around every night but was occasionally relieved by a colleague. Sister Allen appeared to be always on duty too, but must have had some time off when Staff Nurse Hull and Staff Nurse Morgan were in charge to organise the many student nurses. Frank Rackham and Ben Smith oiled the wheels. I never saw anyone but members of this new 'family' because of the risk of infection but today was to be an exception.

When I was returned clean and sweet to the iron-lung, Sister said, 'There's someone to see you.'

A quiet man came up to my iron-lung and introduced himself. 'I'm the chaplain. I thought I'd come to see how you are.'

I was horrified. Why have they brought the chaplain, I wondered. Don't they expect me to live? But I only answered, 'I'm very well thank you. And you?'

He replied, 'Fine, thank you. Is there anything I can do to help?'

What did he have in mind? I asked myself. *The last rites?* He wasn't looking at me as though he thought I was dying.

Slowly, I replied, 'I don't think so, thank you.'

I wasn't quite sure what one said to a hospital chaplain in such circumstances. I needed an instant miracle – but felt it would be rude to say so. I could have coped adequately had I been on my feet talking face to face with him. In the iron-lung I was out of my depth.

The chaplain, being a professional talker, had no such inhibitions. He told me that he had lost a leg and so understood how I felt. In the privacy of my mind I doubted whether he did – he was not an absentee mother of small children – but he must have had his own difficulties to contend with as his leg could not grow again. He would never be any different but I would be better soon. Not knowing quite how to go on, but feeling sympathetic towards him, I said, 'It must be an inconvenience to you.'

He replied, 'Oh, I'm getting used to it now, although at first I could not see why it had to happen. Don't you wonder why this should happen to you?'

I answered, 'No, I know why it happened.'

He looked surprised 'Do you?'

'Yes, polio attacked me.'

Once again, I felt I had said the wrong thing but could not think what it was he wanted me to say. I tried to please him more as I thought his job must be thankless and it was very kind of him to come and see me. I said, 'I'm most grateful for your visit. I expect you're kept very busy in a place like this.'

He answered, 'Yes, there is always plenty to do. I make a point of visiting everyone who is admitted to the hospital. I must go now but any time you need me, just ask Sister to give me a message.'

As he said goodbye, I felt puzzled by my inadequate response to him. I wondered why I hadn't told him that I was a confirmed Christian. Perhaps I had wanted to think the essentials out for myself first.

I was glad he had not suggested saying any prayers. I did not expect God would mind that I could not go down on my knees nor even put my hands together in prayer, but *I* minded it very keenly and had to adapt to my situation by reminding myself that everything we do is a prayer. It struck me that the whole hospital was doing God's work. The entire staff seemed to be performing prayers in action as they went about relieving suffering. Each one was a Good Samaritan and the words *When I come again I will repay thee*, echoed in my head. In my heart I felt sure that if there was any justice they would all be well rewarded for the tender loving care that they showed to me, and so many other people.

As the chaplain walked away, I remembered the harvest loaf that I had baked for Brian's school festival. I had made it from a recipe from my *Good Housekeeping* book and had been very proud of it. It was decorated on top with little loaves and small fishes with a plait around the outside. It smelled delicious, the crust was crispy and had turned a lovely golden colour. I had sealed it in a cellophane wrapper and although it looked very appealing I had assumed sorrowfully that it might be used only for display.

Now as I thought about it my blood ran cold. I felt like a leper. I realised that I had made the loaf when I was probably incubating polio. The little loaves and fishes would have fascinated the children. They might well have pulled them off and eaten them, putting themselves at risk. At this very instant, their mothers could be coping with their daily tasks not knowing that their little ones wree about to be struck down by this dreadful virus.

I remembered that Sister Allen had reassured me about the bread pudding. She had said that it was safe because it had been cooked. The harvest loaf had been cooked too. But supposing Sister Allen was telling white medical lies to keep me from worrying about the children? Would she really do such a thing, I asked myself? Would *I* do that to anyone? I knew in my heart of hearts that I would . . . and she would too. I felt sick with fear.

By the time that Ken came to see me, I was almost demented with the thoughts of what could have happened to Brian, Andrew and the other children round about.

I told Ken my fears and added, 'I can't believe you, whatever you say. You're bound to try to protect me. If anything had happened to Brian and Andrew, you wouldn't have told me. I know you wouldn't.'

'I needn't bother with explanations,' he answered. 'I shall get photographs of both of them and prove that they are fit and well, thank God. As for the other children going down with polio, don't you think the news of your illness has gone round the town like wildfire? All the mothers have been watching their children for the least sign of their being off-colour. Any poor little soul who sneezes or looks tired is sent to bed at once just in case he is sickening for polio.'

I wanted to hug him for taking the terrible burden from my mind. I wanted him to hug me too, but all I could do was lie like a lemon in the lung.

Ken said, 'Don't worry any more. I promise I'll tell you if anything is wrong.'

'Couldn't I come home and be with you all?' I begged him. 'Then I could see the children every morning and know how they are. I shall be out of quarantine soon.'

'Of course you can't,' he said. 'Don't let's start that again.'

'I shall go crazy just lying here with nothing to occupy me. I try so hard to be cheerful and patient but I'd get better much more quickly at home. My mind would be well stretched there, sorting out the problems.'

I was so desperate to be with my children that I continued to make Ken's life very hard by my insistence on returning home. I refused to believe that I could not manage to run our affairs from an iron-lung or that I was not strong enough to do so. I kept saying, 'They don't know how strong I am. I can solve anything if only I put my mind to it.'

Eventually Ken said, 'That's the trouble in this situation. You must understand that there are things in life that you can't solve by just thinking about them and this is one of them.'

I was furious with him. I knew he was telling the truth but I did not know then about the concept of disability denial. Had I understood that it is normal to respond to disablement by denying its effects, I might have had a better grasp of the new situation and been able to accept that I couldn't think my way out of the disabilities. Without an instant massive increase in our income, it was impossible to arrange for the help needed to replace the things that I usually did as well as to do the hundred and one things for me that now needed doing. I could not relinquish my pre-polio picture of myself as being superbly confident and competent or my beliefs that all problems have solutions if only we can find them. I thought that Ken was wrong in assuming that I could not find an answer to the present predicament. Blindly, I failed to realise that the only answer was money – a lot of it and for as long as I should live – for the inescapable and punishingly regular weekly bills that had to be paid. Ken was too kind to tell me that.

We said goodbye lovingly, each trying to understand the other's difficulty, but his words smouldered in my mind when he had gone. I had thought that he had shared the same convictions but polio seemed to be changing him. I felt that now a terrible gulf lay between us. I muttered to myself, 'I will get out. *I will get out.*' I could not lie around in an iron-lung supported by strangers – nice as they were. I had to get out, hold my home together and care for my children. If that must be through other people's hands at first, so be it. I would soon be up and about again as I had the greatest stimulus possible – a husband and children who needed me as badly as I needed them.

Although I had held my husband and children in my arms for the last time, mercifully I did not know it. My chances of returning to them were against such odds that no bookmaker on Newbury racecourse would have taken a bet on it.

Chapter 6
Anticipation

Sometimes at night when I was awake with the pain in my back and neck it was difficult to distinguish the hours of the dark winter days from the nights. When I woke up I could not tell if it was five o'clock in the morning or five o'clock in the afternoon and whether it was time to be awake or time to be asleep. The light was always on and I would gaze up at the cracked ceiling feeling like the only person left alive on earth. The entire population of the hospital and the outside world seemed out of reach. There was no guarantee that they were even there and I was reluctant to ring my bell to find out.

Pictures would come into my head to remind me of the kind of life I should be leading. It was natural for me to be active. I was certain to be so again. I would see myself being woken up by Ken with a cup of tea and Brian and Andrew leaping on me or climbing into bed for a cuddle. I would shoo them into the bathroom to wash and dress before sending them downstairs and claiming the bathroom for myself for a while. They would help to set the table while I prepared breakfast and the smell of the sizzling sausages or bacon crept upstairs and summoned Ken down to join them at the table.

The role of being in charge of the hustle and bustle of our domestic routine was in sharp and painful contrast to my role as passive patient. If I had ever imagined that it would be lovely to stay in bed for an extra half hour on a cold morning while somebody else took charge, I now knew how lucky I had been in the bosom of my family and after this enforced long lie-in I would always be glad to get up and get going.

As the hospital pattern became routine and impinged itself on me, the demarcation line between night and day was heralded by the arrival of the day staff. The lively voices of the young nurses echoed along the corridors. Cleaners clattered their mops and buckets. The German ward maid, Trudi, exchanged greetings with me, coming straight into the ward before she started work to say 'Morgen. Wie geht es?' for the sheer pleasure of speaking her own language although my knowledge of German was very limited.

Eileen Morgan always arrived early, bringing a generally cheerful atmosphere to the ward. She hustled about assembling my breakfast things and telling me her latest news. Eileen was a very experienced nurse. As I began to know her better, she told me that she was in fact fever-trained and met her husband when he was admitted with polio to her first fever hospital. He recovered sufficiently for them to marry and set up home. I met their lovely little girl Jennifer through photographs, just as Eileen met my children through their pictures in my locket and photographs which Ken brought occasionally to show the progress Brian and Andrew were making.

As I could no longer cope with a cooked breakfast, Eileen fed me drinks in quick gulps through a pliable plastic straw from a cup held at the side of my mouth. Food that could not be swallowed easily was liable to catch in my throat between breaths and cause a choking fit. I had no coughing muscles to help me cope with that, nor could I hold my breath or swallow hard. Eileen had to plunge a rubber tube down my throat to suck out the food that was choking me. I loathed this procedure. I did not realise that my swallowing difficulty was due to my condition. I assumed it was because my iron-lung was tipped at an angle, so that my head sloped towards the floor and my feet pointed towards the ceiling. I did not see how I could swallow properly with my head below my body. It meant trying to swallow upwards, working against the force of gravity. One should use gravity, not fight it.

One morning, when I was still coughing and spluttering, Dr Graham walked in and said, 'Good morning, what's this I hear about your wanting to leave us?'

'Nothing . . . personal,' I gasped, between chokes. 'Needs . . . must.'

'You haven't given us much chance to help you yet.'

'I have been here two weeks. I should be home by now, cooking breakfast for my family, not lying around being waited on.'

'Don't you like our cooking?' he joked.

I was grateful for his sense of humour, knowing that he understood better than anyone how I felt. He usually chatted away about seemingly inconsequential things but I guessed from the intelligence in his eyes that he was shrewdly assessing my condition. I wondered whether he resented the fact that, despite his newly-acquired skills and the advances in medicine, he had not been able to prevent the polio virus fastening me down with its invisible and immovable chains.

Sister Allen collected her team of nurses to begin my morning nursing routine. I had been promoted to being enthroned on bed-pans on request. Despite Sister's philosophy on incontinence, I was consistently constipated. She did unspeakable things to me, removing little bullets of excrement manually and pressing my abdomen to empty my bladder. I felt tremendously grateful for the relief but I loathed this humiliating treatment and tried every way I knew to throw off my weakness.

I hated having to think about these intimate matters. I was desperately anxious to return to everyday life where bodily functions were so normal and easy that they did not warrant a second thought and were never mentioned in polite conversation. Even my small children would take themselves off to the bathroom without any fuss or comment. Now my alimentary system assumed an importance out of all proportion to the rest of me and, what was worse, it had become the focus of other people's attention several times a day.

I longed desperately to be able to go to the lavatory in the usual way but this was out of the question because of my physical condition. To make matters worse, I discovered that my bed-pans had to be kept separate from everybody else's. They and their contents were specially treated because of the riks of infenction. I felt more like a leper than ever and wondered how long I would remain contaminated.

I found my inability to cope with this part of my helplessness utterly incomprehensible. I tried to accept my unwholesomeness and my dependence with good grace and made every effort, for the sake of the staff, to appear nonchalant at the repeated degradation but I often felt tears pricking my eyes and had a terrible struggle not to cry openly.

I discovered a little somebody sobbing inside me. It was as though this little somebody kept running up and down, up and down, desperately trying to make this bit of me move or that bit feel a little easier. When the silent sobbing stopped I came to know this little somebody as a companion for my mind, an independent spirit full of intuition and incredible staying-power, so different from the calculating, logical part of my brain-bound mind. Gradually I found enormous strength that had nothing to do with my physical or mental conditions which were pretty ropy at times. I discerned by experience which bits of my mind and body had autonomous activities as well as those that I tried to direct consciously.

I discovered that no matter what happened to me to strip away my vitality and defences, life went on. My mind ran unbidden along its old lines, reassuring itself and reconnoitring the ground for new ways of going on. I could hear Churchill's booming phrase 'Never surrender' echoing in my head. I thought of Lord Montgomery, whose birthday was the same date as mine. His words, 'Know your enemy' haunted my brain. I knew that my enemy was my helplessness and put my mind to thinking how I could fight it. I could not rely on my own pathetic physical resources. I had to get help from every possible person I could muster. It seemed imperative that not only should I know my enemy but also that I should really know my friends.

When I thought about it, I knew quite a bit about the effects of polio but I did not know much about how to fight it. I wondered who could help me. I remembered there had been a Sister Kenny who had revolutionised the treatment of polio, first in Australia, then around the world. Her patients had made spectactular improvements. Could her methods strengthen me, I wondered. It would be easier to judge if I knew exactly what was involved. Dr Graham would know and with great anticipation I waited for his next visit.

When he arrived I plunged straight in with my request for treatment such as Sister Kenny gave her patients. I pleaded my case by saying how desperately I wanted to try every possible thing. I did not care how hard I had to work as I so badly needed to get better and go home.

'When your temperature is down permanently, we might try some physiotherapy,' Dr Graham said.

I felt thrilled at the idea. This was what I needed. 'When can I start?'

He replied, 'If you don't fret about going home, your temperature will probably fall. If that happens, you could begin quite soon. Just a little at first, to see how you go. I'll ask Dr Harris to see what he thinks about it.'

I thought to myself that if only I could get breathing again, I could live out of the iron-lung and do more to help myself. Once out of the lung, I could get off my back to give it some relief. I could have a bath. I could be turned and moved so that I could be placed in different positions – perhaps on my front or on my sides . . . maybe even propped up into a sitting position, eventually to stand and walk again. It would be hard at first but was bound to become easier as I persevered. So I continued speaking to Dr Graham. 'What about Dr Andrews, the Consultant Heart Specialist?'

'I expect Dr Harris will discuss it with him.'

'I am sorry to need so much help but I am determined to help myself too. I have never met anyone with this sort of polio so I do not know much about it. I have only known people with non-respiratory polio like the children at the end of the ward. Do you think I could catch that sort of polio from them too and be seriously ill again – on top of this sort, I mean – and could the children catch respiratory polio from me?'

'Lightning seldom strikes twice in the same place.'

'It struck Ken twice. Here am I like this and his only sister had polio when she was a little girl. She was about five, I think, very cherished and well cared for. 'No one else in London had polio at that time.'

'How did it affect her?'

'She complained her leg felt empty after an apparent dose of flu. It was diagnosed by their family doctor who recognised it immediately as she happened to have been treating children with polio in the north of England before moving to London. Ken's mother devoted herself to exercising Beryl in hospital and after-wards, as prescribed by a specialist who was badly handicapped by polio himself. Now you would not know that Beryl had ever had it. She wears ordinary shoes with a special small support under her instep. More recently we had a friend who had polio. It left him with a limp.'

'How long ago was that?'

'Oh, earlier this year.'

'Much earlier?'

'Yes, it must be months ago. He was very bitter about it which upset everyone, including his wife and his mother who were marvellous to him. I don't want to become bitter like that. That would mean polio had won and I can't concede victory to a mingy virus. I want things to do to occupy my mind. I've got too much time on my hands. I want to work and work and work until I fall asleep from exhaustion and don't have to take any more sleeping draughts.'

Dr Graham said, 'I don't know that we would allow you to work and work. But we will help you to build up your strength gradually.'

His words pleased me and I was convinced that I would be up and about again soon. I anticipated that one night I would surprise Ken by walking down the ward to meet him. There would be no hanging on to the furniture to support myself, nor any halting or stumbling. I would walk normally and confidently right up to him and say, 'Come on – let's go places.'

The next time Ken came to see me he enjoyed a refreshing change. I did not pester him with my usual question about whether he had managed to arrange for me to come home soon. Instead I told him about my conversation with Dr Graham and how I felt sure that he meant me to start physiotherapy almost at once – perhaps in a day or two. I was certain to make such fast progress that I might even be up and about and home again for my birthday. After all, it was still a couple of weeks away.

Ken was very relieved to find that I had settled to stay in hospital for a little while longer. The idea of setting myself a definite date to go home seemed impossible to him but he said nothing to discourage me. My recovery might just happen that way and it would not be the first time that I had bounced back from a life-and-death situation with seemingly more zest for life than ever before. He understood the sort of active optimistic person I was and knew my capacity for hard work in impossible circumstances. He left me my illusions and when he was about to go home he said that on his next visit he would bring a few things that would amuse me.

I asked him what sort of things. He laid his finger along his nose to remind me not to be so curious. Then I thought about my birthday, but reflected: he won't bring me my birthday present now. He's always such a stickler for keeping presents until the right time and anyway I should be home by then. However, I blurted out, 'Is it a present?'

He countered with, 'What have you done to deserve a present?'

'I've survived,' I claimed. 'Perhaps I'll have a survival present.'

'We'll see,' he teased and left me wondering what surprise he had in mind.

The next night Ken struggled in with a huge parcel. He put it on the floor very carefully. I was in a dither of excitement to find out what it was but Ken seemed to take ages undoing the string. He is always very meticulous. He never cuts through string but unties knots carefully. At long weary last I learned what he had brought. There was a thrill of music in the air and Gigli's vibrant voice singing, 'Your tiny hand is frozen, let me warm it into life' from *La Bohème*. Ken put his hand through the iron-lung porthole and placed it on mine.

'Is this my present?' I asked. 'A record?'

Ken nodded and said, 'Yes – your present. Your first record. You can choose the next one and the next and the next as the record player is yours too.'

I was delighted and asked him, 'How can I think of a better

record than this? You know it is my favourite and it seems very appropriate at the moment.'

We relaxed together and listened to Gigli as we shared our present pleasure as well as the memories that the music evoked. The feeling of happiness was magical. I felt my spirits lift. I was truly joyful and not having to act an emotion for the sake of others.

I whispered to Ken, 'Music therapy – we can both benefit from it.'

Ken squeezed my hand gently and joked, 'I am glad I have done the right thing, for once.'

'Oh yes, you have. I'm so gloriously happy, I can't bear it. This record takes me back to when we met ten years ago. It makes me forget I've been ill and helpless.' If only time could have stood still for us.

Then I remembered Brian and Andrew and I did not want to be nineteen for ever and unaware of the fate that awaited me. Although a dose of severe respiratory polio was a heavy price to pay for having Ken and our sons, I knew that I would rather be me there in the iron-lung than anyone else on earth. At least I was alive. I had fantastic memories. No one could take them away from me. Please God we should enjoy some happier times together from now on.

Ken played the other side of the record. Gigli continued with 'Return to Sorrento', 'O sole mio' and other Italian songs. Unknown to us, an audience had gathered outside the ward. The men patients from the other half of the pavilion had gathered at the door to listen to Gigli. As Ken was allowed to stay until the night staff arrived, it was after visiting time. When Night Sister walked in, she announced we were playing one of her favourite songs 'Mattinàta' and told us about the audience that was listening silently outside the ward doors.

That night I slept happily, what with thoughts of impending physiotherapy, going home soon and the marvellous music therapy that I would enjoy from now on with my new record player and the Italian songs.

I was awake early the next morning. I hoped that Dr Graham had spoken to the other two doctors about my physiotherapy sessions. I could hardly contain my soul in patience as I waited for the doctors to do their rounds. When Dr Graham and Dr Harris arrived, they brought me not one piece of good news but two. The first was that my physiotherapy was to begin the following Monday. The second was that I was out of quarantine. I was beside myself with delight. Now, I thought, I will show them how strong I am and how unnecessary it is to over-protect me.

As the doctors had donned gowns and masks for their visits while I was still in quarantine, I had only been able to see their eyes. Now they all turned up wearing their white coats over their ordinary clothes. Dr Andrews sported a very cheerful line in ties and I caught myself staring at the front of his shirt and thinking what a nice change it made to see a crisply–ironed shirt set off by a contrasting tie, instead of the creased old gowns.

I apologised, 'I didn't mean to stare or be personal but I couldn't help noticing your tie. It goes so well with your shirt.'

He looked surprised and asked, 'Do you really like it?'

'Yes, very much.'

The next time Dr Andrews walked into the ward he came straight over to my iron-lung and said, 'What do you think of this tie?' Once again I had to say I was cheered by his choice of tie. For my part I had begun to wear blue or pink scarves to stop the draught from the iron-lung blowing into my eyes and Dr Andrews admired them. One day our little ritual of compliments was extended as he had chipped his tooth on a piece of toast at breakfast. He bent down and grinned to show me the damage.

On another occasion, he spoke enthusiastically of salmon fishing and promised that when he went to Scotland again he would bring me back an enormous salmon.

With so few opportunities to relate to a range of other people, such incidents helped make my days in isolation memorable. Visitors were welcome events and even a short exchange of greetings left me elated. A state approaching euphoria reigned over me and I told everyone how lucky I was to be coming out of quarantine and looking forward to physiotherapy.

Another result of coming out of quarantine was that Jill – one of the other patients – was allowed to come and see me for short visits. As a vet, Jill was fascinated by the different ways in which we had succumbed to the various forms of polio. She remained incredulous that all my will-power could not throw off an underlying physiological limitation. She was furious that I should have been left so helpless through polio when – as she put it – I had been so sweetly reasonable throughout my severe attack. She thought it was most unfair that the people who had to put up with the worst doses of polio were also left with the most disablement and the hardest and longest fight to throw it off.

I was thankful that Jill was able to throw off the effects of her dose of polio and in being glad for her I was blessed with a share in her happiness. As she had not had respiratory polio she could breathe under her own steam and as she had not had paralytic polio she could walk about and move all her limbs.

Jill's anger with my sort of polio drove her to do what she could to help me. She would bring her copy of *The Times* and read out the light-hearted pieces from the features and letter pages and ponder on the crossword. One day she brought a book she had been reading, *King Solomon's Ring*, and described the imprinting of Konrad Lorenz on his family of orphaned goslings.

Jill was a marvellous tonic. She brought me so many diverting little titbits that she had read that I longed to tell her something in return. I very rarely could but she did not seem to mind. My news about my impending physiotherapy sessions seemed to burn a hole in my tongue as I waited for her next visit. She was thrilled and we shared a total conviction that it would only be a matter of time before I walked down the ward and out into the sunshine.

Chapter 7
Complication

A fleeting fear that my luck was too good to hold darted into my head but I dismissed it quickly. There was no point in steeling myself against disappointments should my physiotherapy not strengthen me quickly. It was up to me to make it work. Preferring to be cheerful, I revelled in my increasing buoyancy.

My brain seemed to have turned into a balloon full of happiness which kept me drifting over beautiful prospects, taking me too far from the dark and devastating things to be bothered by them. Suddenly the balloon burst. I plunged back down on to the hard boards of reality.

The atmosphere in the ward was made bitter-sweet. We were shocked and saddened by the admission of a new young patient with respiratory polio, Peggy. She had come from Newbury too and her husband, Dick – captain of the Newbury footbal team – showed me a photo of their lovely little girl, Lyn. When Peggy was put into an iron-lung, I dreaded witnessing minute by minute her enduring a similar ordeal to that through which I was graduating. I felt desperate to help but as I could not get up to do anything for her, I prayed to be able to assist her carry her suffering in some way. Seeing someone else in the same boat also brought my own ordeal home to me.

My experiences had drawn a mental map of what she might have to go through. Would she discover as I had that no orifice was sacred, that with or without vacuum pumps, tubes could be inserted into any part of you? At least blood sampling and injections were surface matters and therefore acceptable, but the intrusion of obnoxious tubes into one's interior was a loathsome intimacy. There were so many openings to one's person that were normally regarded as private and to which no one had the right of access, but in the hospital situation sovereignty was sacrificed for the sake of survival. In the new complicated way of life where my missing muscle power was compensated for by electric pumps, I had tried to regard my living body with its sentient responses as just another piece of equipment for the sake of the peace of mind of those who were caring for me. But how I hated catheters being plunged down my throat to stop me choking or pushed up my nose because I could no longer blow it or sniff. My dislike of these procedures was emphasised when I was faced with someone who did not yet know what she had coming to her.

Now I was to have an enema and I was not happy about it. I thought the practice of enemas being automatically given to women in labour must have been started by a man who hated women in general and mothers in labour in particular. It occurred to me that I might not get colic from an enema now that my muscles were so useless. My optimism was short-lived. When the enema was given and the hot soapy suds rushed into my colon. I felt the same sense of churning and outrage. I was very concerned that this should not become a regular procedure for myself or for Peggy.

Now that Peggy was in the ward with a more recent dose of infection we had to go back into quarantine and it was obvious that my isolation would be prolonged. I assumed other people in the outside world would also be incubating polio and would be admitted to the ward, bringing fresh infection and putting visitors at risk. When Ken came to see me that night I was filled with anxiety. I looked again at the white gown he was wearing and the mask through which he spoke to me and kissed me goodnight and wondered how effective they were in protecting him from this horrible virus.

I was too frightened to voice my fears. I had worried about him through all his visits, dreading he might catch polio from me or from the children to whom he read and told stories. The next time Dr Graham had a few moments to spare and leant over the iron-lung for a quick chat, I asked him how safe the barrier nursing procedure was for staff and visitors alike.

'If precautions are taken, the chances of not getting it are good.'

'How can you dare to run such terrible risks when we are here in front of your eyes as a perpetual warning of what might happen to you?'

'Of course the thought does cross your mind at first but you have a job to do and you get on with it. If you do worry about it, you are more likely to get it. It's best to rely on good preventative procedures.'

'Surely,' I insisted, 'without any immunisation available, the more different polio patients you attend, the more risk there is of catching it?'

'It just doesn't happen that way,' he said.

Now that Peggy had been admitted, I wanted to keep Ken out of the ward entirely. Even if he did not catch polio himself it might be that he could carry it to Brian and Andrew. I asked Dr Graham if Ken was very vulnerable.

He replied, 'I can't tell, but if he didn't catch it from his little sister, he may be immune.'

'Could he carry it to Brian and Andrew or anyone else?'

'He could, but it would be highly unlikely and I know he is very careful about taking precautions.'

As I was listening I suddenly became aware that I could not breathe. I could not understand what was happening to me or rather what was not happening. There was a sudden awful nothingness that was filled with a feeling of urgency. Dr Graham, seeing something was wrong, instantly stopped explaining about polio infection and demanded 'What's the matter?'

'Can't breathe,' I gasped.

He speedily checked that the iron-lung motor was working. It was, but my eyes swivelled into my head and I lost consciousness.

Later I learned I had become intensely cyanosed. My acute respiratory obstruction had caused a panic. Time was of the essence. Dr Graham whipped me out of the iron-lung onto a bed, tipped my head down, turned me on to my front and hammered on the back of my chest, summoning help the while. He eventually managed to dislodge a large semi-solid plug of mucus and my airway was cleared and restored.

The staff threw everything they had into an unremitting effort to revive me. A specialist was called. His knowledge of my respiratory plumbing was to save me from drowning in my own secretions. He did a bronchoscopy, diagnosed pneumonia and pushed a thick rubber tube up my left nostril, down into my lung and sucked out the mucus from my collapsed lung. He intubated my right lung in the same way and attached that tube to a positive pressure machine to breathe me. These tubes tortured my face.

That evening, when Ken walked into the ward with a large bunch of yellow chrysanthemums, he saw my iron-lung standing open and empty and stood stock-still with horror. He knew that I could not breathe without a mechanical respirator and the shocking thought flashed through his mind that I had died, just when things were getting better.

Before he had time to think any further, Sister Allen noticed him. She hurried over and apologised for not meeting him before he came into the ward. She took him into a side ward where I was being constantly monitored by the staff nurses, regularly turned from side to side and sucked out. She told him of the battle they had fought to revive me and that I was so weak and ill that only a miracle could save me. As she was just going off duty, she collected her nurses together and hurried off with them to chapel to pray for my survival.

I did not know about any of this until a long time afterwards. When I died clinically, I did not even know that I was dead. I found myself travelling at tremendous speed in a state of ecstasy and expectation. I was not aware of my body and may not have had one, but I must have had some sense of colour as blind people do, as I seemed to be journeying through a green place that inspired a feeling of peace and delight such as I had never known on earth but which I took for granted as my natural state. Strangely enough I seemed to know exactly where I was going. Everything was familiar and as it should be. I was aware that I was homing on to a way I knew and loved. As I sped happily through this green place, I realised that once I had passed through it I should know this joy and peace for ever.

Death is one thing. Life another. Until you die and realise that life is inextinguishable. Death is not the opposite of life but merely the name we give to a process that enables us to pass from our earthbound state to the eternal. This was how I saw life and death when I regained consciousness. The memory of being transported elsewhere remained, intense and persistent. But at the time that I was making the discovery it was merely an experience and it happened too fast for me to do anything other than register my awareness.

I heard my children's names being called loudly and urgently. I stopped and listened. At the point of listening I heard their names again and again. In that moment of moments, when I was being born into eternity, I decided I must turn back. It seemed impossible to force myself free from the gravity-like pull of the direction in which I was moving but after a frantic battle I managed it. I immediately regretted it. Suddenly I was blinking under the harsh light of a fierce naked electric light-bulb which seared through my eyes. I could not raise my arms to shade them. I was back in my agony-racked body and contained in my physical self in the new suffocating and terrifying way that had just been inflicted on me. I found I was no longer in the iron-lung but lying on my side on a bed and boxed in by pillows.

There was a sharp pain across my eyes and nose as though an

axe had been struck into my face up to its hilt. I could do nothing to stop the agony, not even speak as the breathing and drainage tubes into my lungs separated my vocal chords. I felt like Gulliver but with more reason than he had to break my bonds and escape from the aliens around me. I could not move my head to see who was bellowing my children's names into my ear. There were various doctors, nurses and other people around me, thumping my chest, pinching and rubbing my limbs and trying to stimulate a response. I was livid with them all when I realised the condition to which I had returned. Soundlessly I spat my words at them with all the venom I could muster.

'You fools. Go away – leave me alone – I'm going to die . . . again.'

But although I tried so hard to die, I could not find the way.

Sister Allen was highly delighted to see me showing such fight, although she knew the tremendous difficulty I had in trying to form even one word. She said later, 'As soon as I saw your eyes flash, I knew we'd got you back. After that it was up to us to make sure that you stayed here.' She had not been able to hear a word I had said as the two large endotracheal tubes down my nose and throat had robbed me of my voice and made my feelings unintelligible.

Although I was still alive and being kept breathing, I was critically ill. I did not much care whether or not I ever talked or breathed again. I just wanted to go to sleep and never wake up. In this place of safety, people who felt kindly towards me had hurt me badly. They were fighting for my life but I was deeply afraid of them and desperate to escape the routine procedures which revolted and tortured me with no hope of a way out, except in death.

When first intubated, I had tried to form the words to ask Dr Graham to be merciful and end it all. I had no means of compelling his attention. I could not clasp his arm or raise my voice. I just had to hang on to him by my eyelashes and keep contact with him with the expression in my eyes, willing him to interpret.

I was vividly aware of my intense suffering. Perhaps the pain acted as a stimulant. I remember thinking disgustedly of stories of people who pass out when pain becomes too hard for them to bear and presumed that it must happen only in books. As the depth and hardness of my pain made me want to scream and scream, the little somebody inside joined me in protest and kept saying, *no, no, no*, as if in the most urgent, shocked and desperate resistance to the Fates. No sound escaped me and the term 'dumb animals' leapt into my mind. I felt at one with all the animals who had ever suffered in silence, especially the dogs whose vocal chords had been cut so they could make no noise during laboratory experiments.

I could not think what was happening to me. I was completely baffled. It seemed there was a lot I ought to know but could not quite grasp. The little somebody inside me kept saying, *Stop it, stop it, stop it,* but no one stopped it, except when Dr Graham came from time to time with an injection of Pethidine. Even Ken, who had always been so marvellous to me and met all my needs instinctively, did not seem able to understand what I thought I needed.

Ken watched helplessly. It seemed to him my flesh melted rapidly from my bones, turning me into a skeleton. By association, he kept thinking of the skeleton of St Cecilia curled up on its side in the catacomb in Rome. He rarely left me, except when Sister Allen forced him to get some sleep.

Sister Allen or Staff Nurse Hull or Staff Nurse Morgan were with me all the time. It seemed that every few minutes someone pulled the littl plug out of the drainage tube where it emerged from my nose and inserted a catheter to suck out the mucus. This was a ghastly experience. The minute the plug was removed my air supply disappeared completely and the awful sensation of being throttled returned again and again and I felt as though my eyes and throat must burst.

I just did not know what to do. I was in an impossible situation but could not escape from it in any way whatsoever. I could not stop anyone robbing me of my air supply nor had I the power to brace any muscles to relieve the pain and panic. I tried to remember how prisoners under torture had ended their sufferings. I think I must have gone quite out of my mind for a time. I prayed harder than I had ever prayed in my life. I seemed to be arguing with the God that was inside me as well as 'out there'. After all, I protested, Jesus Christ hung on the cross for only three hours before He died and His whole suffering until He was risen was ended in three days. The thought had scarcely entered my head before the question came, *Do you really believe that Christ suffered only once?* With a terrible insight, I knew that the Crucifixion was not God's only agony and that the God in each of us suffers interminably. We are all God's children and cause suffering each time one of us is injured. I could hear the groans of God. They were so terrible that I feared for those around me.

There was a heavy feeling in my chest. It seemed as though a solid weight was lying immovably behind my breast-bone. I remembered expressions of hearts being 'heavy and broken with grief' and wondered whether there was a physiological foundation for what I had always assumed to be figurative terms. If intense grief and pain could contract or distort the heart, would its changed texture feel abnormally rock-like, provoking an image of one's heart as heavy as lead or stone?

I remained critically ill for some time but eventually Dr Graham returned me to the iron-lung and pulled out the tubes that had been helping to breathe and drain me. They were fixed to my face with sticky tape and Dr Graham started to pull it off by easing the corner gently.

He said, 'It would be less painful if I pulled it off quickly.'

I could not wait to be free of the tubes so agreed that he should rip it off. When the tubes were pulled out, great clots of blood slid down the back of my throat, almost choking me before I managed to swallow them. I reflected wryly that they were the first nourishment my stomach had had for ages.

Now that the tubes had been removed I could talk again. I was filled with gratitude for Dr Graham I felt I wanted to acknowledge a little of the debt I owed him. The depth of my regard for him had increased immeasurably with the knowledge that I owed my life to his skill, determination and courage, even though he had gone against my wish to die. How does one address a man who has refused to let you die?

I began to call him 'Taffy' to make him more of a friend and brother than a physician.

'You mustn't call me that,' he said, but I did not feel like being formal any more and compounded my transgression by greeting him as 'Taffy Bach'. He soon forgave me. He seemed to understand my deep need of people I could cling to psychologically in complete confidence in this isolation hospital to which I had journeyed with such hope and trust.

I asked Taffy if I could see one of the photos that he had taken while I was out of the lung. He said, 'I don't think you would want to see it if you knew what it was like. It isn't very pretty.'

'I don't want to see it because it's pretty but because it would be interesting,' I said. He brought me instead a photo of a tree without leaves, its bare branches silhouetted skeleton-like against a Welsh winter sky. The picture carried an atmosphere of wildness and loneliness which was completely in tune with the way I felt.

Once I was back in the iron-lung the whoosh-shoosh of its motor took over, giving me the impression of being at sea again. I felt as though I had battled through one mighty storm after another, only to find myself at the end of it not triumphant on dry land but drifting further away from home than ever. I felt spent, battered and cheated. I had struggled on obediently, trusting in the God that had shielded me during the war, only to find that my faith had fled or, if not my faith, then the object of it.

I remembered seeing a film called '*Captains Courageous*' in which Spencer Tracey, for some reason or other, has to go down with his ship to save the further suffering of a small boy. I now felt that I had to be left to drift into oblivion for the sake of Ken and our two small sons. My own misery was more than enough to stand. I could not bear to think what they were going through and I endured their unhappiness added to mine.

When I was more rested, a Roman Catholic nurse said to me, 'God must love you very much. It is a privilege to be allowed to bear such suffering.'

I did not think much of her idea of God's love but I said nothing – she was trying to be kind and I did not wish to offend her.

Sister Allen said, 'You were always so lucid when you were conscious. It was difficult for us to remember that you were so close to death.'

So close to death – so close to everlasting life. I came to regard time as a force, like gravity, which held me to this planet. As I looked back in my memory to that green place where I had been so vibrantly happy, I longed to return. I saw death as a cervix through which I must be born to find my way again to eternity – just as I had been born through the neck of my mother's womb into this world. If only I had passed through the gate, never to return. That little wooden gate of the Cross that led to eternity. I continued to puzzle over matters of life and death, from my new standpoint. I knew I was desperately weak and vulnerable and those around me knew that I knew. Trudi said, 'You see I am careful not to knock your iron-lung as I clean around it. You have been so ill. I think you feel a little better now, yes?'

Sister Allen was a woman of tremendous faith. She was convinced that her prayers had been answered. She encouraged me to pit my diminished resources against the onset of permanent weakness. I found myself reflecting with wonder on the spiritual strength around me.

I suggested to Sister, 'I expect many patients have died in your presence. Have any of them told you about finding a place of peace?'

She said that they had and that sometimes at the end their faces had lit up with joy as though they could see something wonderful that she could not see. I continued by saying that I thought I could not live very long now. I supposed that I had learnt something that I had no business to know and therefore coud not stay with other human beings who knew nothing of the green place of peace from which I had returned. I felt that this knowledge had made my life forfeit and was happy that this should be so as I was filled with a terrible nostalgia for that life beyond death.

Sister said confidently, 'You'll live.'

'What makes you so sure?'

'God loves you. He will help you.'

'But there are millions of people round the world dying and being born every day,' I answered.

She explained, 'We prayed just for you. We want you to live. Ken and your boys need you.'

'It would have been kinder to them to let nature take its course.'

'Nonsense! God means you to live, otherwise you wouldn't be here now.'

'How can God be said to decide the moment of life or death when men control these things with machines?' I asked.

Sister Allen answered, 'Of course God decides. We wouldn't have the machines if God hadn't given us the wherewithal to develop and use them.'

When she had gone away her words kept coming back into my mind. The matter of life and death was a subject about which many people around me naturally held very strong views.

A Roman Catholic doctor was annoyed with me as I was so determined to die again. He told me I was ungrateful and did not deserve the gift of life or the heroic efforts with which the staff had fought for my survival and revitalised me. He said that if he could, he would turn me over and spank me. My fury returned. I did not hold my words back for him as I had with the nurse. I thought to myself that no one has the right to inflict suffering that he so obviously could not bear himself. I had been reading a book about the Inquisition just before I had polio and to my regret I found myself saying 'This isn't the Inquisition. Go away!'

Ken was living at the hospital again. God alone knows what he went through. To make matters worse, Andrew had been pining and my mother had taken him back to Newbury. Jeff, Ken's colleague, and Jeff's wife Ruby, who were childless, offered to help. They kept Andrew for us while Ken was staying at the hospital. They were very, very good to him and tried to compensate for the temporary loss of his family, but I worried about

Andrew being left completely with strangers as he was a shy little boy. When Ken was allowed to leave the hospital again, he worked out a routine in which he collected Andrew from Ruby and Jeff's house every morning, took him to the local nursery school and left him there all day. In the evening he collected Andrew and took him back to his colleague's house before coming on to the hospital to stay with me. I don't know how Ken managed to cope. I was not much help. I was very very tired and as weak as a kitten for a long time.

Revitalisation was not enough. It added to the quantity of my life perhaps for a few days, a few weeks, a few months, who could tell? I had no idea how to improve the quality.

Chapter 8
Exhaustion

Apparently, banks of birthday flowers wilted in the central heating, reflecting my own unhealthy way of life. I do not remember my birthday. I only remember my gradual mental withdrawal from the otherwise inescapable hospital world.

The iron-lung was tipped up even further than before, to help drain my lung and to ensure that the saliva ran down out of my mouth and not down my throat to drown me. Anyone who went by picked up a piece of gauze and wiped the dribble from my face. I hated this. I felt sure there must be pneumonia infection on these swabs but I could not make anyone stop doing it.

Ken and Mr Rackham were constantly mopping me up and I could not see how they could avoid infection. Sister and her staff nurses were repeatedly sucking me out with a vacuum pump. Night Sister battled with the gubbins that collected while I slept, pushing the tube further and further down my throat, removing the stuff I could not cough up but which would drown me if she didn't clear it. My senses reeled. I detested all this treatment and would have given anything to slip quietly away.

I was reminded again of the Inquisition and the way heretics were garrotted almost to death, revived and garrotted again. I was grateful to everyone, but wished they could be merciful and end it all.

Night Sister was an incredible woman. She could unscrew my equipment efficiently and reassemble it so that it worked better. I often admired her as I watched her clever hands manipulating tiny screws with the rounded end of her nail-file and always felt secure when she was around.

I had a particular reason for wanting her to be on hand every night. The hospital could not afford two positive pressure machines. Peggy and I had to share the same one. Nothing could be done about the obvious danger of cross-infection. A token gesture was made by providing us with our own mask each and separate valve. This meant that each time we were attached to the machine, the masks and valves had to be changed.

With Night Sister there was no problem. She could have done the change-over with her eyes shut, but once, when she was off duty, a locum took charge of my out-of-lung-routine. She put the mask and valve together the wrong way round and as I turned blue and my breathing difficulties became apparent, she pushed me back into the iron-lung. After that there was no other defence but to play possum. The next time I knew that she was coming, I pretended to be asleep. I found it very difficult to keep my eyes shut and still with the lights on as usual and my face in full view. I felt nervous that she would see my eyelids twitch or think it strange to find me always sleeping. When I heard her say to the nurse who was specialling me, 'Oh, she's asleep. We'll leave her,' I was filled with relief but did not dare open my eyes for ages.

Most of the staff were so highly trained and instinctively aware of the meaning of my being unable to move that my condition was very rarely made worse by anyone. Their firm but gentle hands eased my pains and I looked forward to the relief that their ministrations brought me. There was a general attitude of kindness and concern. By sharp contrast, individual aberrations of some nurses taught me valuable and unforgettable lessons.

Sister Allen had been unable to put the feeding tube down into my stomach as my throat had been blocked by the breathing and drainage tubes. She had tried to give me a drink by mouth, but it had gone straight up the back of my nose and caused choking spasms. The skin on my lips soon cracked. Sister Allen was too kind and experienced to do anything but leave well alone but one of her nurses terrified me, although she was only trying to help. She said she would cut the skin off my lips where they were split and peeling. I could not back away from his nurse who peered short-sightedly at me through her glasses. I just kept saying, 'No, no, no. You mustn't' as she approached me with the nail scissors.

My neck was still rigid. I could not turn my face away from her. She cut away the dry skin and then accidentally snicked my upper lip, making it bleed. Instinctively, I turned both lips inward and pressed them together hard to stop the bleeding. This stopped her from cutting my lips any more and I wished I had thought of doing this sooner.

Shocked, I uttered, 'You have made me bleed,' but she remained unconcerned. I pressed my lips inside my mouth again quickly, in case she made another attempt, but she merely answered, 'I've cut enough skin off. We can leave it now.'

As I was tipped up to my limit in the iron-lung, much of my

weight was taken by my shoulders, I had lost every scrap of surplus flesh that I possessed, but I did not know this. The pressure in my iron-lung had been turned up to give me more help and this caused friction burns on my shoulders. One incredibly insensitive nurse who was helping Sister Allen suddenly said to me, 'You are always asking to be made cooler. How's this?' as she sloshed surgical spirit straight from the bottle on to the raw flesh on my shoulders and began to rub hard. A kind of squeaky groan burst out of my throat and Sister Allen said sharply, 'Stop that. What do you think you're doing? I'll see you afterwards.'

On another occasion when my unbroken pressure areas were being rubbed through the portholes of the iron-lung, a nurse passed the spirit bottle across my face to her colleague on the opposite side, spilling some of the spirit into my eyes. I could not turn my face to let the spirit run out or let the tears run away as my eyes brimmed with water. Night Sister brought some lotion and washed my eyes as she instructed, 'Never, never, *never* pass things across a helpless patient.'

I began to realise the full meaning of polio. I learned through experience how vulnerable I was to the thoughtlessness of others. I began to anticipate trouble and to be very wary of those who had caused me pain. I did not bear these nurses any ill will. I was in such a wretched condition that I was grateful for any attempts to help me. I never felt able to complain about the things that were done to me unnoticed. I did not want them to get into trouble. Many were nearing the end of their SRN course and were burdened with a great deal of study outside their hospital duties. I felt that they were truly sorry for unwittingly causing me distress. I was too exhausted to make a stand.

I welcomed visitors, staff or lay, as an insurance against mishaps.

Jill was determined to see me. She told me later that she had been too keen for her own good. While my nurse's back was turned, Jill sneaked into the doorway of the side ward and had been shocked to see that I was intubated. I imagined I must have looked repulsive and recalled that Taffy had refused to show me the photographs that he had taken, but I did not realise for some time the cause of his reticence or of Jill's concern.

Jill renewed her efforts to amuse me but could not stay long because I now tired quickly and my vulnerability to further infection had to be weighed against the value of her visits. She told me how concerned the other patients had been while I had been so ill in the side ward.

'How did they know?' I asked her, thinking that hospitals were like naval signal stations and that one did not repeat what one saw and heard except in the line of duty.

She answered. 'Oh, news gets around. Several of us have had polio. One girl was pregnant but polio killed her baby before it was delivered.'

I told her how sorry I was and sent a message of sympathy back to the girl. I fell to thinking about my own first baby. He had been born dead, despite regular and apparently satisfactory antenatal check-ups.

I was lucky. I had subsequently managed to produce Brian and Andrew. It seemed such a waste to have made so much effort to produce them, only to be whisked away at a time that could damage them permanently.

The saying 'As the twig bends, so shall the tree grow' kept coming into my mind. Brian, at five, had at least started school and would be occupied much of the day. But Andrew, who was only three, was more vulnerable. I had read too much Dr Spock and too many books on psychology to rest easy away from my children.

Miss Carrington, the headmistress at the nursery school, very kindly wrote to me and assured me of Andrew's well-being. I was most grateful for her letter and read it over and over again, trying to glean from it more about Andrew than could ever have been put into it. I was pleased that he was at the nursery school but thought he was too young to be there. He still needed mothering. He was not like Brian who, being older, was venturesome and would talk to anyone at great length. I also felt it was wrong that Brian and Andrew should be apart. They should at least have each other, even though they couldn't have their parents with them. They should live in the same house, play together after school and sleep under the same roof. Their intelligence and sensitivity laid them wide open to all kinds of hurt in my absence.

I tried to be philosophical about the split-up of our family. After all, the Queen travelled around the world and left her children at home. But royal children were properly cushioned against the absence of their parents by the presence of familiar proxies.

I kept trying to be cheerful as I felt instinctively that this would give me the best chance of recovery and a quick return home. I kept feeding my mind with clichés such as 'children are resilient', 'children suffer less than adults', 'none of us is indispensable'. I kept telling myself that I must be grateful to my in-laws for caring for Brian and to Ruby and Jeff and Miss Carrington for helping Ken and Andrew. I truly did appreciate their kindness and realised that things could have been much worse for the children had they been taken into the anonymous care of a local authority. The pressure on me to recover quickly was so great that it caused utter exhaustion.

To make matters worse, the nurses were talking about a woman who had fallen down a well in a village pub near Newbury. She lived there and had walked backwards and forwards across her kitchen floor for years, not knowing that the well was waiting, silent and sinister, beneath her feet.

I asked the nurse, 'Isn't it strange that no one knew that the well was there especially one that was big enough to kill a woman?'

But the nurse replied, 'There are dozens of old wells around here and no one knows about them until a cow or horse or something falls down one.

I was horrified. So many hazards seemed to be lurking in the smiling countryside. First polio and now the danger of hungry well-shafts. I was frantic to stop my children from becoming their next victims.

My fears for my children obsessed me. Feeling so low in health and vitality, I could not summon the energy to think positively about them. The recurrent theme of my thoughts was that if only I could go home I would somehow be able to organise a way of life in which we could all be together. Then our children could grow up secure and happy. I begged to be allowed to go home and I confided in Eileen Morgan, 'Oh Eileen, you know how it is. You have a little girl. You know how you would feel in my place. Please explain to them why I must go home.'

My words moved Eileen deeply but she did not show her feelings. Her eyes were always gentle and concerned and I knew that if she could find a way to advise me she would. I felt that I could say things to her that I could not tell Ken because he missed the children as much as I did.

Each night, when Ken came to see me, there was some little bit of gossip for me to exchange with him. He would tell me what was happening to Andrew at nursery school and Brian in the infants' class at Stevington village school. I would recount the latest hospital happenings. But gradually, the world outside became remote. The hospital world became my world.

Eileen often handed me over to Ken as, although she worked most days from nine until four, she also worked occasional evening shifts. She told Ken that she was worried. I had always managed to regain my buoyancy quickly but now she felt I needed some kind of distraction to keep me from fretting for the children.

Ken brought in a wireless which was a great source of joy but the thought behind its appearance was therapeutic too. Even so, the agony of being separated from my children made me turn increasingly to my escape. I began to withdraw more and more into a fantasy world of snow and ice. I would just stare at the white ceiling until it melted and I was exploring the next part of the adventure in my mind about which I would tell nobody.

Life went on – nursing routines, the hours of nothingness. The ward was very hot but there was a cold draught on my face from a window high up. It remained open the whole time because the cable for our two iron-lungs had to be fed into the ward that way.

One night, while waiting for Ken to arrive, I suddenly couldn't breathe and the iron-lung started making terrible screaming noises. After a few moments, Mr Rackham entered the ward and recognised the sound. There was an obstruction in the air supply pipe of the iron-lung. The corner of one of the pillows which cushioned my feet had been sucked into the pipe. As my face turned blue, Mr Rackham rushed over to the lung, rammed his arm through the porthole, grabbed the pillow and pulled it away. The alarming noise stopped and the iron-lung resumed its old familiar whoosh-shoosh regular breathing sound.

When the emergency was over. I felt wildly elated. I came so close to death that it seemed it was only a matter of time before I slipped through their fingers, and my fears for my family would end.

But I under-estimated the tenacity of those around me.

Chapter 9
Reflection

Visiting-time had become a social occasion. Ken and Peggy's husband, Dick, relayed conversation between the two iron-lungs. It was impossible for Peggy and me to talk direct. Our voices were not strong enough.

During my stay in the side ward, Peggy had made rapid progress. Now Sister Allen told me Peggy was going to another hospital for rehabilitation; Jill and the others were going home. My X-rays showed that my left lung had reinflated and I was fit to be moved to another ward where there would be no cold draughts and I would be given extra attention. There might also be more mobile company as it was a women's ward and some of the patients were up and about.

Although I was delighted about the progress the others had made in my absence, I knew I should miss Jill's visits very much. I was also very anxious about being shuttled across to a new ward, especially as all my confidence rested in Sister Allen and Taffy. I tried to go along with what was being suggested but it worried me so much that I spoke to Taffy about it. He said that he would still be keeping an eye on me as he was not attached to just one ward but generally circulated around the hospital.

The next day the Sister from the new ward came to tell me she was looking forward to my transfer. Although I could not see how anyone could give me better care than Sister Allen and her crew – after all, I owed them my life – I realised the arrangements to move me were for the best. I had to get a grip on myself and face the inevitable.

Sister's visit helped me greatly.

The actual move was a safari-type expedition. Mr Rackham organised electricity leads and sockets so that they could be changed at various points to keep me breathing all the way to the new ward.

As we emerged from the hot-house conditions of Sister Allen's ward, the air struck cold and sharp in my nostrils. I caught my first glimpse of the outside world for many weeks.

We made slow progress as the iron-lung, with me in it, was trundled across from one pavilion to the other and as we passed under a tree, we had to pause while the electricity plugs were changed over. I looked up and saw a tiny bird fly on to a high branch.

While watching it, I realised that for the first time in my life I could see a small bird sitting in a tree. I had always been too short-sighted to see such a thing before. Now something miraculous had happened. My eyesight had improved. Such excitement. I kept repeating, 'I can see a bird in that tree. I can see a bird in that tree.' Everyone was amused, being used to seeing birds in trees with their good eyes, but when I explained to Sister what a new and thrilling experience it was for me, she was delighted too. She said that the muscles around my eyes must have slackened through being paralysed and this had lengthened my sight.

I would be shortsighted no longer. I found myself thinking: '*Then* I saw through a glass darkly, but *now* I see face to face.'

In the new pavilion I was made very comfortable indeed. I was put into a ward with a staff nurse to special me. There were several women patients in the other ward that made up the pavilion.

Sister kept me busy deliberately so that I should not miss Sister Allen or the patients who had left. Taffy called in to see me and told me that I was to start physiotherapy as soon as I was settled. I felt apprehensive. The last time I had heard those words I had had pneumonia.

As Taffy leant over my lung, I told him of my improved sight. He asked if I could move my eyebrows. I thought about this for a minute and tried to move them, not having realised that I could no longer do so. I found myself looking towards my eyebrows and blinking as if I were trying to feel or move them with my eyelashes.

I said to him, 'I expect I can, but I can't think how to do it just now. Can you move yours?'

He raised and lowered his eyebrows so fast he looked like Groucho Marx and I couldn't help smiling.

'What are you grinning at?' he demanded.

'You look so comical.'

He insisted, 'Now you try again,' but I could not manage it so he said, 'That will give you something to do while I'm away.'

'Will you be seing Sister Allen before you go?' I asked.

'Yes, I am just going over to David Ward now.'

'You won't forget to tell her I can see better now, will you?'

'No, I'll tell her. Is there any other message?' he asked.

'Has anything else happened to me that I haven't realised?' I wondered aloud.

'Can you wiggle your ears?' he enquired. I tried to wiggle them and said, 'I used to, but they don't seem to move now. I expect I'll move them again when I'm stronger.'

'Well, practise that too, and tell me when you can manage it.'

'I'll make it part of my daily exercises.'

When Taffy had gone, I thought to myself, Fancy not being able to move my eyebrows much, or even wiggle my ears properly. I will soon alter that.

I hated admitting that I was now a physical wreck. I reflected on Sister Allen's words: 'God wants you to live and we want you to live'. It seemed that I was not going to be allowed to die and I could not find a way by myself. I made up my mind that if I was going to be made to live, it had to be on my terms. I had to find a way of life that was worth living.

I took stock of my situation. My body was a write-off, but I had to look for my assets. I had a very strong will, a good mind and a well exercised spirit. I determined to concentrate on reinforcing my mind.

I was having difficulty with my mind. Frequently I found it very hard to speak. I practised exercises from old half-remembered speech-training classes.

This practice helped with the mechanics of speech but I often felt confused and desperate when people came to talk to me. I could listen to them and follow what they were saying but if they asked me a question I sometimes found I could not answer them as I wished. A reply would come into my mind but before I could grasp it and speak, it would dissolve maddeningly as though its words were composed of rapidly disappearing smoke. I imagined I must seem quite stupid but was unable to explain my problem and felt rather ashamed that I could not manage to answer simple questions that should be well within my capability.

Bewilderingly I would reach an oasis of lucidity from time to time from where I could manage to hold a reasonable conversation with myself and others.

Sometimes, by myself, I would begin a train of thought and suddenly realise that I had lost it. I could not catch it again, no matter how hard I tried. I used to tell myself I must concentrate harder. Chunks of school work would pop up into my mind, even bits of French grammar or maths lessons . . . I ignored the complicated stuff and turned my mind to the simple things. I clung to the alphabet to guide me systematically through a simple exercise as if I were a drunken man hanging on to railings to get home.

When I said my prayers, I used the alphabet again and thanked God for Andrew, Brian and Ken. I used to cheat when I reached the letter C and pretended it was K so I could bring in the three most important people in my life – Andrew, Brian and Ken – at the beginning.

I always meant to put things right by putting C in place of K when I came to it, but I never managed to reach that far.

Sometimes I played counting games. Letters and numbers became mind-savers as I emerged from my great fog of fatigue. I never once doubted that all would come clear if only I persevered and did everything I could to help myself.

I desperately longed to read. To see letters and figures on a page in front of me, instead of always in my head.

I mentioned to Taffy how much I missed reading and was overjoyed when he suggested fixing up a transparent bookshelf.

'How would that operate?'

'It would be attached to the lung. Books and newspapers can be placed face down on it so that you can just look up and read.'

'Do the pages turn over?'

'No, it's not mechanical, though we could obtain one that is. It's merely a sheet of perspex to support the reading matter at a comfortable distance from your eyes.'

'I can't keep asking the nurse to turn the pages over, can I? That would be a full-time job. I read so fast.'

He promised, 'We'll all turn the pages for you when we go by. I think we might have a mirror somewhere, too.'

'I don't want to see myself.'

'No, not for looking at yourself. It's for fixing at an angle on one side of the front of the iron-lung so that you can see who is coming or is standing behind you. I'll have a word with Mr Rackham and see what he can produce.'

I felt delighted to think that I was being allowed to read. My idea of heaven was a library in the sky. It would be filled with every book that had ever been written or thought about. I would be able to understand every word and idea so that nothing was hidden from me because of language differences.

When I was whisked into hospital I had just finished reading John Buchan's '*Blanket of the Dark*.' What an expressive title, I thought. How well it describes the darkness in my mind when I had lost my memory. It had been as though a blanket had hidden everything from sight. I felt very grateful that the things in my memory had not been lost permanently, but had been waiting behind the blanket of the dark ready to be revealed again. I had been haunted by the words at the end of the book, 'Where is Bohun? Where is Mowbray?'

I wondered whether the book had been returned to the library and was spreading polio infection. I hoped whoever was reading it did not lick his fingers to turn the pages and so pick up the polio virus. I must remember somehow to ask Ken to see what had happened to my library books and warn the librarian.

How lucky I was to be a bookworm and to have fed on thousands of books in libraries up and down the country. I was musing on the books I had read when Frank Rackham and Ben Smith appeared and set about fixing the mirror and shelf that were to widen my horizons. We experimented with the mirror. Frank stood in different places until Ben could find the best angle and position in which to fix it permanently.

Sister produced a copy of *Reader's Digest* and said, 'When you've finished this one, I've got dozens more in my office.'

Frank opened it and put it on the perspex sheet, moving it higher and higher until we had the best reading position, and Ben screwed the clips in. I had great difficulty in tearing my eyes away from the printed pages to say my thanks and goodbyes. They were both highly amused at my absorption in the magazine.

I said, 'Look what you've found me to read.'

Frank turned the book over to see what he had given me. It was an article about a Swedish woman who had been helped to overcome her disablement by horse-riding.

Frank said, 'Poor Dr Graham. I can see what you'll be asking him to arrange next. You'll want a blooming horse in here.'

Ben added, 'Plenty of room in David Ward, and the kids would love it.'

They chuckled at the vision of the children enjoying therapeutic gallops around the ward. They turned my page over again before they left. I was torn between watching them in my mirror as they walked away and reading the next page in my *Reader's Digest*.

When Ken came that night, I was able to watch him walk towards me. I caught his eye in the mirror and smiled my greeting. He spent the whole evening turning the pages of my books. He hardly had time to keep pushing drinks into me as usual.

Sister kept me supplied with a succession of magazines. They were easy to read but I hated having to ask for my pages to be turned over. Sister and I made a list of books that would not take up too much room in my locker or drive me mad if I had to stare at the same page for some time. The New Testament was a must, so also was my tiny volume of Keats' verse which had prompted my visit to John Keats' grave in Rome. I wished I owned a copy of Helen Waddell's *Heloise and Abelard*. Another Wren had lent me her copy when, as a very new Wren, I had arrived at Western Approaches – just eighteen and unable to appreciate the implications of the book. I should understand them now. A scantily-remembered poem from the flyleaf tormented me. It was something to do with hills and fountains or some such and ended with the line, 'Never of what I loved to have delight. . . .' Perhaps I could find a copy now and reread it.

With the promise of books, my way of life became more like that of the other patients, if only in a limited way. At last I could listen to my records or wireless with someone else's help. Now I would be able to read also. The thought of books and music stimulated a constant flow of ideas. I thought of many other people who had been confined and who had battled their way out of their predicaments. I was surprised how many characters entered my head from time to time to inspire or amuse me.

I imagined Noah cruising along in the Ark with only his immediate family and the animals. I could guess how isolated he felt as he scanned the limitless depths of a worldwide ocean before releasing the raven, never to see it return. I appreciated the contrast of the extreme joy he must have known when he sent out a dove and she came flapping back with an olive branch in her beak.

I remember thinking about the ancient Pharoahs. I recalled standing inside the burial chamber of the Great Pyramid. I had thought how dreadful it would have been to be placed there, not quite dead and unable to get out. It must have been a comfort to know that when you died you were to be disembowelled and embalmed with no chance of being walled-up alive. The same eerie feeling must have struck the original architects of the pyramids, compelling them to include a tiny hole to the outside world, high up in the chamber, so that the spirit could pass in and out.

One day as I watched a tiny spider spinning his web on the front of the lung the family name for spiders, arachnid, popped into my head, triggering off the tale of Arachne who had woven such a beautiful tapestry that she had angered the goddess, Pallas Athene. She was punished by being turned into a spider – thus condemned to weave throughout eternity.

By association Robert Bruce seemed to follow Arachne naturally and I tried to imagine what went on in his mind when he was trapped in a cave, watching a spider as it tried again and again to start weaving its web. Had he thought of Arachne, I wondered. He could not have guessed that years later children would be told stories about him to learn the lesson of his resolve from his words, 'If at first you don't succeed, try, try and try again.' I remembered the book in which we had read about him at infants' school. I could see the picture quite clearly in my mind's eye.

It was in a similar book to the story of Sir Philip Sydney who, when he lay dying from his battle wounds, was brought a drink of water by his servant. Sir Philip had heard another poor soul crying for water and had said to his servant: 'Give it to him. His need is greater than mine.'

Also poor Monsieur Manet, in Charles Dickens' *Tale of Two Cities*, was imprisoned for so many years in the Bastille that all he could remember was his prison number. How easy it was for a brain to deteriorate with no mental stimulus. How depressing! Poor Lucy, to see her father in such a terrible condition. Brave Sydney Carton, going to the guillotine in place of Lucy's husband and saying, 'It is a far, far better thing that I do than I have ever done.'

Gosh, I thought, no wonder I find it so hard to ask for what I need. How vigorously and thoroughly I have been conditioned to be modest, patient, persevering, long-suffering and self-denying. Don't I know any characters who were a bit more human?

With relief I thought of the Count of Monte Cristo and his terrible determination to escape from his unjust imprisonment in the Chateau d'If and exact revenge on his malefactors.

There must have been more happy prisoners who escaped. Ah yes, there was Alexander Selkirk whose story was written by Daniel Defoe and called *Robinson Crusoe*, describing how he survived on his island in complete isolation until he found Man Friday. I had always longed to find myself on such an island and to be challenged by the need to survive by my own resources. I had not reckoned on being isolated without the use of my very capable and agile physical self.

Then there was Scheherazade whose own resourcefulness at story-telling had so spellbound her captor that he had become her prisoner, enmeshed in the threads of her intricate tales of Sinbad the Sailor *et al*. Finally, after 1001 Arabian nights, she had gained her life and her freedom. I wondered what had happened to Scheherazade, after that. Had no one written *What Scheherazade Did Next* or *Son of Scheherazade*? I would have to find out and fill the gap if there was one.

I recalled the children's favourite books. There was *Snow White and the Seven Dwarfs* in which Snow White, despite being poisoned by the crimson apple and contained in a glass casket, was reawakened by the prince's kiss ... weren't they all? Just like Sleeping Beauty in the other little book, with a picture of a fair-haired maiden dozing by her spinning-wheel. Brian and Andrew always pointed to her and called her Mummy, not, I supposed, because she had fair hair but because she had fallen asleep. They used to wake me up every morning. Her prince had to hack his way through high hedges and thorn thickets to snap her back into action.

The next time I am able to read these books to my children, I thought, I will be able to turn the pages myself. We could all cuddle up together on the settee and read and read and read to our hearts' content. I looked forward to that time with great optimism. The pysiotherapist would be coming soon with her skill and knowledge, the keys that would help unlock my imprisoned self and rub away the ache to move.

All the staff turned my pages and helped to keep me occupied. A Scottish nurse, who paused with my book in her hands while turning my page, told me she adored looking after me as she had never had the chance to care for anyone in an iron-lung before. I wondered to myself: Well, how do I answer that? But before I could reply she continued, 'You ought to write a book yourself about your life in the lung.'

I thought of my ten fingers lying useless by my side, their shorthand and typing skills held fast until they could be freed by the physiotherapist. I told the nurse that our move to Newbury was supposed to give me time to write a book and Ken to paint.

The nurse asked, 'What kind of book had you in mind?'

I replied, 'About how simple it is to communicate with people, particularly children, even if you don't speak their language. This struck me when I was in the Mediterranean and discovered, much to my surprise, how much at home I felt with everybody there, especially in Italy where gesticulations speak volumes. I would rather continue chewing over that idea than write about the miseries of hospital life.'

She said she thought the hospital story would be more inspiring.

The words 'inspire' and 'expire' triggered thoughts about the relevance of my present experiences in an iron-lung. With no iron-lung to provide the vital artificial mechanical respiration, people whose breathing failed, inevitably died. They expired. Strange that the word expire should mean to breathe out for the last time. To die, in fact, as well as to breathe out just one more time in all the millions of times that a person may expect to breathe out in a lifetime.

Odd that inspire should mean to breathe in as well as to infuse thought or feeling, especially of divine or supernatural agency. It was inspiring to reflect that my iron-lung inspired me. I was grateful for the inspiration that had enabled the inventor to create the iron-lung. Had he not been inspired, then I could not be inspired physically by his invention now, or further inspired mentally and spiritually by the people and books around me. But there was more. Had electricity not been discovered and the necessary inspiration led to its harnessing and distribution, my iron-lung would not be inspiring me now.

I dragged my mind away from its preoccupation with the words 'inspire' and 'expire' and tried to concentrate on what the nurse was saying. She said, 'I think a book about being in an iron-lung would teach other nurses things they wanted to know if they were going to nurse patients in lungs. I could not find any books in the library written by people in iron-lungs and I can only guess how it feels to be totally enclosed up to your neck in a box and unable to move or sit up.'

'Are there any other iron-lungs here?' I asked her.

'Yes, there is a spare one at the end of the ward,' she answered.

'Why don't you try it?' I suggested.

'I have', she replied, 'I climbed into it the other night and I didn't like it one bit, especially when it was fastened down and I knew I could not get out of it by myself. I knew it was only temporary, of course, and I could not really tell what it was like to *have* to live in a lung day after day.'

'I know what you mean'. I said. 'Just before I had polio I helped collect money for blind people and became very involved. I used to shut my eyes tightly as if I had suddenly lost my sight and feel my way from room to room. But I didn't dare keep my eyes shut when I went out of the house. As soon as I was outside the front-door, I just had to open my eyes and I remember thinking: Thank God I can see. It must be dreadful to be permanently blind.'

She answered honestly, 'Yes, pretending to be handicapped cannot be the same as the actual experience.'

'I expect someone some day will write about being in an iron-lung,' I said, 'but it will have to be someone more clever than I am. I don't think I could write such a story as I can't think how to keep the story moving when all I do is lie still all day.'

'But,' she said, 'how do you feel about it? You must have feelings.'

78

'I can't afford to think about my feelings very much. If I wrote a book I'd write the first page, setting the scene and saying how the days just went on and on and on. Just as the time must seem to go on and on for whoever is specialling me. I think I'd use the same three words 'on and on' over and over again for a hundred pages, just to show how the unrelenting stillness goes on and on and on and on and on.'

'You must put that in,' the nurse exclaimed.

'I'll see.' I smiled back at her, grateful to see that she was at last turning the page, ready to put the book back on the transparent shelf where I could read someone else's words for inspiration.

Chapter 10
Realisation

Sister, in her wisdom, introduced me to the people on the new ward only gradually. This helped to establish some sense of security and blocked my fears.

Not all faces were new. Taffy, true to his word, seemed always there. Dr Harris visited twice a day or whenever Taffy called him. Dr Harris still came in twice-weekly.

The first time I experienced coming out of the iron-lung on the new ward I was a bit apprehensive, to put it mildly. It was so easy to stifle or hurt me. But I need not have worried. Taffy and Mr Rackham took over my breathing and I listened gratefully to Taffy's singing and humming quietly behind me. Sister and her team carefully and painlessly carried out my treatment.

Although my arms and body behaved as if they did not belong to me, Sister turned me from side to side expertly. She rubbed and restored the circulation to my skin and pushed and shook my chest with her cupped hands so that no secretions could collect and lurk where they should not, to harbour infection. All my itches and worries were soothed and smoothed away.

Tranquillity restored, the trolley with me on it was slotted back into the iron-lung, the hatch pulled down and sealed around my neck with the rubber collar. The locks would be fastened and as the iron-lung motor was switched on again the familiar whoosh-shoosh of the iron-lung announced that it had taken over once more the job of inspiring me and the positive pressure mask was removed from my face. The nurse would be left alone with me until the next out-of-the lung session.

To avoid the fragmentation of being nursed by too many different nurses, I was cared for mainly by two staff nurses who came on duty in the day-time only and stayed for most of each day. One was Eileen and the other was Ruth, who was German – fair-haired and blue-eyed. Ruth could have been my sister. As she spoke of her childhood, roller-skating around Berlin, I thought of my own London childhood where we were taught in school to hate the German enemy. How strange that Ruth was now caring for me.

A nurse who had worked at an ophthalmic hospital took care of my eyes with great gentleness. She removed the lashes and other debris which fell into them and floated about irritatingly, making me feel very helpless indeed. It had not occurred to me before but once again I was reminded of the appropriate design of our physical selves. It had been much easier to stop things falling into my eyes when I had been upright or able to lean forward normally.

One day she saw another nurse rubbing my eyes vigorously to remove the sleepy-dust from the corners. She warned, 'Our Ophthalmic Specialist said you should never touch your eyes except with your elbow', meaning that you should wipe them with the greatest care as they are irreplaceable and much too valuable to be poked into thoughtlessly.

As my confidence grew, my sense of well-being improved. I began to feel more normal. Although I was not generally allowed any visitors other than Ken because I was so vulnerable to infection, a particular visitor was allowed in for a few moments one day. She was a young woman who had suffered from polio herself and had called in at the hospital for her check-up. She had very kindly come along to encourage me. She was perfectly sound in wind and limb except for her arms which she could use in every way except one. As she demonstrated, she could not raise her arms above her head and so could not stretch them up to hang the washing on the line or reach for anything above shoulder-height. She thought she was very lucky to have gained such freedom.

I really did not know what to say to her as she was so proud of her achievement. It seemed incredible that if she could do so much she could not manage to try just a little bit harder and get her arm right up. I was assuming quite unconsciously that I should attain perfect recovery and so should she. I felt sorry for her. I thought she must have some sort of fixation about her condition and could not throw off her last limitation. I was still denying my disability as a permanent state. Seeing myself and others pass through different phases of helplessness I assumed we all had the potential of becoming perfectly fit again.

One day Taffy arrived with two physiotherapists, Miss Clark and Miss Crabtree. I was very keen to start some disciplined exercises to get me home, perhaps for Christmas or at least the New Year.

Not having experienced physiotherapy before, I did not know what to expect. I shall never forget my long-awaited first session.

Miss Clark lifted my right arm up straight, supporting it at the wrist and elbow. I looked up at her hands as she raised her arms and observed her holding this skeleton arm. I could see its bones – the humerus, ulna and radius – quite clearly through its tightly stretched skin. There was no other covering, no muscle, no fat, just the bare bones of an arm that would have been a gift to anyone studying anatomy. I saw the claws on the hand. They looked like the talons on the end of a chicken's foot. The fingernails were humped and brown. Their overgrown ends curled completely over the tips of the fingers. The chicken-foot hand was covered with brown scales.

Suddenly I realised with horror that it was *my* hand and *my* arm up there, being supported by Miss Clark. My blood froze. It must be a dream. A nightmare! Some dreadful spell had been cast. I had been turned into a repellent reptile or a witch from the pages of *Macbeth* or some other obscene outcast, no longer fit to care for my children or anyone else.

Because I was always lying flat and could not see myself, I began to imagine what the rest of me must look like. I supposed my left arm to be equally repulsive. I expected my neck, trunk and legs to be cadaverous too.

For the first time I realised that when I was lying in the iron-lung I had no clothes on nor any bedcovers and that the people who came up and looked in at me through the portholes could see this stark ugliness.

I wanted to run away and hide.

When Sister came to talk to me, I did not know what to say to her. I had been so shocked at the appearance of my wizened arm and hand that I could hardly talk to anyone. She said that she wanted to start to build up my diet and that she would get me anything I liked. I had only to name my favourite food and she would cook it with her own hands.

The thought of putting flesh on my newly-exposed bones to cover them was enough motivation for me to say, 'Could I have some bacon and eggs for lunch please?'

She was delighted, and was soon shovelling a small portion of bacon and egg into me. Fortunately, this proved to be something that could slip down easily.

When Ken came that evening I asked him, 'Why didn't you tell me I was so horribly emaciated? How could you bear to keep coming here? How could you bring yourself to look at me or touch me while I am like this? How could you kiss me? How could you leave me uncovered so everyone knows how disgusting I am?'

Ken said, 'You've been very ill. Everyone here understands. Don't upset yourself. Now you're getting better you need all your strength for your physio.'

'How can I put my mind to physiotherapy when I look so appalling? Can't you cover me up with something?'

'I'll ask Sister,' he said and handed me over to Eileen who had just come into the ward with a plate of mince.

'Will you have mince, chicken or fish?' she asked.

'Whatever you say,' I answered, thinking that I could only put flesh on my bones if I managed to swallow more.

'I think the mince looks the most interesting dish tonight. It made me feel quite hungry and you'll be lucky if I don't absentmindedly start tucking into it myself while I'm feeding you,' she said.

I caught her eyes in the mirror and asked her, 'Why didn't you tell me I was skinny like this?'

'I didn't realise you didn't know,' she replied.

When I had gone down with pneumonia, Eileen had been on a rare weekend off. She had gone home on the Friday when I had been very cheerful, talking about physiotherapy and how important it was to get moving again. Returning on the Monday she too had seen the empty iron-lung and, like Ken, had been filled with fear for me. She had been shocked and horrified when she found me in the side ward. She had never seen anyone go down so rapidly. She used to go home and have a good cry.

Of course she did not tell me this just then. Instead she forked minced meat into my mouth and said brightly, 'I see your friend has sent you some more Newberry Fruits. Have you started them yet?'

'No,' I replied, trying to be as bright as she was being. 'You'd better help yourself and keep your mind off my minced beef.'

'Oh thanks, I'm starving,' she said opening the box.

'Don't eat the orange or raspberry ones,' I insisted. 'They are for me.' Ken came back with Sister then and Eileen swallowed her sweet quickly.

Sister said, 'I don't know what to give you to wear but I thought I'd make you a vest of Thermogene wadding. Do you think that's a good idea?'

'I'd wear a hair shirt if I had to. Anything to cover me up.'

She pushed the Thermogene through the porthole and covered my chest with it.

'How far down does it come?' I asked.

'Waist-level,' said Sister cheerfully.

'What about the rest of me?' I asked.

They looked at one another, knowing that any proper clothes would be difficult to put on me and the creases would quickly make me sore. I did not know about the difficulties so I asked Ken to bring me some knickers.

Before he left I decided that I must overcome my diffidence and have a look at my face. After the shock of seeing my bones I dreaded the thought that my hair might be white and my face deeply marked with suffering as all the novels would have it. And no one would have thought to have told me. I asked Ken to turn the mirror so that I could see my face.

He altered the mirror without saying anything and watched me as I looked back into my face. I did not recognise it. I found myself looking at a stranger and thinking, 'That must be my face so I ought to recognise it. I don't remember looking like that before but then I don't remember how I looked before anyway. I found that my mind could not fasten on any details that were very different. My hair was slightly darker than I imagined it would be and greasy through not being washed for a couple of months. My skin was dry and very white, making my hair seem slightly red against it. My eyes looked back at me without any sign of recognition and I was surprised to see that they did not have any lines etched around them or any signs of suffering as I had supposed.

'That's enough,' I said to Ken, 'I don't want to see any more. But I think I should have some lipstick on to brighten up my face a bit.'

Ken found my lipstick in my bag. He said, 'I'm not sure that I'm going to be very good at this,' as he started to apply the lipstick to my upper lip.

I did not believe him as I had watched him painting with his very sure touch on many a canvas. I merely said, 'Don't forget to try to cover up that snick in my lip where the nurse cut me.'

'I'll do my best,' he said as he completed his task. He turned the mirror towards me once more, 'Will that do?' he asked.

'Thanks, I couldn't have done it better myself,' I said. 'But please turn the mirror back now. I've seen enough.'

Ken said, 'Try not to worry about it. We'll soon fatten you up. Get all the sleep you can so you can benefit from the physiotherapy sessions now that they've finally started.'

After the first shock of seeing my arm I stopped thinking of it as being repellent and thought about it only as it would be when my food began to fatten me again. I could not swallow bread or potatoes at all as they seemed to be the stickiest foods I was offered.

The physiotherapists came twice daily for ten minutes at a time.

They were very kind indeed and found me an oblong papier-mâché bath that could accommodate one arm at a time so that the warmth of the water made it easier for the physiotherapists to bend my arm at the elbow and wrist.

This repeated soaking gradually stripped the layers of dead skin from my hands and fingers and my nails were kept short. I discovered that we all grow extra protective skin very rapidly on our hands but we wear it away constantly when our hands are in use. When our hands are stilled the layers of skin keep growing. I would never have thought about this had my own layers of skin not continued to grow and split into scales. I was constantly being reminded how well designed we are and how provision is made by nature to compensate for wear and tear without our having one conscious thought about it.

The physiotherapists also put their hands by the side of my chest just above waist-level. They manually pushed the breath out of my chest to empty my lungs as much as possible between the mask-given breaths. They would help to make a coughing spasm in my chest by shaking my ribs with their hands as they breathed me out.

I realised that most of my movements, although out of my control, were not beyond the scope of other people's hands. With help my fingers could be separated and bent and so on. My arms could not be rotated as they had become locked with my palms face-down. I could move my legs apart but could not bring them together again. I could bend my knees but not lift my legs up. Finally I discovered that the more I could keep my legs bent the less out of breath I became.

I wondered whether to try to learn more about my own muscles to help my recovery but decided against it. I knew quite sufficient about my skeleton and the various systems of my body. To go into any more detail would almost certainly ensure a state of chronic hypochondria. Even so, my mind dwelt on my physical self and was able to see it in a more detached way now that it could not move itself about. I had to think about the actions it could not perform. If I did not think about it and obtain the help that was needed, the part that required attention did not always get it. People are not generally psychic.

I found it easier to separate the entities of mind, body and spirit and had a revelatory impression that each and every one of us is a blessed trinity, a three in one, a body, mind and spirit closely combined. As my weight was about four and a half stone, I thought about the little amount of the earth's resources that was sparsely contained in my skin. I was intensely aware of my oneness with the whole of creation, because somewhere half my molecules were being absorbed by other living entities. Eventually I would almost double my weight again from unknown atoms that were at this moment directed towards me from around the world. In water from everywhere; bananas from Africa; oranges from Spain; apples from Tasmania; peaches from California and so on. I felt very humble about my place in the scheme of things, about the food I was being fed and the things that were being done to keep me alive.

Now that I was permanently stilled, I became very aware of the movements of other things. I felt like a train that had been shunted into a siding. Before I had polio, when I had travelled in a train and gazed out of the window it had seemed as though streets and houses had sped by, but when the train had stopped at a station, it became obvious that the buildings had not been moving at all. I had been flying past them in the train. Now that I had stopped, I could see time in a different way. Time did not seem to fly by. Instead, in stillness, I was aware of moving through time.

I realised that I could alter the nature of time if I kept myself occupied. I found I seemed to get through the day more quickly than if I had not made the effort but had allowed time to hang on my hands until the high spot of each day – visiting-time.

Ken's visits were magical. My time with him seemed enchanted. He would arrive every night and play our records. Usually he was humming 'Stranger in Paradise', the theme song from *Kismet*. It was on everybody's lips. Taffy incorprated it in his musical repertoire for when he was sitting by my head holding the mask in place. Taffy mentioned that he preferred Borodin's *Polovtzian Dances* in the original.

In the midst of these valiant people, who had risked life and limb in the absence of any polio immunisation. I began to realise my potential. I wished I could find a way in which I could tell the world the story of these unsung heroes and heroines who, with the strangers who were entrusted to their care, created a kind of spiritual paradise in which deeply-damaged minds and bodies were given the very best possible chance to mend.

Chapter 11
Celebration

As Christmas approached, a feeling of hope and festivity began to gather in the ward. The nurses told me that the patients were being kept busy making almond and cherry blossom as all the wards had a competition at Christmas to see which one had the best decorations. Ours was to be a Japanese garden.

No one in his right mind would want to spend Christmas as a patient in hospital but no one could help joining in the spirit of things when the hospital staff took such great pains to celebrate Christmas joyfully. The atmosphere on the ward by the time Christmas Eve arrived was one of anticipation and excitement.

Nurses who had been shopping for a variety of items for the patients smuggled them in and joined in the conspiracy of getting them wrapped and labelled. Christmas cards arrived through the post in shoals and the sound of chatter arose as memories of old friends and other Christmases were recalled.

Everyone on two legs and with two good arms was recruited to collect long twigs and branches from the park. Patients were conscripted to transform these bits of trees into boughs full of almond blossom and cherry blossom with pink-and-white crêpe paper. Those who preferred could make lanterns.

Staff and patients alike sang snatches of carols. It was all excellent occupational therapy and the thoughts of our aches and pains hardly had a moment to themselves as the glory that was Christmas began to shine around.

Even Mr Rackham took a rare afternoon off. As so many patients had been discharged and my new routine on Elizabeth Ward seemed to be settled, he set off to see his local football team playing at home.

We were all particularly happy to know that a young woman who had been admitted a few weeks earlier with multiple sclerosis was going home for Christmas. This made it matter less that the rest of us could not make it. Of course we were all sad about that, but we managed to squash thoughts of our own frustrated longings into the backs of our minds and give precedence to the happiness we felt that at least one of us would be home for Christmas.

This patient had endured a trying time for several years. Sometimes she was fit and well for months on end and then quite suddenly she would be assailed by a terrible weakness. When it happened, she could not get out of bed. If she tried to pick up anything she dropped it. She would then go into hospital and after treatment would gain a remission which enabled her gradually to pick up the threads of her life again. As she walked through the ward everyone called out 'Happy Christmas.' Their greetings carried a very special wish for her and a dream of their own home-going. As she left my ward the door stayed open and a crescendo of sound wafted through. I could hear the Christmas jollifications and preparation. Then, just as the excitement and activity reached fever-pitch, there was a disturbance in the ward that caused more than the usual pain-in-the-heart concern for another poor victim. A young woman who had attempted suicide was rushed in.

Poor Mr Rackham had not been at the football ground long when he was paged on the Tannoy system. He jumped on his motorbike and raced back to the hospital where he grabbed his emergency case full of life-saving equipment. Then he and the flying squad rushed off, to return very quickly with the young woman. Now a policewoman sat by her bed as a suicide attempt was then a criminal offence.

The presence in the ward of a young woman who had been desperate to die was very disturbing. My own intense longing for death was still in my mind. I could not bear to think that some poor soul was rejecting life although in full possession of arms, legs and so on and able to breathe and fight back if anyone tried to inflict physical pain on her.

I thought if only I could make her see what tremendous treasures she had in her possession perhaps she would feel better. I could not go to her. Feeling useless, I asked Sister, 'Will she live?'

She answered, 'She will now.'

'She must have been very unhappy indeed,' I said.

'Christmas is awful for some people. They have no one to love or love them and suddenly the sight of everyone else being happy together is too much.'

I continued thinking of the young woman with arms and legs that she could move which seemed worthless to her. I thought of myself, useless and causing much trouble to those I loved and who loved me.

Then another patient was admitted in a hurry. She was a very large elderly woman who had suddenly become paralysed, though nobody knew why. She was put into an iron-lung with great difficulty as the lung could hardly contain her. She had no chance of survival. Her weight was against her. She was especially distressed because she was not allowed to wear her false teeth in an iron-lung.

When Ken came, he soon discerned the gloom that overhung the ward, despite its abundance of coloured lights, lanterns and decorations.

'I haven't sent Brian his present,' he said. 'If it is all right with you I would like to go to Mum's on Boxing Night after I've been to see you in the afternoon. I'm taking Andrew with me and I'll give them both their main presents at the same time. I've brought them a cowboy outfit each – hats, holsters, jackets and scarves – I'll take some photos of them.'

He had brought my presents – all neatly wrapped – and left them in my locker as he would be back to tea on Christmas Day with me and would open them for me then.

I said to Ken, 'I can't bear the thought of you, Brian, Andrew and myself all living in different places at Christmas. I've decided to divorce you. Make a clean break, then something will have to be done to get you, Brian and Andrew back together again where you belong.'

'Don't be daft,' Ken said. 'We married for better or worse. Life has its ups and downs and if it's worse now, then it must get better soon.'

'I'm serious. The longer our children are parted, the harder it's going to be for them.'

'Don't talk about it now. I expect you're tired and it's very depressing to have two very ill patients admitted, especially as one is suicidal.'

I persisted, 'Don't you see, I must divorce you. It's the best Christmas present Brian and Andrew could ever have. This Christmas must be the last that they are separated. From now on, they must spend every day together, as other brothers do.'

'You could be home yourself for next Christmas.'

'I'm not so sure. What if I get pneumonia again and again? It's best to make the break now.'

'I disagree. This isn't much of a Christmas present for me, you know.'

'It is, if only you can see it. You would be free to marry again.'

'I don't want to marry again. I married you. We're staying married and I want no more talk of divorce. I've brought you a record, so you can listen to this instead. You can hear some carols on Christmas Eve as you can't open your presents when you wake up.'

He put the record on and there was dear old Bing Crosby crooning 'Silent Night' and 'Oh Come All Ye Faithful'.

'Why must you make my life so hard?' I said. 'I don't want to fight you at Christmas. I won't, but if I'm not home for next Christmas, that's it.'

'That's better. You'll see things in a different light later. I must go now and put a few knick-knacks in Andrew's stocking. He'll be awake at the crack of dawn, looking for it.'

When he had gone, I wept. But not for long. When you are lying face-up and unable to turn your head left or right, weeping means that your tears run down the side of your face from the outer corners of your eyes and into your ears, where the salt stings and you cannot wipe it away. Everyone who comes along can see that you have been crying. There is no private life in a hospital, no matter how long the stay becomes nor how many times your spouse comes to see you.

Sister was right. Christmas could be too much for some, not only for those who felt they were unloved but also in spite of or even because of the privilege of being much loved.

When I woke up on Christmas morning, a nurse was standing behind my iron-lung with a lovely little boy in her arms. He was wearing a red dressing-gown. We all grinned at one another and the nurse made a game of dodging the child backwards and forwards so that he and I could glimpse each other in the mirror and play peep-bo.

The nurse ruffled his curls and said: 'This is John. He won't be seeing his mummy today. As you won't be seeing your little boys either, I thought the two of you should get together on Christmas morning. Say bye-bye. We mustn't stop. I shall be in the most dreadful trouble if I'm caught.' She picked up a blanket and said to little Johnny, 'You're going to be Christmas parcel again.' She wrapped him up, plonked another blanket on top of him and hurried from the ward.

As the nurse disappeared with her precious bundle I thought of the living gift wrapped in the blankets, wondering how his mother felt without him. I thought of his little life and how glad his mother would be that he looked so well. I felt sure she would have given anything to have suffered instead of him. I was so thankful it was me in the lung and not Brian or Andrew. They would not have stood a chance with such a dose of polio.

That Roman Catholic doctor had been right. Life is a precious gift no matter how hard it becomes. Without life we could never ever get back to our nearest and dearest. We would be as helpless to reach them as a moth trying to get into a well-lit room through a closed window.

But I wanted to see Brian and Andrew's eyes grow large as they helped me to dress the tree and put up the decorations around our house. I wanted to help blow up balloons and fill all the corners and doorways with mistletoe and holly.

I wanted to be wrapping their presents myself, filling their stockings with nuts, tangerines and little gifts, watching their faces on Christmas morning when they dashed into our bedroom and hauled everything on to our bed with an urgent 'Look what Father Christmas has brought' as though we had never seen any of it before.

I wanted them to enjoy *my* mince-pies, *my* snow-laden cake. I wanted to pull their Christmas crackers with them as we sat side by side in front of a log fire. I wanted to take them to church for the Christmas service as usual. I kept telling myself, *It doesn't matter. They'll have a lovely time and hardly miss you. Ken will see to that.* But I felt full of rebellion and had to battle for a grip on my emotions.

I thought about the Holy stable family – Joseph, Mary and Jesus – who were the focus of Christmas. I turned my mind back two thousand years in imagination to hear Mary telling Jesus that God was his father. I remembered teaching my own children to pray to God their Father, using the very words 'Our Father' to begin their prayers, as many Christian mothers down the ages and around the world had done. My mind travelled back to the shock of seeing Michelangelo's Pieta in St Peter's in Rome for the first time. The poetry of grief on Mary's face as she held the broken body of her son had haunted me ever since.

I watched in my mirror as Miss Holly, the Matron of Prospect Park and Miss Aldwinkle, the senior Matron of the Reading Group of Hospitals, walked towards my iron-lung. Miss Aldwinkle had as a nurse cared for Douglas Bader. Tears of weakness were streaming down the sides of my face and into my ears. I could not reach my handkerchief to wipe my eyes so I apologised and said, 'I'm not crying really. It's only weakness. It happens now and then.'

She said, 'Oh my dear, don't apologise. If I were in your situation I would cry all the time.'

Her honesty lifted my spirits. As the two Matrons left, my tears flowed freely. I felt completely overwhelmed with longing for the sight of my children.

After my Christmas morning nursing routine I was dolled up and pushed into the small ward so that the special lay visitors – the Mayor and Corporation, the hospital managers and so on – could pop in to see me during their Christmas rounds. My hair was brushed and arranged in a bun on the top of my head, Japanese-style, with bits of blossom pinned around it. Boughs of blossom had been fixed to the iron-lung and a name-plate which Ken had made with bamboo-type letters spelled out 'Lotus Wun Lung'.

The Mayor of Reading came up to my iron-lung with his entourage and bent down to look at me eye-to-eye in my mirror. He said, 'Dear, dear, dear. What a fix to be in at Christmas-time.'

I reassured him, 'It's only temporary. I'll be up and about by next Christmas.'

'Is that so?' he asked. 'I'm glad to hear that. I wish you as happy a time as possible this year.'

He continued on his way.

The next event of the day was Christmas dinner with a doctor dressed as Father Christmas slicing the turkey. Sister said, 'I'm going to serve your Christmas dinner with a little bit of everything except potatoes. Do eat as much turkey as you can manage – it's so nourishing – but I wouldn't advise you to have sherry or any other intoxicating drink as it might not agree with you in your condition.'

'Don't worry. I'm quite capable of being inebriated on my own high spirits.'

Eileen fed me and we toasted our absent friends with a glass of Lucozade each. I thought that Eileen should be at home with her husband and little Jennifer but she told me that it was hospital tradition for all the staff to come on duty on Christmas day. Because everyone did it, nobody minded.

After lunch and the usual routines, Eileen began to read *Reader's Digests* to me as a Christmas treat for half an hour. It was so much better than having a book on the perspex shelf and having to wait for the pages to be turned. We became so absorbed in our reading that we were surprised when it was suddenly tea-time and visitors began to arrive in time for tea with the patients.

Usually the hospital had a party and concert for visitors but so many patients had been admitted that the staff were frantically busy and no entertainment was possible that year. Instead, visitors came for extended hours and to tea on Christmas and Boxing Days.

When Ken came he told me how Andrew was enjoying his Christmas. Then he helped Eileen push my lung to the doorway of the big ward. Dr Harris walked over to Eileen and said, 'Don't bring the lung too far into the doorway. The risk of infection to her is too great.'

Too many visitors had been coming backwards and forwards into the ward, all of them automatically stopping to speak to me out of the kindness of their hearts. Eileen felt dreadful and immediately said to Ken, 'Let's push the lung back a bit. I'd never forgive myself if anything happens through my fault.'

Dr Harris looked at me and noticed that my face had been made up for the first time. 'Very pretty,' he commented and then added to Eileen, 'This make-up is not a good idea. It would conceal signs of her becoming cyanosed.' Eileen looked at me, nodding her head in agreement with Dr Harris. She said that she would keep a special eye on me.

Now that I realised that my lips turned blue from time to time, I was very anxious to cover them up for vanity's sake and to begin to wear lipstick again. It would be a sign to those around me that I was better enough to care what I looked like, even if I could not do very much about it.

After my lung was pushed further back into the side ward, my mirror was arranged so I could see into the big ward. The patients there called out to me 'Happy Christmas' or some such message. In the side ward Ken hung our Christmas cards in strips down the wall – hundreds of them, not only from our families and friends but also from people I did not know.

He began to open my presents for me. He had brought me a small musical box which tinkled out 'Moonlight and Roses'. I had several scarves, including one from the hospital staff, tins of talc and tablets of soap as well as two copies of Paul Gallico's *The Snow Goose* and a box of Newberry Fruits from Eileen.

By the time Night Sister arrived, I was thoroughly tired and ready for sleep. Ken had just left, after reminding me that he would be calling in briefly on Boxing Day as his father was coming to fetch him and Andrew. Sister said, 'Ken told me you were depressed last night but you look your old self now. You've forgotten about divorcing him, haven't you?'

'Did he tell you about that?'

'Yes, he wondered where the idea came from. I told him that it wasn't from me.'

'No, I'm the guilty one.'

'It might seem a good idea to you, but he'll never part from you. He cares for you too deeply.'

'That makes it a thousand times worse.'

'Your divorce idea makes life harder for him too. Do you know that he asked if he could give you the motor nerves of one of his arms?'

'I didn't know, but it wouldn't surprise me. It sounds like him. Don't let him do it.'

'It's not possible, although he meant it.'

'Yes, he would. He means what he says.'

'Not many men would make such an offer.'

'I know. But don't you think he deserves his freedom?'

'He doesn't want it.'

'But he needs it.'

She looked around the room. 'What a selection of Christmas cards. May I look at them?'

'Yes, please do. You may know the people who sent some of them. I don't know all the signatures.'

'There are no two cards alike.'

'No, no two cards alike but I've had two copies of *The Snow Goose*. Would you like to borrow one?'

'I mustn't read it before you do. If there's time later perhaps I could read you a page or two.'

The night brigade arrived and carried out my settling-down routine.

The pavilions were creaky places and at night, when things were quiet, floorboards squeaked and evoked Christmas ghosts of old-time nurses back from the Crimea, carrying their lamps through eternity. As I drifted off to sleep, memories of other Christmases stirred in my mind – Christmas dances, pretty dresses, lively music and happy chatter haunted me from the past. Suddenly I longed so intensely to be dancing in Ken's arms again that in my imagination I ran out of the lung and Ken and I were dancing. Filled with great happiness, I fell fast asleep.

I was lucky to wake up at all on Boxing Day. The minute I became conscious I was aware of a very strong smell of gas. Sister was sitting by the side of my face writing her report. The gas had seeped into the side ward gradually and she had not been so aware of it as I was when I woke up suddenly. But at the same moment that I noticed it, she smelt it too. She looked at me and we both chorused the same word, 'Gas'.

She leant over and said, 'I'll just get someone to stay with you and go to find out what is happening.'

She called a nurse in from the ward and hurried into the kitchen. As Sister went through the kitchen door she saw a woman patient standing by the gas stove. There was a kettle on the stove but the gas had not been lit. The gas was hissing from the jets as the tap was turned full on. As Sister hurried across the kitchen towards the patient she called out, 'What are you doing?'

The patient replied, 'I'm waiting for the kettle to boil. I'm going to make the tea.'

'The water won't boil like that.'

'But I've turned the gas on.'

Sister stretched out her hand and turned the tap off quickly. 'Gas can't boil water unless it's lit.'

'Oh, I'll light it then.'

The patient picked up the matches but Sister swiftly took them from her. 'You mustn't strike a match now. You'll blow us all up. Come and help me to open the windows quickly.'

'But I have to make the tea.'

'Come along. Open all the windows at once.'

They threw all the windows wide open to clear the air.

Sister asked, 'Have you ever made tea before?'

'Yes, lots of times.'

'Well, how did you get the water to boil if you didn't light the gas?'

'Oh, we've got electricity at home. All you do is switch it on and wait.'

Although the incident with the unlit gas was hair-raising at the time, I stored it up as a good story to tell Ken at visiting-time.

As Ken was not coming to see me for very long on Boxing Day one of the patients was allowed to visit as well. She was suffering from an over-active thyroid. She was almost as skinny as I was and we both had a battle to put weight on. She was very affectionate and said the most extravagant things for one stranger to say to another. She kept kissing me on my forehead as though I were a long-lost friend and saying, 'We all love you so very much. I'm so glad that I can come in to see you.'

From then on the nurses used me as an encouragement to this patient to eat more. They would tell her that I had eaten steak and chips, treacle pudding and all sorts of other unlikely comestibles to try to stimulate her appetite and to get her to eat far more food than she wanted. She was frequently weighed and was often almost in despair as she put on less weight than a baby. The procedure reminded me of babies in maternity hospitals being weighed and tut-tutted over if they could not gain enough weight to be able to go home. She was not allowed to leave hospital until she had gained several more pounds.

I asked her about the other patients in the ward. I had heard about quite a few of them. She told me about the one with an incurable skin complaint who had been in and out of hospital for years. She was never cured. Sometimes her condition was a little better, sometimes a little worse. I thought it must be maddening for her and exasperating for the specialist.

The patient I worried about most of all was an old lady who had been widowed and did not want to live. She loved oranges, but because of her condition was forbidden to have them. She used to creep out of bed at night and help herself to the other patients' fruit, and eat them in the lavatory. Unfortunately, as oranges have such a distinctive smell she was always discovered.

Eventually, when it was obvious that repeated warnings were not going to stop her from stealing the oranges, sides were put on her bed. When she clambered over those, she was restrained at night. When she refused to eat, a tube was passed into her stomach. She pulled it out, so then her hands were tied down. She then bit on the tube so that no nourishment could pass. I must confess that I was very relieved when she died as I thought the whole process inhuman. I could see that the nurses were dealing with the situation in the best way they could according to their professional beliefs. But I felt very deeply for the poor old woman who did not want to live. I longed to be able to give her a box of oranges so that she could die happy.

Suddenly my new friend stopped talking to me about the other patients in the ward and said, 'Here comes your nurse. I'll be going now. Oh look! Sister has got Mr Rackham to take the fairy doll from the top of the Christmas tree. She is giving it to your nurse for her little girl Jennifer.'

Eileen came in to our ward with the doll clutched in her hands, her eyes shining with pleasure as though she was a little girl again herself. 'Isn't Sister kind to give me the fairy doll? Jennifer will be so pleased. It will be a lovely surprise to take home to her.'

Her joy was infectious. When Ken arrived later, he gave me the long-awaited first-hand news of the children. Dad had driven down with Mum and Brian and picked up Ken and Andrew. Both boys had written little letters which they had sent me with some soap and a beautiful bouquet of freesias which must have cost a fortune.

Mum had asked to bring them in to see me, but of course that could not be allowed so Mum and Dad took the children to look for squirrels in Prospect Park while Ken spent his brief visit with me. My emotions were very difficult to sort out as I thought of my children, whom I had not seen for months and might not see for some time yet, running about on the grass on the other side of the wall. I wondered how Brian and Andrew felt, knowing I was so near and yet so far.

Chapter 12
Resolution

With Christmas over, I put my mind to looking forward as usual to the New Year, determined that 1956 would be my year. I would go home again and reunite the children with us. We would make a new start as a family. We had already lost nearly three months. I could not afford to take too much time to get better now. Of course, it was only the pneumonia that had held me back. Now, with my increasing appetite for food and the prospect of physio-therapy, I felt I could tackle the world again. I would go rapidly from strength to strength. I began my stock-taking.

My mind was my most insoluble problem. I was intensely aware of everything but I frequently lacked concentration. I just had to go over and over everything, exercising my memory, trying to speak more fluently and to find the right words for my tongue to express instead of faltering and fishing around as I so often did in my weak condition. I had learned valuable lessons and realised how lucky I was not to be also mentally handicapped or blind and deaf. I had so much locked away inside me. My memories, my skills, my potential. I could not afford to be upset about anything. I could not risk spending one more day than I had to away from my children.

How differently 1955 had begun! Was it really only a year ago? Then, as an active and able family, we had been looking forward to the best of both worlds. We intended moving away from our London roots to live in the country. We could then travel back to London from time to time to catch up on family news or to go shopping or to the theatre. We already grew our own fruit and vegetables in our London garden and on our allotment. I had become proficient at planting and preserving and looked forward to extending my repertoire. We grew sweetcorn in the garden and I took great pride in losing none of its flavour between picking and serving. I would put a saucepan of salted water on to boil while I went into the garden to cut cobs of corn. On the way back indoors, I stripped them of their leaves and tassels, ready to drop them into the waiting water before they knew they had been picked. I harvested my crops while they were young and tender and had that delicate flavour that is so soon lost. I made almost a religion of feeding my family on fresh fruit, vegetables and salads. I could not think how I had succumbed to polio. We were surely the fittest family for miles. Whoever would have thought that moving into the countryside would paradoxically reduce me in ability and vitality?

It was no use dwelling on the promises of 1955 that had not materialised. 1956 would obviously bring problems of its own. My recovery had been so incredibly slow that I must take stock frequently concerning my condition and potential if I were to find a way to regain my grip on life by 1957.

Different resolutions were called for this year and they must all be directed to the same end: that of satisfying the terrible obsession to bring my family together under its own roof once more.

Had I the use of even one hand, I could start to plan and make notes for my book. When my fingers tired of writing, I could use my good hand to massage the other hand into use. If I could regain the use of my hands, arms and shoulders, I would be able to do so many different things – simple pastimes such as knitting and sewing for the children, writing little letters to them, drawing funny stories with matchstick men and so on. But it was no use looking so far into the future until the practical problem of coaxing even a flicker from any one finger had been solved.

I worked desperately at trying to call up some response from the fingers that I could not see. In my head I kept going through the old touch-typing sentences, *The quick brown fox jumps over the lazy dog* – a sentence which uses every letter of the alphabet. I felt that there should be an automatic response at least of a little feeling at the end of each finger as the letter which it should instinctively move to type became necessary, but of course I could not move my fingers at all, let alone automatically. Instead of being able to ghost-type by instinct, I had to spell out all the words, letter by letter, to try to establish the connection between brain and invisible fingers somewhere inside the iron-lung.

My progress remained painfully slow, until one day my mind leapt forward with the aid of a machine which was as life-saving and inspiring mentally as my respirator was to me physically. To my great joy, a Red Cross hospital librarian came to see me. She brought a reading-machine. It was a projector for which microfilm books could be obtained. My transparent reading shelf could be turned into a screen simply by putting a folded draw-sheet on top of it. The Red Cross lady asked the nurse to put her hand into the lung and place my toe from one button to the other so that I could get the feel of the range of movement that was needed to work the machine.

She then explained, 'All you have to do is press the left-hand button to turn the pages forward and the right-hand button to turn the pages backwards. When you want a page to stop still, you just take your toe off the button.'

It was easier than ringing the bell. I was still reluctant to summon help with the aid of the bell, but I was eager to read.

Having learnt how the machine worked and tried it out, I over-optimistically requested Gibbon's *Decline and Fall of the Roman Empire*. I had wanted to read it ever since I lived in Italy and now that I had all the time in the world, I could make good use of my confinement. It did not occur to me that I was too reduced mentally be able to tackle it. The librarian looked appalled. I thought, Oh dear, I've asked for something that isn't in stock. She had been so kind, I did not want to disappoint her, so I said that anything would do and perhaps I could borrow *Decline and Fall* later if it could be obtained from her headquarters.

She asked what sorts of books I liked to read and I told her I preferred biographies, travellers' tales (particularly sea stories) and almost anything about the Mediterranean. Generally I did not care for fiction but had read all the usual novels such as those by Huxley, Wells and so on. I liked poetry of any length and was constantly searching for new ideas for cookery, gardening, house-keeping, archaeology and so on.

'That gives me plenty to go on,' she said. 'I'll see what I can find you. Are there any things that you *don't* like reading about?'

'Yes, I said, I detest macabre stories – like some of those by Edgar Allen Poe.'

'Don't worry,' said the librarian, 'I won't bring you anything like that.'

On her next visit she fixed me up with a microfilm of *Reach for the Sky* by Douglas Bader, as he had also been a patient in Reading. Later she brought Monica Dickens' *One Pair of Feet* about her experiences in hospital as a nurse and *Cheaper by the Dozen* by Kenneth Galbraith.

As my feet were often in use with the push-button for my reading machine, I thought I could extend my range of activities and do exercises with pressing my feet alternately on the foot-board. I developed an exercise of heels together, toes together in a kind of restricted Charlston step. I fantasised about the other sorts of push-button machines that could be adapted to, or invented for, my needs.

I amused myself and others around me with my ideas. I thought I might find an old record player with its turntable still in working order. I would design and have built on to it a special support to which my arm could be attached. Then my hand and arm could go round and round in a stirring motion and reconnect with my brain. I could not manage such an exercise while I was still in the lung, but I hoped to be out of it soon.

If it was not for my breathing difficulties, I could have a washing-machine for my person, especially built so I could be washed and dried up to my neck at the push of a button. One gadget that seemed more attainable was a ticker-tape machine or teleprinter, which would print in plain language outside the lung the words I sent in Morse code from a buzzer by my foot inside the lung.

Meanwhile, I revelled in the heady experience of using my book-reading machine, watching rivers of print flood on to the screen above me, irrigating the channels of my mind and helping little seeds of ideas and information to grow into food for thought.

One day I was given more food for thought than I anticipated.

A nurse who was feeding me egg for breakfast suggested that I should try a small piece of fried bread. I could not think of anything more fattening, so I was tempted. She said, 'I noticed there was plenty left; I could soon fetch some. The kitchen isn't very far.'

I agreed with her 'My egg does look a bit lonely on that big white plate and I do so want to put on weight.'

The moment the nurse left the ward, I could not breathe. I began to suffocate. There was a feeling as if an enormous weight was pressing on my head and body, as though time itself was sitting on my chest. My eyes and throat felt about to burst. My heart seemed to be beating in my head and throbbing in my ears. The lung was helpless and for once I put my foot on the bell and kept it there, ringing and ringing. The emergency bell on the iron-lung registered the lack of air and also began to ring, both bells being independently wired and battery-operated in case there was an electricity failure.

Unknown to me, Mr Rackman was at the refrigerator changing bottles of blood. He saw the refrigerator light go out, guessed there was a cut and yelled at the people in the kitchen. 'Power cut! Quick – the lung.'

He rushed from the kitchen, burst through the doors and began hand-pumping my lung. His anxiety gave him the strength to hand-pump vigorously while other people went for extra help and phoned the electricty board to see whether the power could be restored immediately for the hospital.

This new terror – that of power cuts – meant that I never ever slept easily again. I was always checking on where people were and making sure that someone was constantly on hand. When the men arrived from the electricity board, Mr Rackham explained the facts of life and death forcibly to them. 'You see,' he said, 'when there's a power cut, it's not just a nuisance to us. It doesn't merely mean that we can't listen to the wireless. People in iron-lungs can't wait until the electricty is restored again. Either their lungs are kept breathing every minute of every day and night or they die. It's as simple as that.'

I don't know whether the lack of any more cuts to the hospital was due to Mr Rackham but we had no more while I was there.

Later, I heard that the hospital had been connected to the emergency grid and I could only wonder that this had not been done before.

One evening the nurse who specialled me arrived exhausted. She had been out with her boyfriend all day and had missed her sleeping-time. In the quiet, deserted hours she became hypnotised by the regular rhythm of the lung's steady breathing. It was so soporific that she fell fast asleep with her face resting on the radiator. I did not know she was asleep until I found that the air was leaking slightly past my rubber collar and blowing in my eyes. The intermittent puffs of air across my face were merely an irritation. My main concern was the slight drop in pressure in the lung, causing my breathing to become shallower. I was terrifed the pressure would drop further if the leak was not stopped. I called the nurse but there was no response. I called again and could not think where the nurse had gone as I was never supposed to be left alone.

Luckily her friend came hurrying in to tell her the latest gossip. The poor girl who had fallen fast asleep inspected her face in the mirror and found she had dull red scorch lines down her cheek. Fortunately, she had been woken in time to avoid bad burns and scars but her skin had been marked and her confidence in herself as a responsible nurse was badly shaken. She adjusted my collar to stop the pressure in the lung falling further and apologised profusely for not hearing my call. As she rubbed some cream thickly into her face, her main worry was that Night Sister should not know what had happened. I agreed she would not hear about it from me. I guessed the girl had learned her lesson.

In the New Year another patient was admitted with respiratory polio. I discovered that her name was Jean, the same as my sister. Naturally I was very concerned for the new girl in the lung next to mine, just as I had been for Peggy, but I wished that there was different hospital procedure whereby people who emerged from quarantine stayed out of quarantine, if only to keep their visitors out of danger.

Jean's husband could not manage to visit her every night so Ken looked after both of us while the nurse went to supper. He would give her drinks, wipe her nose and mouth and generally be exposed to fresh infection. I was again assailed by the constant anxiety of whether or not Ken would pick up polio and we would both be disabled, leaving Brian and Andrew totally vulnerable in our absence.

I realised that the very good reason for her being put in the lung next to me was so that one nurse could care for us both. Our iron-lungs were sometimes pushed closer together and our mirrors arranged so that we could see each other and exchange an occasional few words. Conversation still proved too exhausting as we lacked the puff to talk loudly and our two lung motors drowned our speech with their noise.

The powers-that-be decided that we needed a sink in the ward so that the staff could wash their hands before they left or when their duties took them from one patient to the other. The workmen duly arrived to attack the walls to make holes big enough to anchor the sink, its water supply and drainage pipes. The dust and the incessant noise were a great trial as each blow on the wall echoed through my head, exacerbating its ever-present soreness. I felt as though my brain had turned to crystal and each hammer blow left its mark like a bruise of shattered splinters just above my ears.

Eileeen said to me, 'You can't put up with this. I can't stand it myself and I'm up and about.' So she wheeled both our lungs to the far end of the ward where we were at least out of reach of the dust.

Whoever had the idea originally that there was an urgent need for a sink must have washed his hands of it. The water-pipes were never connected to the mains and the sink was never used while I was there.

We were soon out of quarantine as Jean's comparatively rapid progress followed a similar sort of pattern to Peggy's. Locally there were no more patients with polio and Mr Rackham stowed some of our belongings in the auto-clave to kill any trace of infection. They could then be taken out of the hospital. I sent most of my things home, including my little music box. Someone had overwound it on Boxing Day and I asked Ken to take it back to the shop for repair.

My physiotherapy sessions had not restored any movement to my fingers or arms but I had reached the stage where the mask could be removed from my face for a matter of seconds and the physiotherapist assisted my breathing with a manual technique similar to a life-saving procedure. The few secondary muscles I possessed in my face and neck jerked violently with the effort to gulp in as much air as possible before my ribs were forced together again by the physiotherapist and then released so that my lungs took up their tiny volume of air once more.

I had always thought people could live on hardly any air at all while they were at rest and I was amazed how inadequate the supply was, in spite of my own extreme effort and physiotherapy assistance. The sensation was rather like being frantically out of breath but having to keep swimming faster and faster while being pursued by a shark. Unlike swimming though, you cannot heave your chest in and out to gulp in the air that you need when your diaphragm, intercostal muscles, shoulder girdle and primary breathing muscles in the nose and throat have been put out of action. Robbed of their life-giving purpose, they become instead a death-dealing cage that feels bound by iron bands.

My 'shark' was my fear of not being able to return to my children quickly if I did not somehow make myself breathe. But breathing activity cannot be regained in this way, however strenuous the effort. The motor nerves govern activity and must recover first.

Even so, each day I remained constantly game to try and try and try again. My longing for my husband and children empowered me to endure the terrible fights for breath. Those around me had to watch my condition closely and to clamp the mask back over my nose when I began to turn blue, which happened after a very few minutes.

At first I was given manually-assisted breathing for one minute only. It was a very, very long minute and I had to concentrate with all my might from the beginning to the end of it. Gradually, over a period of weeks we worked our way together from one minute to two minutes, then three, four, five, six, seven and finally a triumphant eight minutes. This was to be our maximum achievement. Night Sister brought me a rag doll to celebrate our eight-minute assisted breathing. We called it Otto.

Sister asked me, 'Where shall we put him?'

I answered, 'In the crook of my arm, of course.' As I registered the weight and pressure of the doll on my left arm, I realised anew my intense longing to hold and cuddle my children.

Chapter 13
Beginning Again

It may sound ridiculous to say that I was happy in an isolation hospital, but I was constantly surrounded by a staff with particularly buoyant personalities. Also because I had battled and won through so many obstacles, I was filled with a sense of achievement when I woke up each morning and found I was still alive. I think it was because of this that I managed to cope with the many failures I had to face. Each morning I felt grateful for the day's inspiration. I also found I had a kind of mental stability that might be part of my heritage as an Englishwoman. I realised that I had been conditioned during the war by the behaviour of the people around me never to accept defeat as total or permanent or damage as irreparable.

When Taffy left, I knew I should have to make a tremendous conscious effort to manage without him. I was determined not to let his absence depress me. I had depended on him medically so much it was hard-going to face each morning knowing that he would not be dropping in as usual. In a strange way, his presence seemed to continue. Fortunately, I managed to win the war for my morale as Taffy was succeeded by a very humorous, tall fair man who gravely assured me that he was half-Russian. His eyes seemed to twinkle all the time so that I was not sure whether or not he was joking. He brought his records into the ward to play – Tchaikovsky, Sibelius, Smetana and so on – and Smetana's 'My Country' (*Ma Vlast*) seemed the perfect music to accompany the cranking sound of my machinery.

His partner was slightly older and said that he was hoping to specialise in pyloric stenosis. I asked him, 'Do you have a soft spot for baby boys?'

'Not particularly,' he replied, 'but how do you know that it is a boy's weakness?'

I told him that I had once worked for King's Fund. My head had been full of diagnoses then.

'What else did you learn at King's Fund?' he asked me.

I replied, 'I learnt how to become a bridge between busy general practitioners and their problems on the one hand and the hospital doctors who coped with these emergencies on the other.'

'I did not know that you had any medical knowledge,' he said.

'I prefer to keep it that way. I have never told anyone else in the hospital about my King's Fund training. They don't even know that I was helping with an iron-lung survey a few years ago, so please don't tell them.'

It seemed to me that I had much to be grateful for in having worked at King's Fund and become used to talking to doctors all day, every day. I expected to be allowed to take an intelligent interest in my own condition and to ask questions which would be answered honestly.

I realised how fortunate I was that such a beneficial relationship with the housemen had become established so quickly, helping to reinforce the sense of security which had developed on Elizabeth Ward and which had sustained me and helped me to keep my nerve each time I was slid out of the lung for my treatment. I felt supremely confident that although I had not made the breakthrough to recovery, it would probably come quickly and suddenly. All I had to do was to keep on trying and to be cheerful about it.

I knew that, at King's Fund, the bible of information that I had helped to start about the health and welfare equipment and services would have grown into a large and useful fund of knowledge on which I could now draw. I could now give information to King's Fund about life on the other side of the sheet, so my exasperation with my condition would serve some useful purpose after all.

Poor Ken's role as the bringer of sad news, when I was moved from David Ward to Elizabeth Ward before Christmas, was merely a rehearsal for another such job.

He was lumbered with the task of telling me that I was to be transferred, not just to another ward but to another hospital. Members of the staff could not bring themselves to tell me. They knew how attached to them I had become and how difficult it had been to transfer my feeling of security from the staff of David Ward to the staff of Elizabeth Ward.

I immediately responded to Ken's news by saying I did not want to go to another hospital. I liked the one I was in. That is, I did not exactly *like* it, but in my vulnerable condition better the devils you know than the devils you don't.

'You're not being sent to any old hospital,' Ken said.

'Do I have a choice?' I answered.

He took the wind out of my sails by saying, 'Yes, you have.

There are two or three orthopaedic hospitals from which you can choose.'

I protested: 'But if I can travel in an iron-lung, why can't I go home?'

Ken said, 'You know you can't go home. There's no one there to look after you. I'd have to go to work all day and the boys will be at school. All our relatives are too far away.'

'Something should be arranged in these special circumstances. It's not right that families are broken up because the mother has to go into hospital. There must be many families at risk nowadays when people live miles away from their relatives.'

Ken agreed. 'That may be so, but it isn't possible for you to come home until you are at least able to look after yourself.'

'I don't agree with this system,' I said. 'I've committed no crime – unless being ill is a criminal offence – yet I can be shuttled around like a criminal from institution to institution. There should be a writ of medical habeas corpus with guaranteed adequate support. If I can be kept in hospital at enormous expense under the NHS, it makes sound economic sense to be cared for at home by the NHS. Far cheaper for the taxpayer than my being here.'

Ken explained, 'You need to go to a different kind of hospital for more physiotherapy.'

'I can have physio here.'

'But not as much as you need. This hospital is meant for people who are acutely ill or have some condition that doesn't require physiotherapy. The other hospitals have swimming-pools, occupational therapy and other sorts of treatment. They're special hospitals with experience of rehabilitating people.

I protested: 'I feel trapped. It's most unjust. I've put everything into getting better. I want to go home but I'm pushed from pillar to post. Even criminals know they will go home one day! They can put their food into their own mouths and scratch themselves where they like and when they like. I'm worse off by having polio than I would have been had I stolen the Crown Jewels.'

'Why keep talking as if you're in prison?'

'Perhaps because I feel as though I am.' I said. '*I* have lost my freedom. *You* haven't. You come and go. You have another life outside. You do work that you choose to do. All I do is watch other people suffer without being able to help them. I hate being shut up in hospital.'

'The doctors and nurses are shut up too.'

'It's different for them as well. They choose to come here in the first place. They help the people here. I can't. Patients have to put up with whatever is decided must be done to them. Doctors and nurses have time off. When they've finished work they go elsewhere, to concerts, theatres or dances. They go on holiday for days on end. Patients suffer a sustained, intensive dose of misery – their own and other people's. They wake up to it, endure it through the day and go to sleep with it. I must get out of it.'

Ken persisted, 'All the more reason to go to a rehabilitation hospital.'

'I know nothing about any of them. If I must be moved, I might as well go to the nearest hospital. It would be easier for visiting.'

When Ken had gone, I reflected: I suppose I must blame myself . . . I have been putting on an act for everybody. I try to impress the doctors with lies about how well I feel in the hopes that they will let me go home. I must just set my mind to making a rapid recovery in the new hospital. I shall soon be home. Brian and Andrew will keep me up to scratch. The pain of seeing everyday jobs being done by other people will keep me stimulated to try to keep fit. Once home, I shall work out ways of fitting up some technical equipment on which I can exercise. I always have plenty of ideas for improving things. Now that so much is at stake, I shall soon find the answers.'

How strange that the last new building I had seen in London was the first purpose-built bungalow for a disabled person! I recalled my neighbour showing me over it and pointing out that there were no steps or other obstructions but plenty of helpful additions such as wide doorways and handles and switches within easy reach from a wheelchair.

As I was musing on my everlasting preoccupation with going home, Mr Rackham came beaming along to the iron-lung. I caught his eye in the mirror and joked: 'I hear you want to get rid of me. I don't blame you. I've been a lot of work and worry.'

'We only want to see you get on,' he replied. 'You've worked so hard, it's only right you should have a better chance to improve than we can give you.'

'I think my best chance is at home. That's where I would be if I could get out of this lung. I hear one old man made a dash for it this morning. He must have felt fed up with looking through the rails of his cot sides like a criminal. No wonder he upped and ran.'

'But they caught him though.'

'Yes, but he'd nearly reached the main road. The nurse thought it was so funny to see him haring along with his split-back nightshirt flapping in the wind. She said his little pink bottom must have been frozen.'

'He didn't know what he was doing,' Mr Rackham commented.

I laughed. 'He seemed to me to have the right idea. But as I can't run away I think I'll probably be going to the same hospital as Peggy. What did you think of it?'

He enthused: 'Oh, it's a fine place. They have a specially heated pool for water treatment, or hydro-therapy as they call it. It's wonderful the way people progress once they've been in the pool a few times. The water supports them, you see, so that it's easier for them to do their exercises. They have a big gymnasium too, with all the latest equipment and so many physiotherapists about the place that you can't move without treading on one of them.'

'I'll miss you all,' I said.

'We'll miss you too, but I'll be backwards and forwards to see you from time to time. Jean will be going there soon after you. That's one certain visit in the near future.'

He began unscrewing the sucker jar. I mulled over what he had said. I heard the ward door open, looked in my mirror and saw the doctors coming in on their rounds. I wondered whether to screw up my courage and begin a battle to stay where I was, but I knew I hadn't a leg to stand on. I thought I had better appear light-hearted.

As Dr Andrews walked across to my lung I observed: 'That's a nice tie you're wearing.'

He explained, 'It's my best one. I am sorry I couldn't bring you a salmon. The water was too cold.'

With visions of fishermen wearing thigh-length waders in deep streams, I asked, 'Do you mean it was too cold for you to go in after them?'

Misunderstanding me, he roared with laughter and said, 'I don't dive in after them, you know. It was too cold for the salmon to bite.' Still laughing to himself, he repeated the joke to Dr Harris as they left the ward together.

One freezing February morning, my nurse woke me up to start my treatment and told me that it was snowing.

I was thrilled, not only because in my fantasies snow and ice had come to mean a source of security for me but also because I hoped that the snow would prevent my going to the Rehabilitation Hospital. Alas, my hopes soon melted away. The huge ambulance that Mr Rackham had managed to track down and borrow for the occasion would have been capable of taking Hannibal and the elephants over the Alps. It had everything except a power supply.

Now that the ambulance had arrived, our departure became imminent. As I waited for it to be made ready, my mind went back to that sunny Saturday morning in mid-October, four months earlier, when I had waited in my bedroom for the Newbury ambulance. I had thought that it would be better to go to hospital at once and cure whatever was the matter with me. How naïve I had been! I had expected to be home within a few days. My high temperature or that headache must have affected my judgement. Gosh, that persistent headache – it had poleaxed me.

But apart from my illness, my general condition had been tip-top. My hair, skin and nails had shone with health. Now they told a different story, reflecting the fevers and deprivations of the past months. I had learned that polio was a very particular virus, choosing its hosts with impressive discrimination.

I pondered on the tiny polio virus and its enormous survival potential and power. I smiled at the irony of my life being so radically changed by a peace-time invasion of my person, after I had survived the hazards of war in London and at sea. Such a deadly enemy deserved the utmost respect and consideration. It seemed to be the veritable king of the disease and disablement jungle – a lion – marking for its prey only tender young children or fit young adults. No weaklings or tough old characters interest this virus. Other, jackal-type infections, such as pneumonia, attack them or lie in wait for the carcasses that the polio virus has reduced and left.

I had taken a long time to arrive at stage two – that is, falling prey to the jackal. And because I was so reduced by the second infection I lost the chance of early physiotherapy that was essential to recovery.

No use worrying over that. Once I arrived at the new hospital I would soon be leaping about again. After all, I was eating and sleeping better now. I had my books, records and wireless to amuse me. The whole staff seemed sure I would do well and I was certain of it too. I would miss them all but I would be back to see them soon.

They were an incredible group of people. They really cared more for their patients than for their own safety. It was impossible not to feel deeply attached and indebted to them. I had missed Taffy when he left . . . and Sister Allen . . . and Staff Nurse Hull . . . and all the David Ward nurses when I was transferred to Elizabeth Ward. I was lucky in a way that I had had time to get used to the new housemen, Sister, and the Elizabeth Ward nurses.

Except that now I was attached to them, it seemed hard to be torn away again.

Dr Andrews and Dr Harris had been constantly around from the beginning, giving continuity, as had Night Sister, Eileen, Frank and Ben. I would never forget these marvellous people . . . or the patients . . . no matter how quickly I recovered. Soon I would be home, reading Brian and Andrew story after story, sitting in front of a roaring fire. And I would sleep in my own bed again, curled up with Ken's arm around me. I would have to turn up the hem of the new green curtains and finish my tweed dress – or had I managed to finish it and forgotten? What a struggle each stitch had been! How stupid of me not to have realised that something was badly wrong. That must have been the first phase of communication failure. The polio virus had begun to destroy my motor controls, cutting off my means of stitching things together, cutting off my means of transporting food and drink to my mouth, cutting off my means of communication with myself and other people. I really was out of touch. Fancy not seeing anyone of my own, except Ken, for four months, not even my children, my parents, my sisters or my in-laws. I would ask the family down for a homecoming party.

There was not much time left to think about the new hospital as people kept popping in to say goodbye and all the equipment was being checked and double-checked for the last time. It had been arranged that I should be hand-pumped all the way. Frank and Ben would form a team and take it in turns. They would pump for ten minutes and then have a break for ten minutes. My nursing requirements were to be covered by Night Sister. It was the first time they had all been involved in such an ambulance journey and there was an air of excitement about the venture.

The electrical lead for my pump would have to be fixed to an extension cable and the cable plugged into the wall socket simultaneously so that I could be wheeled in the iron-lung the whole length of Elizabeth Ward, out into the forecourt of the hospital to the back of the ambulance. The timing had to be accurate, for once we arrived at the back of the ambulance the iron-lung had to be disconnected from its power. It then had to be lifted, with me in it, from the ground to inside the ambulance in sixty seconds flat, and no hitches, while I waited anxiously for my next breath. We had also to load the iron-lung pump, three oxygen cylinders, one spare pump and hose, one positive pressure ventilator to be worked by hand plus the two-stage oxygen resuscitator and three kitchen chairs for Frank, Ben and Night Sister. Strangely enough,

Ann and Ken when their troubles were only little ones.

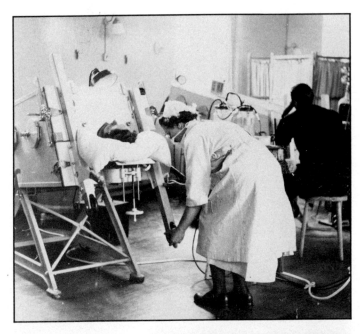

Opposite above: *The last photograph Ann ever took. It shows her husband, Ken, and sons in Trafalgar Square.*

Opposite: *Waiting in Friary Park for Daddy.*

Above: *Ken keeping vigil in the polio ward at Prospect Park Isolation Hospital, 1955.*

Right: *Ann intubated when pneumonia complicated polio. Temporarily out of the iron-lung and kept breathing on a positive-pressure machine.*

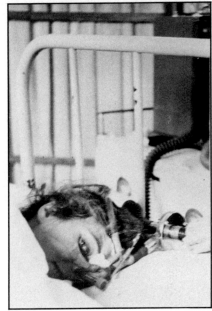

*Oxford Hospital
Occupational Therapy
Department 1957.*

Above: *Ann with
Occupational Therapists
Hilary Schlesinger and Inky
Stevens and a
fellow-patient. Ann is
wearing a jacket she knitted
pre-polio without knowing it
would be the last.*

Left: *Hilary transports a
delighted Ann to the OT
Department.*

Opposite: *The last Oxford
Hospital visit. The final
pose.*

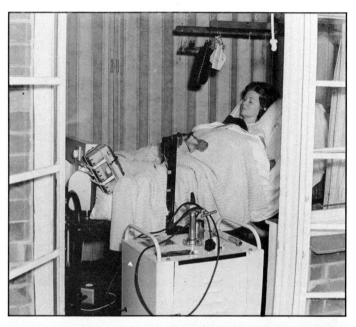

Above: *New machinery for old. The smaller, less noisy, respirator pump fits neatly beside Ann's bed adjacent to the controls for telephone, tape-recorder, radio, light, bells and electric blanket.*
Right: *The converted iron-lung motor, its pipe passed through the wall and attached to the cuirass. In the background can be seen the batteries of the emergency generator provided by the Invalids-at-Home Trust in case of power failure.*
Opposite: *A rare moment out of bed for a brief breath of fresh air with Ken on watch before winter closed in. A Bragg-Paul pneumo-belt, invisible under Ann's sweater, is powered from the domestic electricity supply.*

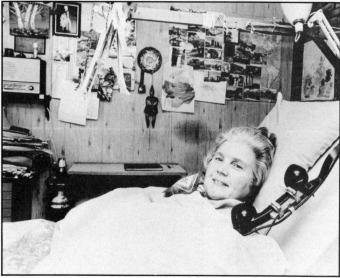

Above: *At the House of Commons in 1965. Ann and Ken made the journey as part of the campaign for the needs of disabled people who live at home. (Thomson Regional Newspapers.)*

Below: *Ann at home. (Kenneth Saunders,* the Guardian.*)*

none of us was worried one bit. We were filled with optimism and a spirit of adventure.

Suddenly there was a cold rush of air. The ward doors had been opened. The ambulance was ready. This was it. Ken wheeled my iron-lung close to Jean's.

'Your turn next,' I said.

'See you soon,' she answered.

'Take care of yourself,' we both chorused.

'Goodbye, goodbye, goodbye.'

Sister said farewell. I called out, 'Goodbye, and thank you for everything. When I'm better I shall come back, walk down the ward and thank you properly.'

She said, 'You will be very unusual if you do. Most of our customers just want to forget all about us.'

I assured her, 'I'll never forget and I'll keep my word.'

Eileen had come on duty early especially to see me set off to the new hospital. She gave me another box of Newberry Fruits. 'Here you are,' she said, 'something to nibble on the journey.'

I wanted to hug her and to express to her the gratitude that I was feeling towards everybody for the comfort and peace of mind that they had all helped me to battle towards.

'I'm not saying goodbye as I know Jean is coming to the new hospital soon and maybe you'll be coming with her,' I said.

'I hope so, but if I'm not so lucky I'll bring Ron and Jennifer to see you anyway,' Eileen answered.

Surprised and touched, I did not know what to say but merely continued smiling at Eileen and everyone else who was making my farewell a cheerful one.

Quickly I was pushed from the warmth of the ward out into the biting cold wind and swirling snow. A snowflake settled on my eyelashes, another on my cheek and my forehead and another on my lips. It was invigorating. I was free at last. I was enjoying a taste of English weather for the first time in four months. I was part of the great outside world again.

Events speeded up. To my regret I was whisked away from the snowflakes. My small craft with me in it was hauled aboard the ambulance and anchored firmly to the floor. Last cries of 'Goodbye, Good luck,' rang out as the door closed and we set off.

Outside, visibility was almost nil so it did not matter to me that I could not watch the passing scenery from the depths of the ambulance. Inside the ambulance I could hear the steady breathing of whoever was hand-pumping my iron-lung motor. Night Sister sat smiling beside me. Everything was running smoothly.

Suddenly, a terrible stink of burning rubber assailed us. My heart leapt with excitement. Something must have gone wrong with the ambulance. We would have to go back to Reading. I felt like a condemned prisoner being granted an eleventh-hour reprieve.

The ambulance stopped. The driver inspected the damage. He discovered that some brake friction on a tyre was the cause of the trouble. He put it right and we were soon on our way again.

There could be no turning back. I was on the road to recovery.

PART II
POLIO WARD

Chapter 14
Road to Recovery

A mean wind was blowing as the ambulance slithered to a stop in the frozen snow. I looked up into my iron-lung mirror for my first impression of the hospital. The mirror reflected only the blinding whiteness of the blizzard. Ken and the doctor, who had followed the ambulance by car, suddenly appeared in the whiteness by the open ambulance doors. Around me I could hear the rest of the staff who had come from Prospect Park Isolation Hospital beginning to start unloading. The doctor went into the Rehabilitation Hospital to prepare them for my arrival.

Frank was breathing hard from his hand-pumping efforts. He asked Ben to go on pumping while he went into the hospital for some help.

'You've both done well to hand-pump an iron-lung for a couple of hours between you,' the Night Sister commented. She began collecting up my possessions including the notes from Prospect Park.

Ken helped her down from the ambulance and climbed up beside me in her place. He grinned and made one of his typical understatements: 'Some journey.'

I agreed. It had indeed been some journey, a transition from isolation to rehabilitation.

'How's the driver?' I asked.

Ken replied 'He's sitting tight in his cab until we find out the lie of the land.'

'It's a whiteout,' Ben commented. 'Lucky to find the place at all in this.'

'I hoped we wouldn't,' I said. 'Then you would have had to take me back to Prospect Park.'

During the journey I had tried to adjust to the pain of parting from the select few who had become my life-support team and had fought for my survival at the Isolation Hospital. None of them had felt able even to tell me that I was being transferred. They had left that job to Ken.

My inability to see myself as permanently and catastrophically disabled meant that I talked to everyone as though my condition were only temporary. I spoke with such conviction about my eventual recuperation that others believed it too. They wanted me to recover and fell into the same trap of denying my disability. All my thought-patterns and plans were those of a competent and resourceful young woman. My conversations with the hospital staff had been carried on as though I was still the same person that I had been before polio had struck. It was true. I *was* the same person. I merely could not move or breathe. Indeed, I now had more experience and understanding of human beings under pressure.

Frank had returned. 'I've found some strong helpers,' he called up to us.

I heard feet being stamped and arms being clapped in an effort to keep warm. For the people manhandling my iron-lung and its heavy pump from the ambulance, the task proved weighty and complicated, even with all the strong arms that had been mustered. All the time they were lowering the iron-lung on the hydraulic lift from the ambulance to the ground, Ben continued to hand-pump from his place in the ambulance. He maintained my air-supply through the long pipe that connected the handpump to my iron-lung. The minute he stopped working, the lung was moved away and the pump rapidly lowered so that Frank could take over the hand-pumping on the ground immediately.

It was a strange procession that made its slow way through the swirling snow. Night Sister had tucked her woolly scarf around my head and protected me with her body from the worst of the wind. On my other side Ken fought to keep the scarf in place and help to maneouvre the heavy lung on its way. Ben put his great strength to moving the pump along at just the right distance so that the air-supply pipe from the lung did not become detached while Frank continued to hand-crank. We negotiated our way past the single-storey hospital buildings while Frank kept up a running commentary on our surroundings without looking up or taking his mind off the mechanical hand-cranking. Our progress was made more interesting by such comments as, 'On our left is the gym. Now on our right is the swimming-pool. We're approaching the covered way . . .' It seemed an endless maze of paths. At last Frank said: 'Ah, here's the ward we want! They're just opening the french windows to let us in quickly.'

Since having polio I had been nowhere but in the Isolation Hospital. Being loaded into the ambulance and transported from hospital to hospital had been an adventure. Being hurried along various hazardous paths was exhilarating.

As we skidded from the crisp cold snow into the stifling atmosphere of a small recovery ward I heard the french windows clang shut behind us. My respirator pump was plugged into the hospital power supply and everyone relaxed. I murmured my thanks to the hand-pumpers and pushers and maintained my smile to greet the new hospital staff.

An immaculate grey-haired woman dominated the room, looking down at me from behind plain horn-rimmed spectacles. Her stiffly starched cap and apron were arctic-white; her belt-buckle told me she was a state registered nurse. I soon learned she was the Ward Sister.

A rapid exchange of information occupied the various people in the room but none of it was addressed to me. I realised it was suggested that I be transferred to a new iron-lung. It was somewhere in the room but beyond my range of vision. Ken was the only person to speak to me. He said that I was to be lifted from one lung to the other and that he would support my head – I still had no control or strength in my neck.

For the last time I was pulled out on the trolley stretcher of the Both iron-lung which had breathed me for four months. Four pairs of hands slid under my head, shoulders and arms, my middle, my bottom, my thighs and my feet. The Ward Sister had taken charge of my shoulders and arms and gave instructions for a concerted lift. As I was raised one of my arms fell down with a sickening wrench, shocking the nerves from my neck to my fingertips. She made a grab and retrieved it. 'Hm,' she commented, 'badly-winged, isn't she?'

The new respirator was more like a flat bed on to which a large cover was hinged so that the whole lung looked like an alligator with its jaws wide open. I was carried over to this lurking alligator-lung and placed in the lower jaw, so-to-speak. The upper jaw was pulled down, snapped shut and sealed fast around my neck. Immediately I realised that it was more comfortable than the Both and breathed me well. That, at least, helped conquer my fear of an unknown respirator.

My notes were handed over. My hospital friends departed with the Both, promising to tell my old Ward Sisters not to worry and that I would soon be back to walk down the ward to see them. I did not realise that their smiles concealed fears that I might be incarcerated in hospital for ever.

Suddenly there was just Ken, the Ward Sister and a casually-dressed woman with greying hair. As they stood by the french windows I could see them clearly in the mirror saying their last few words to the Isolation Hospital staff.

Ken carried my belongings towards me and said, 'I'll put these in your locker for you.'

The two women walked back across the room, passed the side of my lung where I was lying with my head towards the french windows and my feet towards the corridor door. They were out of my field of vision but I heard the Sister say to Ken. 'Time for you to go. Visiting-time is from seven-thirty to eight in the evenings.'

I became alarmed at the uncompromising tone of her voice. Then the corridor door slammed behind them. 'Please don't leave me,' I said to Ken. 'Wait until someone comes to stay with me.'

'Of course I'll stay,' he said, and smiled at me reassuringly. Neither of us had grasped the terrifying situation I was about to face. Ken looked around the recovery room. He began unpacking my possessions, stacking my reading-machine, gramophone and records by the wall behind the lung and out of the way of anyone coming in from the corridor. He arranged my toilet things in my locker and put the wireless on top. Then, noticing that the alarm bell on the iron-lung was disconnected, he reconnected it. He was just connecting the lead from the bell by my foot into the wall socket when the Ward Sister returned.

'Still here?' she commented.

'I'm just waiting for a nurse to stay with my wife.'

'She'll be quite all right on her own,' the Sister asserted.

'But she's always been specialled.'

'That's not necessary here,' the Sister answered.

'She cannot be left alone. She's very nervous about power cuts,' Ken explained.

'She'll be all right here,' the Sister reiterated.

Ken persisted, 'But what will happen when there's a power cut or when she needs anything?'

'My office is opposite. I'll hear if she needs anything and there's a bell into the corridor where people are constantly up and down.'

As I listened to this exchange I could not believe my ears any more than Ken could believe his. If the lung stopped for any reason it had to be restarted immediately or I would die – or worse still, suffer irreversible brain damage. Did the Ward Sister not realise that without the help of the lung I could not breathe at all, nor could I use my own hands or body to restart the lung? She had described me as badly-winged – had she not grasped my total dependence on the iron-lung and the consequent impossibility of calling for help without any breath in my body? Didn't my notes explain that I had lost my ability to cough, sniff, sneeze, even clear my throat should my airway become obstructed, or to help myself in any personal or private way? Even such a simple thing as one of my own eyelashes becoming loose could drive me mad because it would fall back into my eye, instead of on to my cheek in the normal way.

Then the other member of the reception committee reappeared. The Sister said, 'This patient's husband is worried about leaving her with us. I've told him our usual arrangements.'

Ken repeated. 'My wife is very anxious about being left alone in case of a power cut – as happened at the last hospital – or if she needs anything. She has always been specialled.'

'Sister is very experienced,' the woman commented. Ken caught my eye in the mirror. I was greatly alarmed at the thought of being left without help and felt overwhelmed by my helplessness. If only Ken could have picked me up in his arms and carried me away I could have sought security somewhere else. But I could not be picked up by one person, nor two, nor three. I was like a puppet whose strings had been cut. Four people had been needed to move me from one iron-lung to another. Even if I could have been stiffened with splints or plaster so that I did not flop about and risk breaking my neck or back, Ken would still have the task of keeping me breathing somehow all the way home.

It was not feasible to leave without the iron-lung, and with the increasing pressure being put upon him by the implacable Sister it was becoming impossible for him to stay. Even if he insisted on staying now, how long could he manage to remain steadfastly by me? A day? A night? A week? He would have to leave some time.

Ken said to me, 'Don't worry. I'll stay with you.'

The Sister played her trump card. 'You will have to go now. The doctor wants to examine your wife, don't you, Doctor?'

I was surprised to learn that this casually-dressed woman was a doctor. Did that mean she would have more insight into my inability to cope without Ken? Perhaps I could explain my feelings to her and as soon as she heard my medical history she would appreciate my anxiety. Surely she could understand why I needed so much attention, and that someone must be by my side most of the time feeding me, washing me, putting me on and off bed-pans.

Meanwhile an examination by the doctor would take time and I would not be by myself straightaway.

Ken asked again, 'Do you want me to stay?'

I felt confused, but I knew it would be better to avoid trouble at all costs, especially at the beginning of my stay here.

Miserably I said to Ken, 'You go. I'll see how I cope.'

He looked concerned and insisted, 'You're sure you'll be all right?'

'I'll try to manage. You won't be late tonight, will you?'

'No. I'll be back at seven-thirty on the dot,' he said, and kissed me on my forehead.

Sister then noticed my belongings that Ken had arranged along the wall. She interrupted with: 'What are these?'

'They're my wife's things, her gramophone records and so on.'

'They must go,' she insisted. 'Your wife will be too busy to listen to them.'

Ken hesitated as though to say something, then on second thoughts decided it would be better not to argue. If I miraculously recovered I would soon be home. If not, he would bring them back later. He picked up my belongings and walked out into the deepening snow. Somehow he had to carry the wretched things to the bus-stop, wait for the bus into town, change to a long-distance bus that would take two cold hours – or probably more with the state of the roads – and dump them in his office. He would have an hour at the most in which to collect Andrew from the nursery and arrange for him to be cared for, snatch a sandwich and catch the buses back to the hospital to arrive by half-past seven.

When Ken had gone my examination began. As my notes had arrived with me the procedure was a routine check. The Sister noticed the scars on the insides of my ankles. She indicated them to the doctor, commenting 'Cut-down drip?'

The doctor replied, 'While she was intubated, I expect.'

I tried to break the ice by joining in this conversation. I felt I had to try to establish a reasonable relationship with the people running the place that was to be my home for a while. In the most friendly and helpful manner I could muster I said, 'The scars are from the drip that I needed when my first baby was stillborn.'

The doctor looked at the Sister and gave her opinion: 'She doesn't know what she's talking about.' Neither addressed a word to me.

Duly embarrassed, I said no more. I felt totally friendless and unsupported.

They walked to the side of the iron-lung where they were hidden from view. I heard the corridor door open and close and realised they had gone. I was utterly alone. A great wave of panic roared over me. My heart pounded in my ears and terrifying thoughts seized my mind. If there were a power cut or the lung broke down, would anyone hear me through that heavy door? No one could see me from the corridor as I was hidden by the bulk of the lung. Neither could I see the door. I could see only the reflection of the whiteness and the french doors in my mirror. There was no one in sight. It was snowing hard, the flakes were as big as swans' feathers. They made my alien surroundings even more terrifying and unfamiliar than when I had arrived an hour ago. The icy beauty of the scene struck surrealistic chords of terror. The wind was blowing the snow in deep drifts piled high against the french doors. The path outside was completely smooth – all trace of Ken's footsteps had been obliterated.

I looked at my watch that Ken had transferred, with the locket containing the picture of our sons, on to the handle on the front of the new lung. It was about noon. There were more than seven hours of terror to face until Ken reappeared at half-past seven, and twenty-three-and-a-half more after that until he came again the next night. My blood ran cold. I seemed shaky inside. I felt that I was solidifying into a slab of ice. My face, feet and hands froze. I stared into the mirror, desperate to see some sign of life appear outside the french doors, but saw reflected in its cold glassy surface only the wild, wind-driven snow and the widening strip of white on the window-panes as snow piled upon snow.

I had been less than half a day in this hospital which was to be my home for many months, but it had taken me no more than half an hour to realise that the atmosphere of the place was utterly different from that of Prospect Park.

My isolation on that first morning ended suddenly when the corridor door crashed open and a tiny nurse flew in carrying a plate. She looked about twelve-years-old and I was delighted to see her. 'Ready for lunch?' she asked.

I was embarrassed. I was bursting to spend a penny and hated having to ask this infant to help me. But the necessity was urgent. I said quickly, 'Can I have a bed-pan, please?'

She looked shocked and asked, 'What about your lunch?'

'Please leave it there. I'm frantic. I've only just got over being incontinent.'

'Why didn't you go before?'

'I didn't know it was lunch-time. I've been travelling in the cold all morning.'

'You'll get me shot! I'll try to nip into the sluice without anyone seeing me.'

She rushed off and returned shortly with a bed-pan and her friend to help lift me on to it.

'You'll be for it if Sister finds out,' her friend muttered. 'You'd better hide the bed-pan cover.'

The twelve-year-old spoke up. 'Sister wouldn't like a wet mattress, would she? She'd have to part with one of her precious clean sheets.' She settled me on the bed-pan. It was bitingly cold.

Her friend said, 'Must dash. I'll be back to help you take her off when I manage to get away again.'

The twelve-year-old chatted away happily as she fed me. I apologised for being so slow, but said little, for I still felt frozen. I was physically cold, true, but also full of apprehension about this new environment. The conversation of the two young nurses had not stilled my fears of the Ward Sister.

Suddenly the nurse said, 'There's something I should have told you. I was given a message for you.'

I felt intrigued. 'From whom?'

'John. He's next door. He saw you arrive, says he fell instantly in love with you and wants to know your name and all about you.'

'You'd better tell him I'm an old married woman with twelve children. He hasn't a hope!'

'Oh, John never gives up hope. He's a fiery Scot. He caught polio while working for a tobacco company overseas last year, flew home and has been here ever since. One of our staff nurses is crazy about him.'

'Is he hit badly?'

'Can't move a muscle except in his face but he has the most wicked eyes and keeps us all falling over ourselves to help him.'

Another nurse rushed in and gasped: 'Here's the pudding.'

'We haven't finished first yet,' protested the twelve-year-old. 'You'll have to tell Sister we're not ready. This patient eats very slowly. She has swallowing difficulties.'

The pudding-bearer said, 'You're very brave. Tell her yourself.'

'I can't. This is nearly cold already.'

I was about to say I could not manage any pudding when I remembered I had to find ways and means of keeping myself occupied. I asked about Peggy Slade who had recently been transferred here from Prospect Park and heard she was in the room next door but one.

'How is she getting on?' I said.

'Very well indeed. She goes to the gym now and has her physiotherapy there. She also goes to the O.T. Department so she isn't in the ward very much.'

'O.T. Department? What's that?'

'Occupational Therapy.'

'You mean like a workshop?'

'I suppose you could call it that. They do cooking, weaving and that sort of thing.'

'Is Audrey in the same ward?'

'How do you know about Audrey? She flew direct here from Egypt.'

'Yes, I know. Frank Rackham from the Isolation Hospital told us about her. He knew I'd been to Egypt and that seemed to give us something in common. Shall I be moved in with the others?'

'I should think so.'

'Oh good! I shall be glad to talk to Peggy. I never actually saw her before as I didn't have a mirror on the lung. I'm looking forward to meeting Audrey.'

'Perhaps she can pop along to see you this afternoon.'

'Pop along?'

'Yes, she's got up into her wheelchair in the afternoons and she won't be able to go across to the O.T. Department in the snow. I'll suggest it when her occupational therapist comes over to give her her treatment.'

The faithful friend rushed in and helped me off my bed-pan. I had taken ages to eat my lunch although I had declined the potatoes. I now said I did not think I could manage any pudding. I was to regret this later when I found myself alone and terrified again.

When everyone had gone, the eerie quietness began to alarm me again. All I could hear was the whoosh-shoosh of the air rushing in and out of the iron-lung and the underlying thumping sound of the motor as it pounded away in a regular rhythm reminiscent of a ship's engine. The only machinery I could call to order was my brain. That in its turn must be forced to control my emotions. It must not relinquish its obligation to analyse and contain the destructive power of fear. Panic must be conquered. I must keep on keeping on. I must. I must. *I must.*

I muttered and struggled and used all the self-discipline that I could muster. I forced my mind to think about Audrey and tried to picture her. I filled my mind with thoughts of her and my fears began to recede. I was just puzzling how we could manage to communicate without the use of our hands if she did not speak any English when the door opened. Instead of Audrey, the Almoner entered and introduced herself. She brought a form to fill in which took only a little while. Before she left she assured me that there was no need to worry about anything and put a leaflet face-down on my reading shelf. I was intrigued to find it said that I should ask for anything I needed. It seemed a Kafka-like kind of mind-breaker. The stark, ill-timed irony demonstrated no feigned goodwill but instead a complete lack of awareness which I could do nothing to dispel.

When Audrey was wheeled into my room and placed so that she faced my mirror I saw at once that she was as English as I was! She had been in Egypt as the wife of a serviceman, so I would not, after all, have a chance to practise my few Arabic phrases.

We chatted about Egypt, then she asked me how I liked the alligator-lung which she had occupied before me. Audrey's respirator appeared to be in a heavy wooden box which the nurses had dragged in behind the wheelchair. It seemed unbearable to talk about our husbands and homes but we discovered we lived only a few miles apart. Although our speech was soft and slow and tea was fed to us, we covered a lot of ground.

I would have liked Audrey to stay but she was wheeled away to be put back to bed and by four o'clock I was again alone. Somehow I struggled through the hours until Ken could appear, but without my book-reading machine, record player or wireless set, time hung heavily. Different nurses came to feed me my supper and I ocuppied my mind counting up how many people I had seen in the few short hours since I had arrived. It was so confusing after the routines of Prospect Park where the same nurse stayed with me hour after hour.

Ken was late – the snow had held up the bus. We had only ten minutes together. Before he left he told me he had propped the corridor door open with a chair so I could hear and be heard. He noticed that both my bells had been disconnected. He reconnected the emergency bell on my iron-lung which should ring automatically if the pressure inside the lung dropped. The two-pin plug to my foot-operated bell had probably been unplugged from the socket in the wall when the nurses opened the lung to put the bed-pan under me. Ken fixed this plug firmly to the wall with sticking plaster so that it could not be removed.

As Ken left he said, 'Now you will be all right, won't you? To make sure you're secure, just ask everyone who comes in to do what I have done. Check that both bells are connected – the bell on the top of the iron lung and the bell by your foot – and keep the door propped open with this heavy chair.'

After he left the bedtime ritual began. More nurses came to give me a milky drink, clean my teeth and plonk me on the last bed-pan of the day, but there was an interval of about half an hour between each operation, and I kept dozing off. There were two student nurses on duty at night – they started at eight o'clock – and they had twenty-nine other patients to attend to. The elder of them, only just eighteen, was designated 'senior' because she had been on the ward for three months. A peripatetic Night Sister plodded around the far-flung wards; the only registered nurse nearby specialled John and his room-mate and was not allowed to leave their room.

At last I fell asleep and did not wake up until Night Sister flashed her torch across my room. As soon as I realised I was in the polio ward of the new hospital I closed my eyes tightly and fought to shut my mind to the new surroundings.

Chapter 15
Steep Hill

There were gleams of hope, attempts at being cheerful, even in this unlikely setting. Sometimes the very existence of the hospital regime seemed to unite patients and some of the staff in a common bond.

On that first, bleak awakening in my snowbound room a little nurse rushed in with a bright red anemone in a vase.

'It's from John next door,' she gasped. 'You're to pretend it's a red rose. He expects you to know what that means in the language of flowers.'

Mentally I clutched at this straw. I was glad of John's sense of humour and asked the nurse to thank him for his gift. Somehow it seemed to make this strange place more bearable.

One of my early visitors was a young woman in a bottle-green dress with blue edgings. She blew in out of the snow and beamed an introductory smile in my mirror. 'I'm Brenda Stevens,' she said. She seemed more like Miss Sunshine to me! Apparently my room was on a short cut between the Occupational Therapy Department and the main entrance; she could save herself a few yards by coming through it.

I noticed the phoenix badge embroidered on her pocket and told her that in my WRNS days I had been stationed at HMS *Phoenix* in Egypt. 'I think I'll adopt it as my symbol,' I said. 'I've been through the flames and intend rising from the ashes.'

Years later she told me that from our brief conversation she assessed me as being very bright and relayed my words to her colleagues. She did not realise that the happy chatter was a desperate and disciplined attempt to conceal an abyss of misery.

Monica, the chief physiotherapist, also arrived that morning. She gave John his treatment twice a day, coming to me immediately afterwards for a brief five or ten minutes of passive movements. A nurse held a mask over my face to keep me breathing while the lung was open for these sessions.

As I could not talk intelligibly under the mask there was not much verbal communication between us. Instead I tried to read Monica's face. She was extremely glamorous and took great pains with her make-up. She wore a red belt over her white overall and matched her lipstick to it. Her two badges, one from the hospital where she had trained and the other from the Chartered Institute of Physiotherapists, established her qualifications. I was always delighted to see her.

Knowing that I had to knuckle down to the routines of this hospital for the sake of my own progress did not make it any easier to do so. Initially I made many mistakes – as, for instance, on the first morning when I asked the nurse optimistically when I would have my bath. In the Isolation Hospital I had looked forward to my bed-baths in the iron-lung twice every day. I felt much better when I had been turned on my side and generally rubbed and refreshed all over, especially as I had been told that this movement was essential to prevent my muscles wasting and to stop secretions accumulating in my chest.

Now, the nurse informed me, baths were to be a once-a-week treat.

Drugs were another source of potential misery. When the Ward Sister escorted the doctor into my room, an assortment of remedies were automatically prescribed, including barbiturates, laxatives and vitamins. Summoning up my courage I politely offered to forego the barbiturates and laxatives. I was thankful that I was able to agree enthusiastically about the vitamin pills. We were deep in the winter and vitamin C seemed to be noticeably lacking in the solid, stodgy food offered from the hospital kitchens.

The doctor also advised that I must drink several jugs of water each day. I must see that the nurses measured my intake and output 'to avoid trouble with my waterworks', as she put it.

This last prescription proved a great trial. I discovered that if I drank the required amounts I became frantic by the time I was allowed the next bed-pan. I need not have worried. I soon found that the nurses were too busy to have time to record each cup of fluid taken and each outlet of urine. Often they rushed into my room before going off duty and whispered conspiratorially, 'How much have you drunk?' I never knew, so they 'remembered' for me.

In the previous hospital's iron-lung I had been moved at least six feet on the trolley stretcher twice a day when it was unfastened and slid out of the lung with me on it. This gave me a view of a slightly different patch of ceiling. Now I remained fixed in the same spot under the same ceiling hour after hour. My immobility was emphasised by the absence of anyone on call to change the positions of any part of me when stillness became intolerable. These two dimensions of immobility were a terrible frustration for me to face, together with my terror of being alone. Ken's visits were too short to undo the damage.

During the four months I was in the Isolation Hospital, he had spent hours rubbing my limbs, brushing my hair and generally helping to maintain my condition and morale, as taught by the Sister. Now, with the complicated bus journey and the inflexibility over visiting, he endured eight hours' travelling to spend ten minutes with me.

He left his office at five o'clock, caught his first bus for the two-hour journey, raced across the junction to catch the next bus to the hospital gates, then hared along the paths to save precious seconds knowing that visiting-time was already nearly two-thirds gone. He usually arrived about seven-fifty and Sister was adamant that he could not stay a minute longer than eight o'clock.

When he left the hospital he always knew that as he reached the junction he would see the Newbury-bound bus disappearing from sight. There was no nine-thirty bus. The next bus left the station at ten-thirty. It took over two hours in the bitter cold meandering around far-flung villages and hamlets to reach Newbury after midnight. At Newbury he would collect his bicycle from the office and somehow hold on to the handlebars and pedal his way up the hill to home, arriving about one in the morning at a cold, dark, silent house. He would fry himself bacon and eggs and eat them in solitary state before clearing everything away and preparing for the early-morning start back to work.

One night when Ken hurried in he found the emergency bell on the iron lung had been disconnected again. The engineer was coming along the corridor and Ken mentioned it to him.

The engineer agreed with Ken. 'Sister will not leave the bell alone,' he said. 'I don't agree with its disconnection. I keep making sure it works and she keeps making sure it doesn't.'

'What possible reason could she have to disconnect an emergency bell on an iron-lung?' burst out Ken.

'She says it distracts her nurses. They all come running when it rings, only to find someone has forgotten to disconnect the bell before undoing the sides. Of course, whenever the nurse has to open the lung the bell rings as the pressure drops, if she has forgotten to switch it off.'

As I could not see the alarm bell from my position I had not understood this aspect of my insecurity. Now that the increased risk was known to me I could not cope with my fear of brain damage. I wept and could not stop.

Ken went to see the Sister. While he was gone I willed her to understand the hazards and keep my alarm bell connected. Perhaps Ken could help her to see how at risk I felt in my isolation.

I could hear Sister arguing as Ken insisted that the emergency bell on my iron-lung must be kept connected. She totally refused to do this but eventually agreed that I should be moved in with Peggy and Audrey. When Ken told me what had been decided, I still could not stop crying.

I tried to apologise. 'I'm sorry to be a cry-baby.'

Ken wiped my eyes with his handkerchief. 'Don't think about it. It's enough to make strong men weep.'

Once I had moved into the ward with other patients, I felt a new sense of security. My iron-lung was near the door that led to the corridor. Beside me was a dark young woman called Dorothy who had had polio but needed no breathing assistance. Peggy, whom I had known at Prospect Park, was in a similar position and she and Dorothy spent most of the day in the gym or in the Occupational Therapy Department. Both of them expected to be going home soon. Audrey and I were anchored to our respirators so we stayed in the ward on the receiving end of the plethora of nurses with bed-pans, drinks, meals, bowls of water and so on. Morning and afternoon we slogged away at our physiotherapy sessions, hoping that before too long we would be able to join the others. I still imagined that the reason I was making such slow progress was because I had been so desperately ill with pneumonia and unable to start physiotherapy during the crucial weeks following my paralysis.

Occasionally the four of us were joined by two young men, David and Jonathan, who could propel themselves around in their wheelchairs. They too had had polio but had been weaned from their respirators, and could whizz out of our ward and into the Men's Ward when Sister was on her way. We always heard her coming so they were never caught.

Eileen was another visitor who was wheelchair-borne. She was in her twenties and her legs had been badly affected. Frank Rackham also came with the Staff Nurse who had specialled me in Prospect Park. I was delighted to see them, and tried hard not to compare the hospital I had left with the hospital I was in. There could be no going back. I just had to accelerate my recovery and get home fast.

Audrey was got up each day and as there was a distance between her bed and my iron-lung, I noticed in my mirror that she wore a different respirator when she was up from that which she wore in bed. She always asked for her chair to be wheeled to the side of my iron-lung so that we could talk for a while. Our voices were too soft for us to hold a conversation normally, across the room, especially with the noise of the respirator motors in opposition to us.

I was intrigued by this expanding family of respirators and as Audrey had experienced first an iron-lung and now two other life-support kinds of paraphernalia, I asked her to tell me about them.

'What kind of respirator are you using now?' I asked.

'A Bragg-Paul. Have you heard about them?'

I had indeed heard about them when I was working on the respirator survey for King's Fund, but I had not seen one before.

Audrey was wearing a wide, flat, black rubber belt like a cummerbund. It was fastened across her front with chains and hooks and connected to the box by two tubes. Each time she breathed out, the belt was inflated with air supplied by the machinery in the box. This direct pressure squeezed the residual used air from her lungs. I noticed Audrey managed to take in gulps of air by using her neck support muscles. This jerked her head backwards and forwards in a most disconcerting way.

'Does it help you much?' I asked.

'It's better than nothing, but I'm always glad to go back into my cuirass and to let it take over my breathing for me.'

'What's a cuirass? I've never heard of that one.'

'It's a fairly new development of the iron-lung – a sort of shortened version reaching from your neck to your thighs. A kind of tortoise-shell or breastplate is strapped to your chest by a wide belt across your back and breathes you in and out as an iron-lung does. It's even driven by the same motor with a special adaptor.'

'What are the pros and cons?'

'Well, for a start, you can be propped up on a bed in a cuirass. The bed can be wound up to support you in a semi-sitting position so that you can see more.'

I smiled, 'And be got up into a chair?'

'And be got up into a chair,' she echoed.

'If you can sit in a chair with a cuirass, why are you wearing a Bragg-Paul?'

'Well, you see, if you can manage, you can be weaned from the lung into a cuirass, then weaned off a cuirass on to a Bragg-Paul, and then graduate to breathing by yourself. Then you can go home.'

'Any disadvantages?'

'None.'

This information raised my hopes considerably.

The Ward Sister did her rounds early, saying 'Good morning' to everyone and handing out the mail. Later in the morning she escorted the doctor through the surgeons' rounds when the young nurses rushed about even more than usual. Each surgeon had his own patients on the ward. He would arrive like royalty with an entourage of doctors, physiotherapists, occupational therapists and visitors from home and abroad. They would gather around the bed of one of the surgeon's patients, holding an intensive discussion – and maybe giving a demonstration – on the patient's condition. Suddenly the questions would cease, and the surgeon would make his way to the next bed or the door, usually at speed, with his retinue hurrying after him.

As the days lengthened we had a small celebration party for Dorothy. She was due to return home and on her last night, thanks to a friendly Staff Nurse who turned a blind eye, all our visitors joined nurses, physiotherapists and occupational therapists in our ward. 'Rock Around the Clock' was belting out from a record player carried in for the occasion and visitors arrived with cakes, crisps, nuts and even bottles of wine. It had to finish at the usual end of visiting-time, yet such a break in our daily routine was more than welcome.

When Dorothy left, Jean was wheeled in. She was making a rapid recovery and had already graduated from an iron-lung to a cuirass.

I started a new regime of being put into a bed and having a cuirass strapped on to my chest for an hour or two each day. At first I was terrified of being lifted in case I was not securely supported, as I had not forgotten the first time that Sister and her crew had transferred me from the Both and let my arm drop, pain being an effective conditioner. But I loved the freedom of being in a bed again. I enjoyed being able to see the things that were in front of me instead of having to watch events in my mirror. I came to appreciate the process of being moved from the lung to the bed. I had lain in the same spot in the same iron-lung night and day for so long that the very act of being moved was an enormous thrill.

Now I was out of the lung for a short time each day, not only was my view of the world changed but also I hoped to see Brian and Andrew very soon. I had not wanted them to see me while I was still in the iron-lung. If after six months' separation they found me lying in an iron-lung with only my head sticking out, it might be very frightening for them. I was determined to be able to spend at least three hours in my cuirass before they came. I wanted to be propped up in bed with my bedclothes pulled up to my chin and tucked in firmly around me to hide everything abnormal from view. It would seem strange to Brian and Andrew that I could not put my arms around them to cuddle them – it would seem odd and disturbing to me too – but if my arms could not reach out to them, my voice must. We were sure to have so much to talk about after so long apart and so many bizarre things happening to us.

I hoped that my voice would seem cheerful. It was annoying that it sounded weak and faltering while I was depending on cuirass-given breath to power my words. There was nothing much I could do about it except to attempt to discipline myself to a completely new regime of extra exercises to strengthen my physical condition generally and my voice in particular.

Ken arranged for the children's first visit on Easter Sunday. Brian was still living with Ken's parents. He had been with them from the first day that I disappeared into hospital. Andrew had spent the first few weeks of my illness with my parents but now he was living with Ken's sister.

Easter would mark the start of a new life for us all. Surely I would find in the growing warmth the strength and energy I needed to progress quickly from iron-lung to cuirass, from cuirass to Bragg-Paul and from Bragg-Paul to sweet independence and home.

Straightaway I began practising my exercise in my iron-lung, pressing as hard as I could on the foot-board of the lung. I concentrated first with one foot and then with the other until I became too puffed to continue.

I found it needed an incredible amount of effort and energy and had to wait until the iron-lung breathed me back to a better state of respiratory balance. During these, for me, Herculean exertions, every accessory respiratory muscle I could command worked wildly to assist my air intake. The muscles around my eyes, nose, mouth and one side of my neck flexed and extended themselves autonomously.

One day I had just reached a frantically out-of-breath state when Sister walked in with the doctor. They noticed the exertion of my neck muscles moving and came across.

'What are you doing?' the doctor asked.

I was so short of breath that I found it almost impossible to answer but eventually I managed to gasp, 'Exercises.'

'What exercises are they?'

'Walking . . . exercises.'

'What do you mean?'

'Pressing . . . my feet . . . alternately . . . on the . . . foot-board.'

'You'll kill yourself.'

'Don't think so . . . Not exactly . . . LIVING in . . . this state . . . am I?'

'Why are you so discontented?' Sister interrupted.

I replied, 'I've lost . . . my girlish . . . laughter.'

'She's quoting,' the doctor explained. Looking at me thoughtfully, she added, 'I wish I'd married and had children while I was young, like you.'

I felt I had to comfort her and said, 'But you have . . . your career.'

She nodded her head slowly and walked over to Audrey's bed with Sister.

I thought carefully about her warning that I would kill myself if I exercised too ruthlessly. I was not convinced. She was the doctor and knew all the medical theories but I was the person who inhabited my body and could best gauge its needs and capabilities. Moreover, I was the person who had to live with my mind and it was a mind obsessed with making its body work its way home to its dearly-loved and loving husband and little children. All the same I would not take any chances that might just possibly spoil our Easter reunion.

I planned that occasion with great care. I decided I would wear my pretty blue cardigan back-to-front to cover the cuirass in case its black rubber rim was visible above the bedclothes. I would also wear a blue scarf knotted nonchalantly at the right side of my neck. I knew that my hair was badly in need of a shampoo. It had not been washed since I had shampooed it myself the previous October before I had polio. It had grown very long but had kept its waves. As I could do nothing about its condition I put it firmly out of my mind. I never looked in the mirror so it did not worry me. I would wear my Cyclax make-up and Yardley lipstick so that I still smelled the same to my children.

Shepherded in by Ken and his parents, Brian and Andrew walked into the ward quietly and slowly, having obviously been warned not to make a noise. They came up to the side of my bed and held up bunches of daffodils – suddenly I realised I could not take them. Ken rescued me. 'Give me the flowers. I'll put them on the locker where they won't get squashed.'

I found it almost impossible to speak but managed to utter,

'What a lovely breath of spring!' before fixing my face in a cast-iron grin to keep the tears at bay.

Ken lifted up Brian and Andrew and sat one either side of my bed so that they could kiss me hello. We all kept smiling at one another as though we had climbed Everest and were stuck on the summit, not knowing where we could go from there. Fortunately Brian had brought his first school books. He held them up and turned the pages with some difficulty because of the fixed position I was in and my inability to sit myself up or lean forward or generally coordinate with his efforts. Child-like he ignored the problem and, being so articulate, his running stream of explanations about his work melted the tension and we all began to relax.

Andrew, who had been sitting silently on the other side of the bed looking at me suspiciously, suddenly broke in with, 'Why is your hair so black?'

I smiled as brightly as I could and explained, 'Because it hasn't been washed for a long time. I can't wash it in bed, can I?'

He thought about this before nodding his head. He was a man of few words and had spoken his piece.

Brian asked, 'Can I tell you a story?'

Andrew perked up immediately and nodded his head again. Grandma intervened with. 'Are you sitting comfortably?'

Brian continued, 'Then I'll begin. This is a story about Stevington. You remember, Mum – where I live with Nan and Grandad. Well, you know the village cross and how it stands in the middle of the cross-roads? Well, one day John Bunyan walked all the way from Bedford to Stevington and stopped at the cross for a rest. He was hot and tired so he slipped his pack off his back and sat down to rest against the cross. He shut his eyes and did not notice the pack as it began to move and roll faster and faster down the hill towards the river. John Bunyan opened his eyes and saw his burden growing smaller and smaller in the distance. He thought, "That's a good idea to write down in my book. I can describe how Pilgrim came to Jesus's cross and his troubles fell off his back and rolled into the river."'

I could hardly speak. Brian seemed to have remembered the tale word for word and had brought us all the perfect Easter story.

The lady with the tea-trolley arrived and broke the spell. Refreshments were only for the patients, so the grandparents took the children to the canteen, leaving me alone with Ken.

I said to him, somewhat obviously, 'They're growing very fast. It's such a pity that we're missing watching their development.'

Ken shrugged and answered, 'They're thriving, that's the main thing. They were delighted to be coming to see you this afternoon and were taking note of everything.'

'I'm glad I managed to be out of the lung. Don't you think I'm doing well?

He picked up my cup to hold it to my lips but I was anxious that Brian and Andrew should not come running back in and see me being given a drink like a baby.

I asked Ken, 'Can you drink my tea for me? I really don't want it and it'll only be wasted.' I always felt so inhospitable not being able to offer my visitors a drink at my bedside. We were lucky to have the canteen open this Sunday afternoon although it meant one's visitors had to leave the ward. Time in the canteen ate into visiting-time.

Brian and Andrew seemed to be gone for ages but eventually they trotted back into the ward followed by Nan and Grandad. It was time to say goodbye. 'Have you had a drink?' I asked. They had.

Fearing tears, I tried to compensate for having to part so soon by offering, 'When you've gone I'll find a nice nurse to give your flowers a drink. It was so kind of you both to bring them. They'll look lovely on my locker and will last a long, long time.'

Two pairs of small arms were suddenly around my neck from either side of the bed and two fiercer-than-usual kisses were imprinted on my cheeks.

'See you again soon,' I said to them as they were lifted down to start the journey back to the houses they now called home. We were all being very brave.

I thanked my parents-in-law for looking after them so well.

They leant over my bed and kissed me saying, 'Just take care of yourself. Don't worry about them. We'll see that they're all right.'

I wanted to jump out of bed, run to the car and hop in with them, travel to the dear little village of Stevington and tuck up my children in their beds for the night. But I could not even run to the door to wave goodbye. I could not even wave to them from my bed.

Oh arms, I thought desperately. You must move soon! And chest, you must breathe!

Chapter 16
Gear Change

When my visitors left on Easter Sunday I was returned to the iron-lung. It was much easier to breathe there than in a cuirass. It was also less painful. When propped up in a bed I was in a position I could not maintain for myself and as I gradually slumped to one side or the other the elbow that was under pressure became extremely painful. My other arm would flop off its pillow and hang down the side of the bed, hurting me in every joint up to my neck.

Being back in the lung was always a relief but it was a relief I could not afford. I had yet to graduate from lung to cuirass, from cuirass to Bragg-Paul, and from Bragg-Paul to breathing on my own. I had to repeat this to myself every morning if I were to go home soon.

I had to instil in myself a sense of intolerance towards living in a lung and concentrate on its drawbacks. It was such a final encapsulation. I was contained like the little Russian nesting-doll Tasha I had owned as a small girl. I lay rigid in the lung like an over-sized Tasha. The lung stood stationary in the polio ward. The polio ward was approximately one-twentieth of the hospital. The hospital was situated in a town in a county that contained neither my own home nor the houses where my children lived. Put like this, the lung seemed a long way from home and struck me as a most undesirable place to be.

One morning, just after a second visit from Brian and Andrew, I was put on my bed in my cuirass where I was to stay until four o'clock. Jean, Audrey and myself were feeling very restless. I said I could feel the sap rising and hoped that the urge to move meant that a lot of new growth was taking place inside all of us and that our motor nerves were being restored like the leaves on the trees.

At that moment a little nurse ran in with a red flower in a vase. She rushed over to my locker and plonked the vase on it saying, 'This is from John,' as she turned to dash out of the door.

I called as loudly as I could: 'Please thank him for me.'

Jean said, 'Nurse, can you please straighten my pillow for me?'

The nurse bustled over and made a hasty attack on the pillow. In doing so she moved Jean across the bed while leaning on the pipe of her cuirass. The pipes were not fixed – something had to give. Jean's pipe fell out of the respirator connection. The disconnected pipe lay on the floor making an empty gasping sound. We all recognised the sound immediately as air going to waste, yet it held no meaning for the nurse. She was only intent on making Jean comfortable.

'There,' she said kindly, 'I must fly now. Every time I come in here you all want something.'

Jean, with her air supply disconnected, had no breath with which to speak, but Audrey shrieked as loudly as she could in her thin kitten voice: 'Come back, nurse. Fix Jean's pipe into her cuirass.'

I joined my soft voice to Audrey's and called, 'Come back, come back!'

Fortunately she came back and reconnected the pipe. Yet when Audrey explained that the pipe *must* be attached to the cuirass to provide Jean's breathing-power the young nurse asked, 'Does it make any difference?'

When we were left alone again Jean began to react with anger to the panic induced by the incident. 'Does it make any difference?' she demanded. '*Does it make any difference?* Does she think we would wear these things if it didn't make any difference?'

Audrey tried to soothe her down. 'Perhaps she supposes that just having the cuirass strapped on helps you to breathe.'

'Well, she supposes wrong, doesn't she? She shouldn't be allowed on a polio ward if she hasn't been taught what respirators do!'

'They don't learn about respirators before they come on the ward,' said Audrey. 'They are supposed to learn while they're here.'

'Well, I've never seen anyone teaching them. Not anyone whose job it is to teach them, I mean.'

Audrey agreed. '*We* have to teach them if we want to survive but I don't know if that makes us the best or the worst teachers.'

'Are many patients medically qualified to teach?' I asked. 'Do doctors and nurses go down with polio more frequently than other people?'

Audrey thought for a moment. 'It's strange you should ask that,' she said. 'I was so worried about the doctors and nurses in Egypt in case they caught polio from me but I've only known one doctor to catch polio.'

'Badly?' I asked.

'Badly,' she echoed.

'Where is he now?' I persisted.

'He went home just after I arrived here.'

'He could breathe then?' I asked.

Audrey replied, 'No, he was on a cuirass, but as he was a doctor and his wife was a nurse he was allowed to live at home.'

This information struck me as very valuable. If one person had gone home while depending on a cuirass, another one could follow. Doctor or not, a precedent had been established. I must make more effort and stay out of the lung completely. 'What was this doctor's name?' I asked Audrey.

She replied, 'Dr Finnigan.'

'It's strange he's never mentioned.'

'I don't suppose it would do to keep talking about someone who had gone home on a cuirass, otherwise we might not make the effort to progress to Bragg-Pauls and so on.'

Jean chipped in at that. 'You must be joking. Just to get out of here is enough reason!'

'Perhaps they make it unpleasant here so that we don't stay too long,' I added.

The door opened and a stranger entered with Sister and the lunch-trolley. She watched Audrey struggling to feed herself with the help of the springs that supported her arms in slings.

'They work very hard for their food,' the visitor commented.

'I keep them good and hungry,' Sister replied.

That afternoon I kept thinking about my husband and children and myself living our separate lives and sleeping under separate roofs. I thought about Dr Finnigan in his cuirass in his own home, with his own wife, under their own roof. I felt my resolve to stay in the cuirass increasing. I was determined to follow in his wake. By four o'clock I had made up my mind that I was never returning to the iron-lung again. I did not say anything to my room-mates but when Sister arrived with her three nurses to transfer me I summoned up all the command I could muster.

'I do not intend to return to the lung any more, thank you, Sister,' I said.

I was amazed at the imperious tone of my voice. What was more, I was astonished at the way it affected Sister. For once she seemed completely at a loss. Instead of countermanding my wishes she merely struggled to collect herself as she muttered, 'Of course you must go back in the lung.'

My voice remained very quiet but determined as I continued,

clearly and slowly so there was no chance of misunderstanding: 'Surely this must be my decision. I am the one most affected by it.'

'You can't', she objected. 'You are not capable. You must return to the lung.'

I answered, 'I'm more than capable of making my own decisions, Sister, and sticking to them.'

'I can't be expected to reorganise my ward when you want to go back in the lung later on,' she commented.

'I don't think you heard me, Sister,' I replied. 'I said that I do not intend to return to the iron-lung any more. I meant exactly that.'

Sister continued, 'You might think you can manage now but it will be a long night when you find you can't sleep and the night staff won't be able to put you back.'

I persisted, 'I'm not going back – ever.'

She tried harder, saying that the consequences could be very serious.

I agreed and said that I would meet them as they came.

Suddenly she whisked her nurses out of the room. I was relieved and incredulous. Not one of them had tried to disconnect my respirator, pull back my sheet or take away my supporting pillows. My words alone had stopped them in their tracks. I could not believe that the first part of the battle was over. I steeled myself to oppose Sister should she return.

The morning after I had resolved not to return to the lung I woke up with a crashing headache. It was half-past five and the Night Nurse had just flung the curtains back. The sun streamed on to my face as I woke in a bed for the first time since I had polio. I thought the headache must be because of my position. Instead of lying flat on my back in the lung in the darker part of the room, I was propped up beside the window. As I could not move my head I was unable to look away from the light.

The nurse put my tea on the locker. 'Be back in a minute to give it to you,' she said kindly. 'How do you feel?'

'I'm not sure yet.'

The nurse grinned and rushed away. Audrey and Jean, who were usually very sleepy in the mornings, were wide-awake. Jean called out, 'Isn't it great we are all out of the lungs?' Audrey asked me if I was all right.

I thought for a moment, then I lied: 'I'm fine, thanks. I feel drunk with the thought that I made it through the night.'

'Did you think you'd have to ask to go back?' Jean asked.

'Oh no, it's not that. I knew I couldn't give in. I just didn't know whether Sister would be able to get a grip on me and somehow force me to return.'

I fell to thinking about the previous night. I had needed all the strength I could find. Luckily Ken had been at a council meeting and unable to come and see me. He might have strengthened my resolve but, on the other hand, he might have been so concerned about the consequences that he would have tried to persuade me to leave the lung more gradually. I had prayed hard to everyone I had ever heard of, from my own Church of England parents to my Roman Catholic godmother. I had felt like a captain of a ship in distress, determined to stay afloat and get my ship home and calling up every available assistance. I had prayed to God the Father, God the Son, God the Holy Ghost, the Virgin Mary, all the saints – especially St Antony, patron saint of lost causes.

I didn't know where my strength had come from but now I felt so elated that even my bad headache could not take my serenity from me. When the nurse returned I asked her to pour my tea away as it was cold. 'What's the date today?' I wondered aloud.

'It's the sixteenth of May.'

The sixteenth of May! So I must have come out of the lung for the last time on the fifteenth. As I was put in a lung on the fifteenth of October that made seven calendar months exactly.

Suddenly it was time for the surgeon's round. I still felt as though I was sitting several inches above my actual bed while the collection of students gathered around to look at me. Sister was telling the surgeon across my bed in front of the students what an uncooperative and difficult patient I was. She could have been talking about somebody else entirely for all the impact her words made on me, although I found them embarrassing in front of an audience.

The surgeon looked at me inquiringly as I had not bothered to speak. 'What have you to say?' he asked.

'I must go home to my children,' I answered. 'Coming out of the lung is the first step. With your permission I shall stay out.'

'How do you feel?'

'Very well, thank you,' I lied, looking him straight in the eye as though my life depended on convincing him that I could cope on a cuirass.

'See how she goes,' he said to Sister.

Suddenly the surgeon had gone. His rounds were finished. Sister bustled in with several nurses, moved me out of the room and into another, setting me apart from my friends. This had made me break down before.

Strangely, I was now happy to be on my own. I did not know where I had gathered my immunity from fear. I did not know that I was in a state of inebriation caused by the accumulation of carbon-dioxide and insufficiency of oxygen because the cuirass breathed me less adequately than the iron-lung. I only knew I was thankful to be in a quieter room with just one respirator pump going – my own – very few visitors except the nurses and physiotherapists who were actually caring for me, and no room-mates. My head was aching so much that I had no wish to make polite conversation.

Nurses relayed messages from John. Apparently he was delighted that I was now in the next room. Then he asked me to listen with him to Bing Crosby. The nurse switched on the earphones that were always suspended from the back of my bed, and the familiar words rolled around the room:

For you and I have a guardian angel,
Oh high, with nothing to do,
But to give to me and to give to you,
Love forever true.

Shortly afterwards David and Jonathan wheeled themselves to my french window. 'We heard you stuck your toes in and refused to go back to the lung,' David said.

I was astonished they had heard about it so quickly. 'How did you know?'

'It's all over the place. The whole hospital is rooting for you. Keep it up.'

'I'm doing my best,' I said. 'Thanks for coming in.'

'Well,' said Jonathan, 'we couldn't leave you in solitary, could we? See you again some time.' They glided out as quietly as they had glided in.

The first day passed as a dream. When Ken arrived he regarded me with a mixture of surprise, pleasure and concern. We seemed somehow to be very close and each drew strength from the other at the significance of graduating from lung to cuirass.

'Only two more steps to go, from cuirass to Bragg-Paul and from Bragg-Paul home,' I said. What I didn't tell Ken was that I intended coming home on a cuirass if necessary, just like Dr Finnigan. I was sure that Ken was more competent than any nurse.

The nurse who was settling patients down for the night was wearing a mask as she had a cold. Ken began cleaning my teeth for me in order that I should not be so open to infection.

Sister came bustling into the room and demanded, 'What are you doing?' Ken thought his actions seemed self-evident but answered politely for my sake: 'I'm cleaning my wife's teeth, Sister.'

She said, 'There is a nurse on duty to do that.'

'But she has a cold and cannot come near my wife.'

Again Sister backed down, but I was furious at her tone. A year ago when I was up and about no one would have dared to have spoken to either of us in this fashion. Then, my teeth were my own affair. As far as I was concerned Ken still had far more right than anyone else to perform any personal service for me. Yet I knew I must not dwell on it, it was not important. What was important was that I should get better and go home.

When Day One in the cuirass ended, I slept the sleep of the just.

I had a headache when I woke but it was not as bad as the previous day. I confidently expected it to get better and better. I still felt slightly sick and ate very little but I believed it good to fast now and then. Later I learned that my red blood cells had increased phenomenally to help improve the flow of my diminished oxygen supply. I still managed to cope with the usual routines.

Monica, the physiotherapist, brought a ball with her when she came. It had been bandaged firmly into John's right hand to keep his fingers bent and now it was my turn. John said that the ball travelling from hand to hand between us would reinforce the message of the red roses. I had discovered that Monica had a very soft spot for John – she talked about him most of the time. Soon I felt I knew him intimately although I had never met him.

When Monica left, the doctor came into the room on her own. This was strange as she was usually accompanied by Sister. Without any preamble, she began lecturing me rapidly. She alleged that I had complained about trivialities, that I was a perfectionist and that instead of complaining I should think about John. While she was talking nonstop I could not reply. Eventually she paused long enough for me to draw breath and defend myself. Her complaints seemed out of proportion to anything I could call to mind.

I asked her if she had finished what she had to say and whether I was to be allowed to answer. I assured her I had no idea what she was talking about.

'Your husband went to see Sister last night with Jean's husband. He alleged you never get any butter and sugar and so on and you can never find a nurse when you need one.'

'If that is true, it's happening without my knowledge,' I replied.

'Jean's husband must have waylaid my husband after visiting-time, requesting his support. If you look in my locker you will see a row of little pots all brought in from home each week – one for sugar, one for butter and so on. My husband has supplemented my diet without any fuss ever since I came to this place and I expect he will go on doing so, as the food in this hospital is inadequate. That is hardly serious. Nor can I believe that you really regard being a perfectionist as a fault. If it is, then this hospital is the first place in which I have heard such an opinion. When you mention John, I really must protest. I think of John more often than you know, but I do not have the kind of mind or soul that would make me feel better at the thought that someone else is worse off! Thinking of John's predicament only adds to my misery as I cannot jump out of bed to do anything to help him. It is true – we are short of nurses – but I put up with that in the hope that John's nursing needs are met.'

After such a long speech I had become violently short of breath and I had to fight for my words. It must have been obvious to the doctor that my battle to respond to her comments caused my breathing to become distressingly laboured.

I put this matter out of my head but was intrigued at tea-time to find beside the usual bread and scrape and cakes, some sardine sandwiches. I wondered if this was a sign of an improving diet but, alas, this treat was a once-only occasion. Every week a friend sent me half-a-dozen new-laid eggs. Every week I had to give them away to the nurses as no one had time to cook them and feed me. This worried me because I knew from the doctors at the Isolation Hospital that I needed a high-protein diet. The food at the Rehabilitation Hospital was bulky and mainly carbohydrates. It seemed to me that it would have been inadequate for anyone, and it was hopelessly inappropriate for disabled people who were trying to regain their strength.

The next morning the doctor spoke to me again. She said she would not have me upsetting her staff. Naturally, I thought she was still harping on the same subject and that Sister had complained to her again. Wearily I asked, 'What have I done now?'

The doctor replied: 'You said you wished you could take your mind home and just leave your body here for us to deal with.'

I looked at her in amazement. 'Yes, I remember saying some-thing like that to Monica. I said it was a pity I could not take my mind home to deal with the domestic detail. It worries me that my husband has everything to do, with the children in Bedfordshire and his week's work, as well as visiting me, when I would give anything to be home looking after him. I'm sorry this should have upset Monica.'

I was puzzled by this but even more confused when she returned the next morning. This time it was: 'You are taking too much of the nurses' time during your treatment. The nurse was with you for twenty minutes.'

I couldn't think why twenty minutes was regarded as too long, considering everything that had to be done. 'Was she?' I answered. 'She could have been. I did not take stock of the time and she only did the essentials.'

'She cannot be spared for all that time. In future her sessions must be much shorter.'

I was completely baffled and rationalised her changed approach by thinking that maybe she had been overworking.

That night the Night Sister woke me with, 'Why don't you give in to them? They are sure to win in the end.'

As I raised no subject for discussion I could not think what she was talking about. I asked, 'Give in to what?'

'Go back into the lung,' she replied.

'What for? The Professor said I could stay out.'

'But don't you see – it wasn't *their* idea. Why don't you go along with them? It will make life a lot easier for you.'

I could not believe my ears. So far as I was concerned I was out of the lung for ever. No one had suggested I should go back in. Why should a senior member of staff side against her own colleagues and befriend me? Did she really care what was happening to me? Or had the doctor, on finding her tough tactics did not work, asked the Night Sister to soften me up by feigning friendship? Either she was for me or for them. Sincere, or acting a part. I was in no position to decide.

'I'm not going back into the lung whatever happens,' I said. 'I'm on my way home and if anyone obstructs me I shall consult my consultant. Goodnight. I am so weary. I hope you don't mind if I go to sleep now.'

She said goodnight and left me, but I did not sleep for a long time.

I kept turning over in my mind the happenings of the past few days and the behaviour of the senior staff. The Night Sister's words had put a new perspective on things. I had felt free to make my own decision about whether I should stay in the lung but obviously in doing so I had annoyed Sister and the doctor. Oh God, I thought, why have you put me so completely in the power of these women? I do not take out my frustrations on *them*. Why do you allow them to do this to me?

I seemed to get the impression – I can hardly call it an answer – that I was not *completely* in their power; that even stripped of ability and vitality as I was, I still had whole areas of my life that were known to me only. I fell asleep thinking about this.

Chapter 17
Going Places

In June Ken bought a second-hand car. This made the journey to the hospital much easier for him and we could spend longer together – two whole glorious hours on Saturdays.

Together, but not alone. For my solitary confinement had been short-lived. The room I was in would hold only one other bed and locker since my respirator pump took up considerable space. Now patients fresh from the operating theatre were wheeled in one by one. They must have had some strange impressions as they floated in and out of the post-operative fog to the throb of my respirator pump. I always made a point of apologising profoundly for the noise of the respirator. Sometimes my companion would be retching and vomiting, then I always kept my toe firmly on my bell until a nurse appeared to mop her up – although I did not dare ring the bell for my own unscheduled needs.

One of our welcome visitors to the wards was the trolley lady. Patiently she walked from bed to bed with her goods – soaps, toothpaste, stationery, sweets. She was a kind person who would take my purse from the locker, hold it where I could see it and count the money out. She delivered not only commodities to our bedsides but also a joke or two and a giggle.

It was Andrew's fourth birthday in June. Ken had shopped for the present and the card, and I was able to buy little bonus boxes of sweets for both boys. Grandma was giving a birthday party for him and they were all coming to the hospital on Sunday.

When the children arrived they were full of the party and the fun they'd had – it had an extra significance now they were so rarely together. They drank Lucozade that I'd bought from the trolley lady and we shared the little cake that Mum had made. I say we shared, but at this time I still would not allow myself to be fed or given a drink in front of Brian and Andrew. I said I was too full up and would eat it later.

Suddenly it was time for them to go. I gave Andrew his box of birthday sweets and Brian his un-birthday one. They flung themselves on me, planted their two fierce kisses on my cheeks and were gone.

Ken hated shopping, but this year he excelled himself for my wedding anniversary present. He had found a pretty little clock in gold and cream colours with delicate hands and numbers. I was enchanted with my present and would have been delighted had he given it to me silently. But as he stood it on my locker he said, 'This is no ordinary clock. It is a magic clock for a very special person and a very special purpose. This clock makes time disappear. Every time you look at it you will be amazed at how much nearer you are to coming home.'

The clock was a tremendous tonic. It did indeed help me to strive towards going home.

On the fourth of July it was John's birthday and he had already voiced his special birthday wish to Brenda. For his birthday present he wanted his bed and mine to be pushed out of our rooms into the corridor at tea-time so that we could meet for the very first time.

Sister was off duty. Sheila and Mavis were in charge. When Brenda suddenly proposed that we should have a ten-minute tea-party in the corridor Sheila agreed and set about organising it. I was not to be told. I was merely to be moved in bed with my respirator as if changing rooms again.

My first impression of John was a blaze of red-gold wavy hair with a thick matching beard. Beneath his well-marked eyebrows a pair of challenging grey eyes quizzed me. He used his eyebrows expertly to emphasise his words effectively as a Neapolitan would use his hands.

'Well-met by sunlight,' he said, after introductions were completed.

'You have the advantage of me for you saw me arrive and I haven't seen you before. Now I shall be able to picture you clearly when your red roses arrive or the nurse knocks on the wall because they are playing our tune again.'

'I hope you're not disappointed,' John answered. 'I am not quite myself these days.' His authoritative voice sounded wistful.

'No,' I replied, 'you are just as I imagined and maybe more.'

'You too,' he added.

Then, overcome by our mutual admiration, we looked down at our sheets and I suddenly said, 'Sheila, will you be mother, please?'

'Of course,' she said, picking up the tea-pot and handing the birthday sponge to Brenda to cut up and pass round. Brenda fed me and Sheila fed John while they ate some cake too.

John gave me an un-birthday present – a box of Kirsch-filled chocolates. I had sent him a huge tin of Johnson's baby powder as I had discovered this was the kind he used.

There wasn't time for John and me to say very much nor was there any need. We knew we should always be friends. I thought of the doctor and wondered what she would have said.

One morning when I woke up I found that my head was free and that I could lift it back up if it fell forward, with my chin resting on the rim of my cuirass. I could roll it slightly from side to side as though the vice in which it had been held for so long had melted away in the night.

I was so excited I sent immediate word to John. 'Someone seems to have turned my head. I wonder who?'

John had just discovered a tiny useful movement in the index finger of his right hand and, with Sheila guiding him, he wrote a spidery five-letter code: 'ITYAW . . . I Think You Are Wonderful. The doctor, who was not so impressed, merely commented, 'Most people recover some head control.'

I was elated – signs of progress were rare. This one encouraged me in my belief that if I persevered I might be cured after all.

The sun shone all day and I could feel its benefit even through the window. By the time Ken came I had rolled my head on its little path from side to side hundreds of times. Ken was so delighted he looked suddenly ten years younger. I was in such a hurry to get better and my recovery was so painfully slow that I didn't know how to contain myself. Dear God, I thought, if I cannot be helped and strengthened for my own sake – or for yours – then for Ken and our sons' sakes, let it happen.

Summer days sneaked by. On fine mornings our beds were pushed through the french windows on to the concrete path outside so that Shirley, the ward maid, could wash the floors more easily. Sometimes my bed would be parked beside John's for a while. We couldn't turn our heads sufficiently to look at each other so we didn't speak much. We just enjoyed the companionship of being in the same boat.

On one occasion he commented, 'You're not like the others. Quiet women are rare.'

'No need for words between us, is there, John? It's nice just to relax together and enjoy the sight of the sky and the feel of the sun.'

We often discussed hospital practices when outside. I met many other patients who were sometimes wheeled to the sides of our beds. John and I were a captive audience and confided in each other about our favourites. John, being hag-ridden, welcomed another John, also recovering from polio. He was a student who bowled along in his wheelchair and swung alongside John's bed. He was an excellent tonic for John as they swapped yarns about Africa.

These trips outside were mystery tours as we never knew whom we would meet. When you have been isolated and your contact with other human beings has been severely restricted, everyone seems exotic and larger than life. Usually my visitors were other women, but one of the most moving encounters was with an enchanting little four-year-old Spanish boy who was afflicted by polio. His enormous brown eyes lent an expression of anguish to his olive-skinned young face. His black bubble curls bobbed about as he stomped along on his calliper-enclosed legs, swinging his arms with his elbows out in a frantic endeavour to keep his balance. He was also handicapped by the lack of English words at his command. Even so, there was no mistaking his message as his voice fluted out: 'My nurse, come back. I love you.' 'His' nurse was hurrying away from him with her fingers in her ears, trying not to hear him. We were almost in tears ourselves at his helplessness.

As the summer grew hotter so the number of people being stricken with polio increased. Supplies of the new vaccine were so tiny that only special groups of people could be immunised.

By now Audrey and Jean had graduated to wheelchairs and Bragg-Paul respirators. More than that, they could breathe unaided for the best part of the day. They were my favourite visitors. I regarded them as my living guarantees of slow but sure recovery. I never minded that their achievements upstaged mine. I was very fond of them both, as is the way of people who have been through tough times together and then forced apart. However, they could not bring themselves to tell me that they would be going home.

Brenda broke the news to me; I was both sad and glad – sad not to see them but glad for them, that they could begin to pick up the threads of their lives again. I should miss their firm support, but I would be seeing them from time to time when they came to the Outpatient Clinic for check-ups. One day it would be my turn to follow them home.

After their departure I was moved to another room, but John was shifted also and we were still next door to each other. He continued asking the nurse to knock on the wall each time 'True Love' was being played on the wireless.

It was at this stage that Monica decided to try to get me up from my bed into an armchair so I should feel more normal. She put the armchair in position, explained what she was going to do, then whipped off my cuirass, put one arm around my waist, pulled me across the bed and took my weight on the upper part of her body. She slid my feet to the edge of the bed as she moved my floppy arms together by securing both my useless hands in her capable one and with a swift twist and a hauling movement she had me in front of the chair.

I was fighting desperately for my breath, my head had fallen too far forward for me to raise it again and my left foot had fallen across my right foot, trapping it.

I could hear Monica insisting, 'Move your left foot back.'

But I couldn't think how to do it. My left sterno-mastoid muscle, which reaches from the top of the chest to the back of the ear, kept making frantic but feeble spasms and jerking my head sideways as every available accessory breathing muscle desperately attempted to grab a gasp of air.

Monica threw me into the armchair and held the cuirass tightly to my chest without bothering to fix the strap into place. Gradually I began to regain my breathing equilibrium. She then fastened the belt and put my arms on pillows so they no longer hung down beside me uselessly and painfully.

I had been badgering Monica to get me up as a birthday present for Ken and for several days she had been heaving me to the edge of the bed and supporting me as she half-turned me to face the door to put my feet on a high chair beside the bed. I still had the picture of myself as an agile, vigorous young woman and was surprised at the slowness of every movement. Here I was being cosseted and carefully controlled as though my age had trebled and I had suddenly become a frail and senile old woman.

With the sunshine and fresh air I had rapidly turned brown. I felt a sense of well-being which was completely at odds with my inability to move. Gradually Monica managed to get me up for longer periods. At first on every other day, then every day except weekends; ten minutes, twenty minutes, thirty minutes, and eventually two whole hours.

The effort was exhausting. I fought like a tiger for my breath. My motivation was my need to return to my children and I felt I was in a do-or-die situation. If I managed to force some sort of breathing capacity into existence I could insist on going home with my cuirass, as had Dr Finnigan. If I died, then Ken could marry again and make a new home for the children while they were young enough to forget about me.

I was amazed at the strength of mind that drove me on with this battle just as it had compelled me to refuse to return to the iron-lung. One part of the mind said, 'You must be mad.' The other part agreed, 'I suppose I am but it can only be expected when a family is forced apart as we are.'

Brian's sixth birthday was on September the fourteenth – a Friday – and the family were all coming to see me on Sunday for our own little celebration. Last year I had made Brian's cake in the shape of a fort with candles designed like the guardsmen we had seen on our farewell tour of London. I missed the fun of preparing such surprises for my family. Instead, I nursed along my new ability to sit out of bed with the satisfaction that I would present them with a new surprise.

Ken's birthday was on the Monday and I would see him in the evening for half an hour. Naturally my secret was almost too much to contain. He did not press the point or try to guess when I told him I would have something to reveal when next he visited.

I had bought a road atlas for his car. Brenda had smuggled it in, wrapped it up and left it in my locker for me. I tried to think of some way I could write on his card. My head was too wobbly for me to control a pen in my mouth. I kept telling myself, *it doesn't matter really*, but to me it mattered very much. I wanted to write my own birthday message for him to read – not to dictate it to someone else.

When Ken came to see me on Wednesday I was wrapped in an old army blanket. I did not care. I sat in the chair smiling expectantly as though I were a queen. My cuirass was tightly strapped on to me over a large square of cotton which protected my skin from being chafed by the rubber seal. I wore tiny cotton pants but nothing else as the effort of being dressed would have robbed me of the energy I needed for the effort of sitting upright for two hours. The old blanket served not only to keep me warm but also to keep my arms and body together. A woolly patchwork blanket was tucked in around my lower half and folded into a bundle under my feet. My hair was brushed back into the usual ponytail. I never looked at myself in the mirror. I merely imagined that the essential me was somehow visible and that was all Ken wanted to see.

When he arrived he was astonished. 'So this is my surprise! What a marvellous one it is. How long can you stay up?'

'All visiting-time,' I bragged. 'But you know, it's a funny thing. Before I had polio, if I sat down I thought I was at rest and not making any effort. Now I find that being propped up in this chair with everything supported – head, back, arms and so on – is phenomenally difficult to sustain and tremendously hard work. I keep sliding towards the left where the weight of the air-pipe seems heavy. I feel so stupid that I can't support myself. I gradually slide like a jelly. It's most confusing. I expect babies feel like this when they are first sat up.'

Ken spent our visiting-time supporting me in an upright position. He could not put an arm around me because my cuirass prevented it, but at least we were able to be a little nearer each other, sitting side by side, than when I was on my high bed and feeling so remote.

I put so much effort into this daily marathon of sitting up that I was now too tired to talk much when Ken came in the evenings. He would spend the time rubbing my arms, brushing my hair and taking away some of the frustration of not being able to move.

Meanwhile there were changes within the hospital. Polio was on the rampage around the world and as the numbers of victims increased we lent our two most senior therapists to overseas countries. The chief occupational therapist and Monica both flew off to South America. Brenda now had to assume the administrative responsibility of the Occupational Therapy Department, so John and I were kept occupied from then on by a dark-haired girl named Hilary.

Monica had introduced me to her successor by telling me she was also an ex-Wren, Maureen, or as she became in the following months, Fiz. Fiz regarded the world with the same air of detached concern as John and myself: she quickly became a friend and ally.

After these changes Sister went on holiday. Before she left she gave the staff nurses a long list of instructions, the recounting of which caused much mirth.

The first instruction was about a sealed biscuit-tin with a large label on which was printed in block capitals: DO NOT OPEN THIS. No one could ignore the challenge of such an eyebrow-raising label. The opened tin contained a sealed parcel. On top of it lay a sheet of paper with the words: I TOLD YOU NOT TO OPEN THIS. Helpless with laughter, they could hardly unwrap the parcel, but when they did they found Sister had squirrelled away several pounds of butter which had already begun to turn rancid. They sent it back to the kitchen in exchange for a fresh supply.

The second instruction that was disobeyed concerned a stack of blue flannelette sheets which a grateful patient, remembering how cold and shivery she had been, had presented to the ward when she left. These 'cuddles' or 'next-to's' as they were called, because they were tucked in next to us to avoid the chill of the cotton sheets, were becoming discoloured in the airing cupboard while those of us who could not move were feeling the first pinches of the autumn frosts under our threadbare bedclothes.

'Can't let these discolour,' commented Sheila as she tucked the flannelette snugly around our necks and around our feet. We lived in a fool's paradise for a while. When Sister returned from holiday she whipped them from our beds and hoarded them in her store once more. We missed the forbidden warmth. The nip of autumn felt much sharper when we returned to our old thin bedclothes.

As September careered towards October I became very restless. It was almost a year since I had been stricken by polio. I was constantly being reminded of all the marvellous things I had been able to do and vividly recalled those last few weeks while in possession of my taken-for-granted able body. I felt a new sense of rebellion welling up inside me. I just had to summon up more strength from somewhere so I could start going places and never, never, never spend another polio anniversary shut up in hospital.

Chapter 18
Road Obstructed

That autumn I shared my room with other polio survivors and discovered from them what very different forms the disease can take.

My first companion had been pregnant when polio developed. After giving birth successfully she had spent two weeks in an iron-lung. She considered that she had suffered the severest experience that life and polio could inflict, yet her range of movement did not seem to be impaired in any way.

Following her came Margaret, about my own age, who had survived bulbar polio. She could move, walk, use her hands to write, yet she could neither talk nor swallow without tremendous effort. I could understand her speech, but she found coping with the nurses, doctors, physiotherapists and so on, very exhausting. Her husband was in the forces and could visit rarely; when Ken came to see me she would disappear, so conscious was she of her affliction.

My next room-mate – like so many patients in this long-stay hospital – was a long way from home. Her elderly father had to travel all the way from Dorset, so Ken arranged to give him a lift from Newbury. That worked for a while, but this was the autumn of the Suez crisis and petrol was rationed. Many patient's relatives faced problems with visiting. I pretended to Daphne that my only worry was the lack of petrol, but I felt sick at heart. Ken was still on the Naval Reserve List. I could not imagine how I would manage without him. I knew if he were killed or injured I could never bring Brian and Andrew under one roof again.

Even with Ken working in Newbury I did not seem to have any hope of going home. I had arrived in hospital determined to benefit from all the advantages that it had to offer, including visits to the pool, yet I had not been in the water once. Having been so badly battered verbally by the doctor when I decided to stay out of the iron-lung, I hesitated before asking to go to the pool. With the help of Fiz, I was continuing to increase my tolerance of staying out of bed and I was eager to attempt something different. I waited for a day on which I woke up feeling in command of myself and when the doctor came round I asked whether she would consider my going to the pool.

'You cannot possibly cope with that yet,' she said. 'Apart from anything else, you lack the breathing capacity and the weight of the water on your chest will be against you.'

I insisted that I be allowed to try it. 'After all,' I said, 'how do I know for sure that it's beyond me if I never try?'

The doctor said wearily, 'All right, try it. You obviously won't believe me until you do. But don't tell the others. I don't want anyone else to think of visiting the pool who isn't going there already.'

If Fiz was nervous about our pool experiment she did not show it. She dressed me in my swimsuit under my cuirass and, with a porter to wheel and hand-pump my respirator, we set off up the slope to the pool. Fiz gave me a good breathe before attempting my immersion and then, in her practised way, she whipped off my cuirass and had me supported in the pool very rapidly with various buoyant air-rings. Alas, I could not hold my arms into my side or stop my head jerking about in the battle to gulp in some air. Despite our efforts and determination, soon I began to turn blue.

Quickly she fished me out of the pool and had me back on my bed. With no time to dry me she whipped off my costume, covered me with talcum powder and belted me naked into my cuirass. 'Don't you ever ask me to bring you here again,' she said. 'If it doesn't kill you, it will me.'

So there was to be no help from the pool. Then my ambitions to increase my stamina were sabotaged by the good intentions of the doctor. She tried to protect those of us who were on respirators from the worst ravages of winter by prescribing anti-flu injections. Unfortunately I reacted to my dose badly. I ran a temperature and mucus collected in my lungs which I could not cough up. A relay of physiotherapists was needed to help me. They dropped the whole weight of their hands on my chest about eighteen times a minute for several minutes at frequent intervals around the clock. They shook my chest to make the coughing spasm that my own respiratory muscles could no longer produce. I was soon very tender and found their pounding on my sore ribs hard to bear. I did not cry or make any sound except from the back of my throat as I tried to work with the physiotherapists to clear my chest. One of them remarked, 'My God, you're a game one.'

I was surprised by her remark. How could I not make every

effort? I feared that if my chest was not cleared I would suffer another lung collapse – as I had in the Isolation Hospital – and all the ghastly treatment that it would entail. Heartbreakingly, I would lose the stamina that I had so patiently and painfully built up over the past months.

Winter had arrived. October days diminished and November drifted in. On the Saturday before November the fifth Brian and Andrew were to share a bonfire and fireworks at Grandad's house.

I lay in my bed on Bonfire Night thinking of my children and the fun we had had two years earlier in London when we baked potatoes in their jackets and made parkin and toffee-apples. I wondered whether the children remembered it, but guessed their heads would be too full of the present excitement to think of anything else.

A week later when Brian and Andrew came on their Sunday visit they brought home-made birthday cards. The cards were a riot of colour – their minds were still full of bonfires and fireworks. Their presents were some pretty-coloured handkerchiefs that would be easy to find against the white pillows or bed-sheets. I promised not to use them until the following Saturday, the seventeenth, which was my birthday, although I had been allowed to have my presents opened early as this was our only opportunity to be together as a family.

On my birthday morning Fiz rushed into my room carrying a big bag. Daphne, who was always hungry, sat up and asked, 'What's that delicious smell?'

'Wait and see,' said Fiz, as she began to unpack a bottle of sherry, three glasses, and some plates wrapped up in warm kitchen towels.

'Quick,' she said, 'have this while it's hot. You're always talking about toast, so I've made some for a birthday treat.'

On the plates were mushrooms on toast. Somehow, she had cooked them on the electric fire in the Physiotherapy Department.

'I'd forgotten how delicious toast is,' I said. 'It's even better than I remember.'

'I'm very good at toast,' said Fiz.

'You certainly are,' I agreed, adding the accolade: 'I couldn't have made it better myself.'

The quality and quantity of hospital food was such that a great deal of some patients' time was spent in trying to supplement it. One evening when Sister was off duty two women patients wandered into our room.

'I'm Tilly and she's Milly,' said a large red-haired woman, pointing to her thin, yellow-haired companion. 'We're cooking steak. We're starving on hospital diet. We're only just across the corridor so the steak won't burn; we wanted to see for ourselves what goes on in here.'

'We're starving too,' hinted Daphne hopefully. Her words were ignored. Instead of getting the offer of steak, she was asked: 'What are these machines then?'

'They are breathing-machines. They do our breathing for us.'

She was left completely speechless when the reply came as the two drifted back to their steaks: 'You lucky so-and-so's! Fancy even having your breathing done for you. How spoiled can you get?'

I could not help smiling at their abysmal ignorance. What would they have thought about my reading-machine?

Hilary had obtained this through the Red Cross to ease the nothingness of the deep midwinter, without books or records to compensate for my inability to cook, knit, sew or use any of the other thousand-and-one skills that had been locked in by polio. It was different from the book-projector I had used in the Isolation Hospital. This new machine had a ledge on which the book rested and perspex clips to hold the book fast. A long bobbin to the left of the book revolved when instructed. It wound about itself a long line of thick nylon thread, with tiny metal tabs attached to it about six inches apart. One of these tabs had to be fixed to the side of every page separately. To turn the page it was necessary to press a button with your chin or toe, or whatever, to start the bobbin revolving. This wound on the thread and pulled the page over. It was important to keep the tag on the left-hand page. If you accidentally turned the bobbin too many times and pulled the tag off, the page that had just been turned over would infuriatingly turn itself back. Only hardback books could be used as their pages would lie flat. Each time the tabbed pages had been read, someone had to thread up more pages before you could carry on reading.

This was one of Ken's jobs in the evenings – the nurses never had time for anything but essential care. Occasionally Hilary would make a special effort to do it or would find someone else to lend a hand. My requests to the library lady were always for stories of adventure or humour. I blessed the days that James Thurber, Thor Hyerdhal, Jacques Cousteau and company were born.

As Christmas approached, we learned we were to spend Christmas Day in the big ward. On Christmas Eve the festivities began with a choir of nurses walking from room to room wearing their cloaks red-side-out instead of the usual blue. They carried little lanterns and chorused 'Hark the Herald Angels Sing', evoking echoes of other Christmases at other times in other places. My thoughts were with Ken and the children. I imagined Ken creeping into a darkened bedroom and listening quietly to make sure the children had fallen asleep.

When I awoke on Christmas morning and exchanged greetings with the nurse I was deeply touched to hear that Father Christmas had been, as she put it. She showed me a Christmas stocking that had been left beside my bed. Later, during breakfast while she was feeding me, she tipped out the contents on my bed and showed them to me. They were all practical presents. A pretty face-flannel, a tablet of soap, a tin of talcum powder and so on. When I asked who had provided them I learned they had come out of the general fund.

Everyone was very busy, so there wasn't much time to talk. Sister was directing a convoy of beds and wheelchairs along the corridor. Eventually it was our turn to be hustled up the corridor – beds, respirators and all. I was next to an old lady who tried to talk to me, but I couldn't hear what she had said as the sound of my respirator pump obliterated her words. The patient on the other side of me was hidden by a huge bouquet of flowers on her locker. Likewise I could see the people opposite but could not hear them.

At lunch-time Sister pushed in a trolley laden with roast turkey and all its trimmings. It was sliced by one of the surgeons, slightly disguised in a butcher's apron. I could not talk while being fed but the nurse who was feeding me kept up a cheery conversation until she ran out of steam.

After lunch, things were cleared away quickly. The television set was switched on for the Queen's speech. I hadn't seen television since before I had polio, well over a year ago. A general air of gloom settled over all of us as we thought of our nearest and dearest who were miles away. No one was allowed any visitors on Christmas Day. All the nurses were on duty for the whole day and some of them were very, very tired. I found it difficult to believe that, thanks to polio, I was in the absurd position of not being able to see my husband on Christmas Day. The hospital was full of patients similarly deprived. Ken had offered to ferry other patients' relatives to and fro but Sister had been adamant.

'Rules are rules,' she had said. 'Some patients are quite happy without visitors. Not all of them want to see their relatives, and not all relatives want to visit on Christmas Day.'

When Ken had told me about his discussion with Sister he had asked if I wanted to see someone in authority. I had said I thought it best not to bother. I knew the winter was taking its toll of me. I did not have the strength to cope with any trouble – rather, I wanted to conserve my resources to ensure that this time next year I would be home.

By four o'clock it was dark. We were hurried back to our various rooms and reconnected to our power supplies there. I saw Daphne become engrossed in her book, leaving me to my own thoughts. These were quite naturally of Ken and the children – I felt such a terrible longing to be with them.

On Boxing Day we were shuttled into the big ward again. Everyone was tired from the strain of the previous day, but fortunately we could look forward to visitors. They were allowed in from two o'clock, as at normal weekend visiting, and they were to share our tea and entertainments with us.

When we were hurried back to our rooms for the evening my feelings were mainly of relief that my second hospital Christmas was over. Now to get on with the real business of a rehabilitation hospital – getting fit again and able to leave. Never, never, *never*, I resolved, shall I spend another Christmas in this place.

I began to plan my escape.

Chapter 19
Travelling Hopefully

By the New Year my resolutions were made. I would get home if it killed me. I would convince Fiz that I was stronger than average and would encourage her to let me do more. I would ask Hilary to fix up some pulleys and strings so that I could utilise the movement in my feet to help me use my hands. I would plan a bungalow that I could run from a panel of push-buttons that could be fixed to my bed or a chair.

The possibility of my returning home was discussed with the Almoner, who was very discouraging, and our local Medical Officer of Health, who was more hopeful. I reminded Ken of the specially-adapted bungalow that had been built near us in London just before we moved to Newbury. The disabled woman who was to run it was wheelchair-assisted and could move about the whole bungalow with ease as there were no steps or narrow doors. In my head I designed a bungalow that I could manage from my bed and every time Ken visited I discussed it with him.

I told the doctor that I hoped to go home at Easter, stressing the effect of separation on the family and my very, very slow rate of progress. I felt positive that the only way to speed up my recovery was for me to return home to the healing power of normal surroundings and familiar things. The doctor was horrified. She harked back to her old criticism that I was a perfectionist, and said, 'You won't be able to stand watching other people doing your housework! They never see above or below eye-level.'

In reply, I said I thought I might be trusted to run my own home! I had been married almost ten years and could judge the priorities for myself.

When I told Fiz what was in my mind she was completely disarming: 'I'll get you as fit as I can.'

In the January sales Fiz found me a small and light but strong girdle which she would slip on to me before getting me up. This flimsy support helped my breathing. I was not allowed to get up for visiting-times in the cold but, when I was sufficiently recovered from my vaccine reaction, Fiz began hauling me out of bed for ten minutes each morning so that I would not lose any more ground.

Hilary was rather serious. 'Easter doesn't give us long,' she said thoughtfully.

As I explained how I thought I could be kept in some kind of perpetual motion for longer periods each day, she became more enthusiastic. She was soon totally absorbed in arranging my arms in slings which were attached to strings and pulleys that could be operated by small movements of my feet.

The next time I saw Fiz she had worked out a new routine for me. She borrowed a wheelchair to whisk me off to the Physio-therapy Department, where my respirator was plugged in and we were able to spend time and thought on passing electric charges repeatedly through inert muscles, in an attempt to stimulate even the minutest possible movements. I worked long and hard at my new routine but, disappointingly, without results. I was aston-ished, when my first physiotherapist Monica returned from South America, to realise how totally I had transferred my depen-dence to Fiz. I requested that Fiz should remain my physiothera-pist as a change might result in a setback that I could ill afford. About this time I dubbed Brenda 'Inky' as Fiz's influence had revived the habit of giving people nicknames, Navy-style.

Inky had a special stand made that would cover my cuirass. It looked like a lavatory seat and the hole in the middle was just the right size to hold a soup plate. With endless patience, Inky held my right arm and hand in her two strong hands. With one hand under my elbow and another under my wrist, she guided the spoon (which she had strapped on to my hand) from the plate to my mouth and back again. She was very patient and kind and tried to turn my hand as well as lift my arm so that more of my food would go into my mouth and less on the napkin under my chin. Our activities resulted in an increase in the laundry!

The wheelchairs in which I was transported were described by Fiz as 'centuries-old Bath chairs'. Sister had a collection of these relics, all of which were stretched and seated. They afforded no proper support and encouraged disablement rather than assisting recovery. There had been a commotion behind me one day when two physiotherapists tackled Sister about the way in which I was left lurching over one side of a ramshackle old wheelchair. The words I heard were something like, 'Criminal, unnecessary damage – and look what's happened to her spine.'

I was appalled at this new intelligence about my condition and at first too stunned to do anything about it. When I summoned the courage to discuss it with Fiz, she sought advice from the Pro-fessor and others. A stiff leather jacket was made to act as a splint and keep me upright. Getting the jacket made was an ordeal, but I was desperate to try anything that would straighten my back. A plaster-cast of my chest had to be made quickly and cut off rapidly so that the cuirass could be replaced and I could be breathed adequately again. While the plaster was being made, my neck had jerked my head about violently as I gasped desperately to take in enough air. When I saw the finished leather jacket, I was horrified. The left shoulder was much lower than the right. I protested to the doctor, 'I shall be deformed if I wear that! It will permanently fix one shoulder higher than the other.'

I need not have worried. All the effort that went into making the jacket was wasted. So much of it had to be cut away in front to allow the Bragg-Paul to breathe me that it gave me no support at all. It was discarded as unsuitable. The lavatory seat was also dispensed with. My arms were returned to their slings where they dangled uselessly.

Every day Fiz would drag the Bragg-Paul – still warm from John's body – and buckle it on to me. Gradually I acquired the strength to tolerate it for a couple of hours. I began by wearing it while at rest in bed, then slowly became accustomed to wearing it when sitting up in my chair. To my great delight I found that the Bragg-Paul, fitting like a cummerbund below my tiny bosom, enabled me to be dressed in a bra; also a sweater could be worn to conceal the belt. The lower edge left my hips clear, therefore I could wear pants and slacks too. This made me feel a little more feminine and normal than was possible with the cuirass. I could hardly believe that I had worn no real clothes since I went down with polio, now almost eighteen months ago.

Fiz and I worked hard on my breathing, taking advantage of the improving weather. She taught the nurses how to push on my ribs with the palms of their hands, to breathe me out each time I gasped in whatever air I could manage to snatch through the strange contortions of my neck. Looked at in comparison with what I hoped to do, it wasn't much. But at least it was a few minutes' freedom from machinery each day. Gradually the period was extended. I became able to jerk enough air into my body for a few minutes, then a few more, and then a few more with the assistance of occasional pushes on my chest.

One Sunday in March the weather turned suddenly hot. Fiz buckled me into the Bragg-Paul and got me up into a chair. I was hoping to manage the whole of visiting-time out of bed. I felt happy and confident, believing I looked nearly normal in my sweater and slacks. While I was waiting for Ken, a man who lived in Newbury came over to talk to me. He was very kind and thought that news about my home would be welcome. It might have been, but unfortunately he stood on one of the soft air-pipes of the Bragg-Paul without noticing that he had done so. The air in the pneumatic belt froze. I could not gasp any air in. My head jerked about alarmingly as the muscles in my neck made frantic spasms to help me. I struggled to utter the words 'Get off my pipe', as politely as I could. He stared back in total incomprehension. Desperately, I ransacked my mind to think how I could make him move! I could not point or change my position or take any action to help myself. To my relief Ken arrived, saw my predicament, took the man's arm and moved him aside, trying to cause as little embarrassment as possible. Naturally his main concern was for me. He didn't know how long my air supply had been cut off nor how quickly I would recover. As I had already changed colour he pulled me rapidly back into the room, dragged off my Bragg-Paul and strapped me speedily into my cuirass.

From then on I was very, very careful about my air-pipes. My vulnerability in the presence of kindly but untrained people had been brought home to me; I resolved in future never to be left alone on a Bragg-Paul. It was not only less help than a cuirass but also harder work. That, I could endure for limited periods. The snag with the Bragg-Paul was the same as with the cuirass. So long as the machines worked well, they sustained life, but the moment the air supply was cut off they became positively lethal and their weight and restrictiveness were in themselves sources of danger.

Although I forced myself painfully and slowly away from mechanical respirators for short periods each day my horizons remained severely restricted. At last, on the first day of Lent, I was able to make a short journey without being anchored to a big machine. Inky pushed me in my wheelchair to the hospital chapel, stopping now and then to put her hands on my ribs to give my chest necessary pushes to assist my peculiar breathing. Inside the little chapel I closed my eyes, believing God would not mind that I could not put my hands together or go down on my knees to give my heartfelt thanks for the precious gift of life and the strength that was helping me to make some small progress along the road to recovery.

I could not stay long but felt joyful that I had managed even a small journey without worrying about whether there would be a socket for my respirator plug. Inky gave several good pushes on my chest before rushing me back to my room, putting my cuirass back on and plugging me in.

After that, Inky and Fiz between them got me up and took me around the hospital grounds in one direction or another until I could manage to gasp my way through a whole half-hour. When that great day arrived I was whisked to the hospital entrance and across the road to the house opposite on some speedy errand. While Inky was talking on the doorstep to the occupant of the house, I faced the road, looking at the hospital from the outside for the first time.

As I gazed at the long, low buildings I felt intoxicated and did not want to return. I said as much to Inky, who took one look at my face, wheeled me quickly back to my room and immediately popped me into my cuirass. I protested that I preferred to stay out. Inky gazed at me and shook her head. 'You're a very pretty shade of blue now. I'm not sure I should have taken you so far this afternoon.'

'I feel marvellous,' I insisted.

'Of course you do. You're drunk!'

'Drunk? But I don't drink.'

'No, not alcohol drunk – carbon-dioxide drunk,' said Inky. 'It's a very dangerous condition. The worse you get, the happier you feel, the more reckless you're likely to become.'

I giggled: 'Drunk on carbon dioxide and it's free! Unplug me again.'

'Certainly not. You're just beginning to look a respectable colour.'

I was bitterly disappointed at not being able to push my breathing recovery faster. I seemed to do extraordinarily well one day and manage perhaps half an hour, only to be reduced to ten or fifteen minutes for the next couple of weeks. I had to learn that reaching a high spot was the occasional blessing that made the low, sustained achievement worth attempting.

Despite my persistent efforts, I did not manage to go home for Easter. My Easter treat was being able to manage without my respirator while my children pushed my chair along the concrete path to the locked Occupational Therapy Department and back again. I was then wheeled into the ward and plugged in so that I could manage to find enough breath to talk. My complete help-lessness in the hands of my own small sons was totally confusing for me – and no doubt for them. There was no way of knowing what it meant to them – they were thrilled that we had done something other than collect around my bed. I wondered how I could help them understand why our excursion was limited. They accepted without question my need to return to mechanical help with my breathing. They seemed incredibly sensible.

After Easter I said quite plainly that I was going home when the August holidays began. I intended spending the whole of the holiday with my children and husband and we could work out a living routine together before school started again in September.

The doctor put every possible obstacle in my way. First she said the cost of living would be beyond me. It had increased tremendously while I had been in hospital. Secondly, there was no wheelchair available. None had been ordered and I could not possibly move out of my bedroom at home without one. Thirdly, that if I stayed longer I could learn to do more. We both knew that this was unlikely, the hospital had little left to offer me.

I had discovered that hydrotherapy and electrotherapy were beyond me and I was being used more and more as a guinea-pig for X-ray films. This exposed me to cancer-causing X-rays although my family medical history showed clearly that I was likely to be vulnerable to cancer. During these films I felt very much that I was treated as a 'thing' rather than a person. I was exposed alone when the dangerous rays were switched on. Everyone else clattered from the room. During one sequence I was left with a clothes peg pinching my nose so that my inability to breathe through my mouth could be filmed. On another occasion a white liquid was poured up my nose and I had to try to swallow on command while pictures were being taken. The feeling of being regarded as less than human was very hard to bear: I felt insulted.

When Ken came to see me on our tenth wedding anniversary he flourished a bottle of champagne. John, two staff nurses, Fiz and Inky drank with us from thick kitchen cups. Fiz had helped me to be dressed in a pretty white dress so that a photo could be taken on this auspicious day. It was the last dress that Ken had bought me, full-skirted and feminine with tiny tucks in the bodice – a total change from my usual hospital wear. I was rushed in my wheelchair on to the lawn and swiftly tranferred to an easy chair. The back of the chair would support my back, my arms were arranged along the arms of the chair. Ken placed himself behind the chair so that between shots he could give my ribs an occasional push to assist my breathing.

We became adept at posing me in positions which I could sustain just for the sake of a quick snap, as a glimpse of what we hoped my developing abilities would help me achieve. One day,

Ken, Fiz and Inky held me in a standing position. At the last moment they let me go whilst someone's hands kept a grip on my collar from behind. The camera clicked and hands caught me and sat me in my wheelchair, as I collapsed.

On another occasion – when I was in my wheelchair – Ken sat Andrew on my lap. I could not believe the tremendous weight of my thin little son, but we grinned for the snap before Ken snatched Andrew away again.

In an attempt to assist my positioning, Inky brought me a belt with two front pockets stitched into it. She had designed and made it herself. The next time she and Fiz got me up, my hands were put in the pockets to take the weight of my arms, and Fiz held me beside her as I swayed along on two strange feet and legs which did not seem to belong to me and did not want to go. I was preoccupied with the terrible fight for breath. My head was jerking about in a frantic attempt to grab some air for my gasping lungs. I had refused to believe that making myself desperately out of breath would not somehow compel my breathing mechanism to click into place and start working properly. I repeated the experiment before I was forced to admit that I was probably doing myself more harm than good. I hated being unable to use the pockets but Inky insisted they were one of her few failures, and discarded them.

We celebrated John's birthday with a secret lunch in his room. Inky had prepared crab risotto and lemon meringue pie. We enjoyed this feast and chatted about arranging a farewell party when I left the hospital.

'I don't know what I shall do without you,' said John. 'I can't go home – there's no one I can share with.'

'I know one or two,' I insisted.

'I've nothing to offer.'

'You've more to offer than many men,' I pointed out. 'There's nothing wrong with your head or your heart, is there?'

He did not answer but grew very thoughtful. I did not see him for a week afterwards as Inky and Fiz were keeping me very busy. It was a combined effort to get me as fit as possible before I returned home. My chances of survival, removed from hospital care and without trained personnel at hand, had been estimated at three months.

I urged Inky to take me out again but she made me wait until she thought I was absolutely safe. When the time came, we ventured outside the hospital grounds in the wheelchair, then one day I was loaded into the car and Ken drove round the block. Inky sat in the back seat to hold me upright and occasionally press my chest to keep me breathing.

Gradually, over the weeks we increased the distance until we felt sufficiently safe to attempt a longer expedition. Hilary had friends in Oxford who had a little cottage near the river. There was no access problems and a convenient electric socket by a window overlooking the river. They very kindly asked us all – including my machinery – to tea.

I have never enjoyed such a sense of freedom and escape as on that first visit to a normal home. I longed to have a heart attack through sheer happiness. I wanted Ken to be able to tell the children what a lovely time I had had on my first and last outing right away from the hospital. I wanted him to tell them we had been talking affectionately about them. I also wanted Ken to be free to marry while he was still young and while Brian and Andrew were small enough to accept a new mother. I so much wanted these things that I felt sure they must happen. I was filled with joy and serenity. Then I noticed Hilary making signals to Ken and I knew that my elation was not because my wishes were going to be granted but because of the inebriation effect. My breathing power had not been sufficient to cope with the extra excitement and exertion. I was whisked smartly back to my hospital bed to lie quietly in my cuirass and regain my equilibrium.

Next day I met the County Nursing Officer, the District Nurse and a special helper who were being taught at the hospital how to care for me when I went home. The working of various pieces of equipment which allowed me to breathe was explained to them so that they could pass on the information to others. As I listened, it seemed to me that far too much was being left to Ken. On top of his normal job, he was going to have to cope with looking after me, the children, himself and our home for over one hundred and twenty hours each week. It did not seem possible that any of us could survive for very long. The help provided was pleasant but totally inadequate.

When the three of them left, I wept. I cursed being unable to use my hands to wipe away the tears as they streamed down my face but was glad I lacked the muscles to give vent to the good howl I needed to express my feelings.

Suddenly a warm American drawl intruded on my misery. 'Say, what's all this about?' inquired the doctor. 'I've seen you in some tough spots but never known you to cry before. Where does it hurt?'

It was difficult to answer him. My throat seemed to be performing strange spasms as I struggled for control. I couldn't exactly place my finger on the pain. Finally I answered, 'I don't know.'

'*What's happened?*'

I told him how worried I was about the arrangements for going home. I explained that out of the twenty-four-hour around-the-clock care that I needed, less than a quarter was to be provided. We talked for some time, then I said to him, 'I can't go home and be such a burden to Ken! It's too much for any man to cope with. What would you advise me to do?'

He thought for a moment before he said, 'As you've asked, you make sure you get home first, girl. Take whatever help is offered. Once you're home, raise hell until you get what you need.'

Talking my problem over with this doctor was a tremendous help. By the time Ken arrived I managed to be positive about our new way of life, hiding my feelings with a confidence I didn't feel. Ken took his cue from me and we discussed the changes that would be necessary – turning our only downstairs living-room into my bedroom, deciding what kind of heaters to buy and so on. Ken had been advised not to have the children home straightaway but to allow me to settle in first. I agreed reluctantly. I was impatient for our family to be complete again. I believed I could teach the children to be more of a help than a hindrance. I was also convinced that their presence would strengthen my resolve – never to exchange home for hospital again, never to risk another nightmare existence.

When Ken had gone I mused over the two years that had kept me from my rightful place. I recalled being rushed to Prospect Park Hospital with no time to say goodbye to my children or prepare them for the deprivations to come. I remembered how hard I had fought to overcome the devastating effects of severe respiratory polio, the sudden pneumonia, the collapsed lung, my clinical death and ghastly revitalisation and my longing for permanent oblivion. I remembered the new strength instilled in me by Ken and the Prospect Park staff and the transfer to the Rehabilitation Hospital where, in spite of all my own efforts and those of many other people, I could still not breathe or lift a finger to help myself in any way.

It was nobody's fault. The doctor said the polio virus had done too much damage. I could have expected some degree of recovery for up to a year after the attack, then I had to settle for what I had already achieved and learn to live with my handicaps. I did not believe her. I would not. I could not. It was impossible for anyone as strong as myself to remain permanently handicapped. When I reached home, the stimulus of all those undone tasks and the needs of my children must surely trigger some response. The peace of mind and heart would help my damaged motor nerves to recover more quickly than had been possible during the stressful hospital stay.

I fell asleep thinking about the sorts of meals to have on our first weekend at home as well as my more immediate shopping-list. I wanted to buy presents – however small – to express my over-whelming gratitude to all those who had helped me, if not to recovery, at least to my escape from hospital.

The next day Inky pushed me in my wheelchair to some new shops. We bought records in the music shop for the Occupational Therapy Department – I hoped that a record library could be started and that other grateful patients could add to it. Then we rushed along to the china shop where I bought several pieces of locally-made pottery for various members of the staff, not forgetting the Ward Sister. It was difficult to hurry back with so many breakables in Inky's shopping-bag plonked across my lap. She gave pushes to my chest on the way home although I did not request them. I was filled with a sublime serentiy. The next night we held our short but happy party. Several of the occupational therapists, physiotherapists and nurses gave their own time freely and whizzed around with plates of food and cups of iced coffee laced with rum.

I slept very soundly that night and when my home-going day dawned I felt so fit and content that I decided I would do my emergency breathing and use my accessory muscles, relying on Fiz and Inky to give me pushes whenever I needed them. We were to keep my respirator handy just in case I needed to be hand-pumped for some of the journey. There were goodbyes to be said and people popping in to wish me luck. As the door of the ambulance was about to be closed, Sister rushed out with a huge red rose tied with a blue ribbon – from John, of course. Then the ambulance headed for Newbury where Ken and my bed of roses were waiting for me.

PART III
A BED OF ROSES

Chapter 20
Coming Home

I was lying on the stretcher as the ambulance sped along country lanes in the August sunshine, and I could hardly believe my good fortune. Usually people with my degree of disablement didn't manage to escape from hospital, but Ken had fought hard for my release. My physiotherapist and occupational therapist took it in turns to place their hands on either side of my ribcage to press and relax, press and relax, as they rhythmically helped me to breathe. There was no electricity supply to the ambulance. My breathing-machine stood beside me as helpless as I was without any power. If I needed its assistance it would have to be hand-cranked.

It would have been one thing to return home from hospital fit and well after two years' absence. It was a very different proposition to be completely dependent on other people for the essential activities of life and needing a machine to keep my lungs working.

At my side rested the beautiful red rose with the blue ribbon knotted round it. I grieved for John, a captive in hospital with no Ken to come to his rescue. Perhaps later, when I applied my plan for home survival and seen how it worked, I could somehow help John to follow my example. Right now I had to concentrate on establishing my own, new, independent way of life and getting my children back from my in-laws.

I was supposed only to last another three months. There was no time to lose. I had to knit Ken, Brian and Andrew so tightly together that when I bowed out of their lives they would stay together as a family, reinforcing one another.

The answer to my problem would be the entry on to our stage of an unattached, affectionate young woman who would love Ken, Brian and Andrew and take my place. She would have to be someone special. Menfolk like mine deserved the best. They had remained true and loyal to me and to one another all the time; although we each had been living under a separate roof and were able to come together only in a hospital ward.

I had every confidence that our reunion would be a happy one and that we had all developed resources from which we could build a good life.

Two years before, when I had woken to the incredible fact of sudden paralysis and had been rushed to hospital, there had been no time or opporunity to say goodbye to my children. Six months later, when I had seen them again for the first time, they were all prepared and our first happy reunion had been followed by others at intervals of three to four months. But unlike meeting for a short time in a hospital ward, the joy of being reunited under our own roof would not be followed by the pain of parting. I had made it plain that I was never to return to hospital again, not even if my staying at home hastened my death.

Fiz, my physiotherapist, asked: 'Where is Newbury? Are we nearly there, do you suppose?'

'I have no idea,' I replied.

Inky, my occupational therapist, asked, 'Don't you know any landmarks?'

'No,' I said, 'we only moved there three months before polio attacked me.'

Suddenly she said, 'Look, there's a signpost with Newbury on it – one and three-quarter miles.'

My pulse quickened perceptibly, but I tried not to let my excitement show on my face.

'Calm down or I won't be able to keep you breathing to your front-door,' warned Fiz.

I wanted to say, 'I'm perfectly calm,' but my delight at being so near home after such a desperate struggle to get there was almost overwhelming. I had to concentrate every ounce of strength and determination on grasping in the air I needed.

'Try to slow down,' urged Fiz. 'Your breathing is much too rapid.'

I nodded my head in agreement and she moved her hands more slowly, murmuring, 'Press, relax, press, relax, in, out, in, out,' as I fought for slower, deeper breaths.

Inky stood at the open window, watching the world go by. She kept calling out the names of the places we were passing. Most of my mind was committed to the discipline of breathing with Fiz's help. I felt as if I had been running or swimming hard for several miles. I could not choose to stop. There was no option but to make tremendous effort after tremendous effort, breath after breath, minute after minute. One part of my mind was monitoring Inky's commentary on the landmarks we were passing: 'The Fox, The Horse and Jockey, The Clock Tower, The Dolphin, The Lamb.'

My mind snatched at the words 'The Lamb' – the last pub on our route. I knew then I had arrived; another minute or so and I would be indoors connected to my domestic power supply.

Suddenly the ambulance stopped. The doors opened. A crowd of little children gathered to inspect me. To my astonishment I did not know any of them; they would have been toddlers and babes-in-arms when I left. I wondered what else had changed.

'Stand back please, children,' said the ambulance-man kindly.

Ken, who had been waiting at home making things ready for my arrival, was as impatient to see me queening it over my own domain as I was to reassume my sovereignty. At the sight of the ambulance approaching Ken had bounded out of the house and up our front steps and was now on the pavement to help whisk me indoors. I was too happy to speak; besides I had no breath. However, in a matter of minutes I was propped up in bed with my respirator working full-blast. I looked around my own home, taking stock of the room in which I had desperately tried to fight off the effects of those flu-like signs of polio, two years earlier.

There was a window at either end of the room. Only my respirator stood between me and the window on my left-hand side. I watched my next-door neighbour's black cat Tibby climbing up a rustic arch and thought, He's clever to manage that without pricking himself. A pretty pink rose, smothered in bloom, had been trained to climb around the arch. Beside it an enormous Peace rosebush was sporting several large blooms. It was obviously the second flowering of the year. I was lucky to catch them at this stage – they would flourish for weeks yet.

Inky yelled through the kitchen-hatch behind me, 'I've put the kettle on. Where's the tea?'

'In the tin.'

'Which tin is that?'

'In the tea-tin of course.'

'Where do you keep it?'

'On the left-hand side of the second shelf of the larder. There are four tins labelled tea, coffee, sugar and flour.'

She disappeared for a few moments. I heard her looking in the tins. She returned to the hatchway and called out, 'This is the first house I've been in where the tea is in a proper tea-tin.'

I inquired, 'Why, where do other people put their tea?'

Inky laughed. 'In a coffee-, flour- or sugar-tin – *never* in the tea-tin.'

'Too complicated for me,' I protested.

Fiz had been cutting up a chocolate cake she had made especially for the occasion, while Ken unloaded my gear from the ambulance. He brought the ambulance-men in for a quick cup of tea.

'Come along,' coaxed Fiz, 'finish this cake, it's special. I put sal volatile in it.'

'Did you really?' joked Inky. 'I put morphine in mine.'

'No, really,' objected Fiz. 'Sal volatile keeps it moist. The cake is practically solid ground almonds and best butter, real chocolate and thousands of eggs.'

The ambulance-men quickly finished their tea and, brushing aside our expressions of heartfelt thanks for a speedy journey, hurried away.

Ken had begun to hump our things up the stairs. I then enjoyed my cake and tea. I had been too shy to let anyone feed me in front of the ambulance-men.

Fiz would have to leave after supper but Inky was staying until Sunday night. We now began to think in a way that was going to continue for the rest of my life. From now on, in case there were emergencies, it would be essential that I was never left alone. As Inky was with me, Ken would be able to escort Fiz to the station. In future, he would not be able to set foot outside the door unless he arranged a substitute for himself to stay with me. Inky disappeared into the kitchen to rustle up our supper.

Ken stayed with me. 'I bought stuff for a cheese salad. Is that all right?' he asked.

'Just what I felt like,' I answered, thinking what a refreshing change everyday life at home was going to be after the stale routines of hospital.

'I've also bought some new crusty bread. The loaf was still hot when I brought it home. I've asked Inky to reserve the crust for you, unless you would like toast by way of a change.'

Such simple things – crusty bread and toast – but to me they represented the difference between hospital and home. Now I could choose my food and, just as important, choose *not* to eat if I didn't feel like it.

Ken continued, 'I shall be happy to hand over the housekeeping reins to you right now. I'll go shopping in the morning if you will think out a list, or perhaps Inky might like to do the shopping. It will give her a chance to go out. She will probably enjoy poking around the Saturday market.'

He sat down on the chair beside my bed. 'You can't come in yet,' I joked, echoing the old Ward Sister's usual greeting. 'It's too early. Visiting-time is not till seven-thirty.'

We both giggled and felt a tremendous sense of relief and release at our escape from the hospital treadmill.

I looked past Ken to where a delivery man was suddenly framed in the far window. The bell rang, Ken went to the door and returned with a huge bouquet of red roses.

'Best I could do,' he said. 'Next year I will grow you some.'

'Oh Ken,' I said, 'you shouldn't have! Just being home is more than enough.'

'I'll give them to Inky. She was just putting John's rose in a vase when I last saw her. I don't suppose she will mind arranging a few more . . .'

The next thing I knew was when I woke up in the dark and realised I must have fallen fast asleep while Ken was talking to me. I had no idea what the time was, but knew instantly I was HOME.

From my nearer window I could see lights shining from the windows of people's houses. Almost two hundred yards away the main road was lit up for the night. A lighted bus was grinding its way up the hill. It stopped under a street-lamp and I watched several people clambering off or on. Only two years ago I could have been one of the people jumping off the bus and hurrying home on my own two legs – I mustn't think about that. I was lucky – I could now turn my head. I looked out of the other window – there was no one there, only the soft side-street lamplight and my neighbour's living-room light shining through her closed curtains – shining on and on as they had done all those nights that I had been captive in hospital and unable to see them. Never again, I thought. No matter what happens, never again! I am home for good. I knew that I wouldn't be alone. I called Ken quietly. He was sitting behind my bed in the dark, contented that we were together.

He teased me: 'It's nearly time to get up. You've slept all night solidly!'

'I know I haven't. I can see the lights on. Is Fiz still here?'

He grinned, 'I'm just going to take her to the station.'

'What about our supper?'

'We've had ours.'

'I didn't hear you.'

'Inky and Fiz took theirs upstairs. I turned mine into sandwiches.'

'Where's my crust?' I inquired.

'It's ready. Close your eyes. I'll switch on the light.'

Inky and Fiz appeared. 'Heard you talking,' Fiz said. 'Don't mind if I dash off now, do you?'

'Course not,' I replied. 'Thank you for bringing me home.'

'I wouldn't have missed it for the world.'

'And thank you for the gorgeous cake.'

'Don't forget to finish it up.'

As Ken and Fiz left, Inky entered my room with my supper. She had fed me so many times in hospital when no nurse had been available. Now she said, 'As that male nurse has gone out, I'm afraid it will have to be me feeding you again, just like hospital.'

'Oh Inky,' I protested. 'It's not a bit like hospital! I can have what I like – even a clean napkin if I want one.' In the hospital they had been limited to one a week.

She laughed so much the tears streaked down her face. 'I shall miss wiping your bib around a custardy plate just to get a clean one more often than the regular issue.' She mimicked her old wheedling efforts. 'Oh Sister, I'm so sorry! I seem to have dropped my patient's napkin in the custard again.'

She shook with laughter once more and I asked her, 'Don't you think she ever realised that you had done it deliberately?'

'No, my dear, she was too busy chasing everyone about to register what was happening. If she'd really thought about things she would have at least handed out clean napkins after each fishy meal, wouldn't she?'

'But you did it so many times.'

'I didn't always drop it in the custard, though.'

'You didn't?'

'No, sometimes I dipped it in the gravy.'

We both chuckled at the memory of our little ploys.

Ken soon arrived home and began the novelty of tucking me up in bed for the night. He washed my face and hands, cleaned my teeth, brushed my hair, exercised my arms and legs, rubbed my bottom with spirit and enthroned me on a bed-pan. I had slipped down the bed quite a bit. In hospital we had special boards across the foot of the bed. Pillows supported sides and arms to keep us from slipping down. Ken cast around for something similar and saw the bread-board. He slipped it into the space between the bottom of my mattress and foot of the bed and wedged it firmly with two small hassocks I had made for Brian and Andrew before I had polio.

'That will do for now,' he said. 'I'll probably find something better tomorrow.'

He straightened my sheets and tucked them in well around my neck. He put an extra blanket on my bed and hot-water bottles either side of my feet, commenting, 'The nights can be nippy now.'

'Pity I can't put my cold feet on yours, as I used to do.'

Ken smiled as my words evoked the memory of our now absent intimacy. He covered his feelings by saying in mock horror: 'What would Sister say at such an improper suggestion?'

'Sister would say "You cannot have a hot-water bottle. It is the indiscriminate use of hot-water bottles that wears them out."'

Why, I wondered, when I have been lucky enough to escape from hospital, do I keep harking back to the petty irritations? Is it because I cannot believe my good fortune? Do I imagine I am going to wake up in a minute and find I am only dreaming after all? I felt wide-awake. I consciously opened my eyes wider and watched Ken.

Ken collected the towels, bowls and brushes on to the trolley he had earmarked for the purpose, then stooped down to take something from the lower shelf, saying: 'I've fixed up this bell so you can wake me in the night. I'll put this bit well under the bed so I don't kick it in the night when I come running. I've put the push-button on a piece of board to stand by your toe. Just ring if you want anything. I shall be sleeping here on the put-you-up but I'll keep one ear open all night, just in case.'

He kissed me goodnight and I wanted to hug him but my arms still would not move and the dome of my cuirass made an effective barrier between us. The magic of familiar surroundings had not restored even one tiny physical movement but I was confident in my mind that I would mend quickly now I was home.

I watched Ken open up his bed and arrange his bedclothes. This was it. This was our first night together since I was rushed to hospital. No, it was more than that. It was our first night together since he went away to a week's Road Safety Conference in Morecambe.

How had he felt – having left me full of vim and vigour and able to look after our two little boys – to return to find me ill and unfit to care even for myself? How did he feel now as he bravely took on the responsibility of caring for me – without hospital facilities, resident doctors, nurses and other staff on call and a whole back-up of experts and equipment?

Yet emotionally I was exhilarated. I was where I belonged with the man to whom I belonged. Continuously in my brain one phrase echoed: *those whom God has joined together let no man put asunder.*

Chapter 21
Prelude

I slept very heavily that night, waking only two or three times. Ken quickly answered my quiet summons and sorted me out, rearranged me and my pillows and I fell fast asleep again.

Daylight was shining through the curtains when I awoke to the smell of toast. I was home; my first full day stretched in front of me. It seemed crowded from the moment I opened my eyes. Ken made some tea, then spent an hour on my waking-up routine in reverse order to the previous night's tucking-up procedure. He drew my lipstick on, regarding the effect with his artist's critical eye. 'There you are,' he said. 'You'll do until the nurse comes.'

Inky waltzed in with a tray of scrambled eggs and mushrooms and a rack full of aromatic toast.

'Good morning, Moddom,' she called out. 'Will Moddom breakfast with the slave? I have tasted the mushrooms and made sure they aren't poisonous.'

'Morning, Slave,' I greeted her. 'I don't remember clapping my hands for you to appear. Perceptive, aren't you?'

'Perceptive my eye,' she retorted. 'I'm jolly hungry.'

'Is Sir having breakfast now?' I asked.

'Sir's plate is too heavy to carry in so he is tackling it on the kitchen table,' she said. She settled herself on the edge of my bed and with two forks fed us both from the one large plate.

After breakfast, Inky set off with her basket and shopping-list. Ken sailed through the washing-up.

I could see him reflected in the mirror that was suspended above my bed. Ken had fixed the mirror so that I could see through the hatchway behind me and into the kitchen. I could be seen from the kitchen side of the hatchway. We were able to keep up a conversation without holding up the work. We speculated about what Brian and Andrew might be doing on a Saturday morning.

I looked up and saw the District Nurses coming down the steps from the street. I recognised them as being Peggy and Ruth whom

Inky and I had met when they had to come to the Rehabilitation Hospital. It was obvious that their introductory visit would help us all during the first nursing session in my own home.

The nurses popped their heads around the door of my room to smile hello before disappearing into the kitchen. In my mirror I watched them looking round to see where they could keep my nursing essentials.

I am not sure what I had expected to happen at the sight of our own front-door the previous day. I think I had imagined that it would be a symbol of such potency that I would miraculously find my strength and coordination returning. The magic of familiar things would restore me completely. This frame of mind helped me to accept that I still needed the support of a hospital bed with special sections to be wound up and down so that my head or knees could be moved to different levels. Being raised and lowered mechanically would soon teach my muscles to respond to my commands when I grew stronger. At last the nurses entered my room and put their navy blue uniform coats down on my sofa. Ruth remarked, 'We ought to ask for some newspaper.'

'What for?' I inquired.

'To put our coats on.'

I was astonished: 'But my sofa is perfectly clean!'

Peggy laughed. 'I am sure your sofa is all right, but I am not so certain about our coats.'

At a loss, I asked, 'Do you really want newspaper?'

'No, that's all right,' Peggy answered, 'but it's what we are taught to do in our Queen's training.'

'What does Queen's mean?' I wondered aloud.

'It means Queen's Institute of District Nursing Service.'

'How long do you train?'

'Six months – on top of our three years' State Registered training. Then we did another six months to become certified midwives.'

'Are you both midwives?'

Peggy replied, 'In theory, yes. But I don't practise any more. Ruth here has delivered most of the babies on the estate.'

Ruth added, 'And there are plenty more to come.'

'Do you mean that you can be up all night delivering a baby and then turn out to nurse other patients in the day-time too?' I asked.

'Frequently,' said Ruth.

'What an Amazon you are,' I exclaimed.

We all laughed and I felt relieved at their friendliness. It was refreshing to be with competent women who would help me to help myself and not be bossed about and humiliated as I had been until yesterday.

I shut my eyes while the nurse cleaned my nose. Even the little gift of being able to sniff or to blow my nose had not been restored. I accepted the ministrations of the nurses on a temporary basis. Somewhere at the back of my mind I probably explained to myself that I could not expect any immediate recovery after a long and debilitating stay in hospital, but that if I remained good and patient and kept up my constant efforts to make myself strong, I would eventually land on my feet.

Peggy and Ruth chatted happily about their training in London teaching hospitals. Ruth had decided upon nursing at St Thomas's Hospital after her WRNS service. This made an instant bond between us as I had joined King's Fund straight from the WRNS and was constantly in touch with the major London teaching hospitals. She was interested to hear that Fiz was an ex-Wren too. Peggy described laying out a dead patient during night duty on a haunted ward at the Westminster Hospital. She warned me never to use white toilet soap as this reminded her of those creepy times.

'Do you want me to put some by for three months' time when you lay me out?' I joked.

I felt that I had to bring my short expectation of life out into the open. I was no more convinced that I would live for only three more months than I believed I would stay catastrophically disabled. My determination to live long enough to settle my children into their own home would surely give me super-human strength.

Peggy and I discussed the doctors at St John's Surgery. We had registered there as a family when we arrived in Newbury but until my sudden attack of polio I had not met any of the doctors.

Now, two years later, I still did not know them and wondered whether I should contact them while I was fit or wait until my disability was complicated by some kind of illness.

I asked Peggy what people usually did in my circumstances. She grinned in reply, 'Most people in your circumstances don't come home, do they? I expect your hospital notes have been posted to the surgery. Probably Dr Scott will call in later. He's the senior partner and will want to see things for himself.'

I thought about this before asking, 'Will he want to call in regularly or do you suppose I can carry on as usual, calling in the doctor when necessary? Routine calls will make me feel like an invalid, won't they? Do you think Dr Scott will mind treating me as normally as possible?'

Peggy said, 'Mind! I should think he'll be delighted that you feel so confident. He'll soon tell you how often he wants to come. There's no beating about the bush with Tom Scott.'

'We heard of his reputation before we registered with his surgery,' I said. 'That was why we chose him, especially as he is good with children.'

It was children that were uppermost in both our minds. Peggy told me about her husband and little daughter Jill and I told her about my family. I was so impatient to see Brian and Andrew. I felt sure their demands upon me would stimulate the required responses.

I fell once more into the old trap of talking about how I would soon jump into my own shoes and clothes and run my own home. Also my children needed me. I was certain about that. I could not imagine they were better cared for by their kindly aunt and grandmother than I could manage. In the fifties it was thought that even an inadequate mother was better than a surrogate.

I pointed out my curtains to Peggy. I had hung them at the windows to allow the material to drop, intending to take them down and turn up their hems after a few weeks. But I was snatched away into hospital and had been unable to finish them. Now, almost two years later, the curtains still hung accusingly with the rough edges of their hems beginning to fray. They remained a microcosm of my life and its unsewn seams, its unknitted garments, its unshopped-for and uncooked meals, its uncared-for children and husband.

The mother in me knew that fresh rituals and routines must be established in less than three months to keep the family together should the doctor's prognosis prove correct. The urgency of my need to see my children in their own surroundings was strengthened by earlier experience. A wartime child, I remembered calming my little sisters although my vivid but unspoken nightmares had been that our home would be blitzed and our parents killed.

News of my homecoming spread around our small town like wildfire. A kind of politeness paralysed us and made it difficult to turn away people who arrived unexpectedly. Gradually we grasped the situation and made our own rules for survival's sake. We told everyone about the danger of infection – even of a simple cold – and it became known that in order to avoid exhausting me, only people who knew the situation and had some business at the house could be seen. In this category were the official special helpers who varied widely in their circumstances and experience. Among the first – arriving late and harrassed – was a mother with six children to get off to school every morning. It was obvious she was going to need help herself.

Another helper, June, was an ex St Thomas's nurse and a cordon bleu cook. One day when I exclaimed, 'What a pest I am to need so much help,' her usual smile turned into a frown.

'Please don't say that,' she said. 'You provide work that many of us badly need and you do it in the nicest possible way.'

I was on nodding acquaintance with my nearest neighbours, most of whom had kept in touch whilst I was in hospital; having known how active I was before, they accepted my condition on a temporary basis as I did and made no undue demands. We all looked forward to my recovery and the return to normal neighbourly relationships.

My nearest helper in the early days was my next-door neighbour Norah, whose fat cat Tibby I had seen climbing among the roses during my first moments at home. Norah's husband Cyril, being a television engineer, was very knowledgeable about my equipment. Our houses were semi-detached. He drilled a hole through the party wall and fixed an alarm bell in his house for us to ring if we were in trouble. This meant that if something went wrong with my breathing-machine and Ken could not leave me to fetch help, we would not feel alone. My neighbours would realise there was a power cut as they would hear my machine stop. While it was running it was audible in their house. Norah described the noise graphically as 'like a giant breathing'.

Other people soon came to my aid, among them the Red Cross volunteers. Nellie Brown, the Commandant, sometimes minded me while Ken was at a meeting and together we answered the outstanding mail. Nellie penned letters for me in her beautiful copper-plate hand. Gradually other people joined in this task. When people heard from me they did not instantly recognise the letter as mine because of the unfamiliar handwriting. To complicate matters further, the writing was frequently that of several different people in succession. I often wondered what it must be like to be on the receiving end of my letters in which the turns of phrases were familiar whilst the handwriting was constantly changing.

One amanuensis had handwriting so like my own that when Ken first saw a page of it he wondered where I had discovered some of my old papers. I found it a very disturbing experience to see a page of writing that looked and sounded as though my hand had written it when I knew it had not.

Another Red Cross volunteer, Margaret, was also pressed into writing letters. Soon we were corresponding with faraway friends, MPs and organisations which had been set up to help disabled people. We consulted enormous tomes of Acts of Parliament. We wrestled with the words in the National Assistance Act and the National Health Service Act and although these long-winded statutes seemed full of loopholes, we decided to work towards improving the care for handicapped people in our society.

Nellie and Margaret became – and remained – faithful friends. Many of the nurses who have ministered to me over the years have also become friends. They form a continuing, but changing, part of my life. Sometimes family commitments took them away, or maybe a new job attracted them elsewhere. But whatever the reason for their departure, an alarming number of nurses kept in touch with letters and messages through the bush telegraph that exists among medical personnel. I choose the word 'alarming' very carefully. I have no fear of nurses, but I dread seeming ungrateful through not being able to keep in touch with all those who have been kind to me. It has been impossible to write to every nurse who has written to me, even with the faithful help of the Red Cross volunteers.

When I had been home a month and Ken's birthday was approaching, Norah and a few of our other neighbours helped me to prepare a small party for him. Mick brought her Mail Order Club catalogue so that I could choose a small garden shed for Ken. It was difficult to keep such a big present as a surprise, but everyone joined in the conspiracy and assembled the shed at the last moment. Ken was amazed and delighted.

The party was a very happy one with food in abundance and drink flowing freely. We all aired our funds of stories and party pieces. After a while the conversation turned to the night that Ken came home with the news that I had polio. As I listened it seemed as if I was watching an old film that I had only heard about before. Although it was the first time they had spoken of their horror and fear of their children and themselves being 'crippled' (as they put it), their responses were very like I had imagined them to be.

I knew I was very, very lucky indeed to have friends and neighbours who, although they had known me only briefly, had responded to my incarceration in hospital with such sympathy. Now I was home they were diverting me with visits and keeping my room full of flowers.

To amuse me a neighbour gave me two goldfish in an aquarium encased in an impressive box with figures of London Zoo's two famous polar bears, Brumas and Ivy, decorating the top. I put this in my front window so that my neighbour could see it when she passed my house.

Mick brought me her beautiful blue budgerigar named Bill. He had no tail – he had a bad habit of pulling his feathers out from boredom. He was very energetic. He would hop from perch to perch in his cage, ring the little bell and knock hell out of a weighted doll which stood on his cage floor.

I used to ask for the doors and windows of my room to be securely closed and for the door of his cage to be propped open. Bill would fly to my shoulder, peck my ear or keep worrying at my hairslide until he pulled it out of my hair, or fly on to papers above my bed and begin to tear them with his beak. When he felt brave he would fly up to the top of our big mirror and admire himself, saying 'Pretty boy' over and over again. Without his tail-feathers he did not fly very well. He also loved to bath but was afraid of the water. To lure him into his bath we had to place a lettuce leaf on the bottom of it. As Bill stood on the leaf, it would gradually sink until covered by about a tenth of an inch of water. He would then flutter his wings and thoroughly enjoy himself, spraying everything and everybody.

I don't know who was more frustrated. The fish swimming round and round, circling their square aquarium, Bill battling with everything in sight except himself, or me anchored to my one corner needing desperately to be up and about.

I said to Mick, 'You are all so good to us, although we were your neighbours for such a short time before I was rushed away.'

She answered, 'Don't forget we had a special kind of atmosphere here, because the rest of the road wasn't built. No shops, mud everywhere and all our children being little together. Besides, I remember when my Bobby fell out of a tree and broke his arm and I brought him back from the hospital. *You* sat *me* down and made me drink hot sweet tea.'

'Reciprocity?' I queried. 'I think it's more than that. You keep helping me now, although I cannot do anything for you.'

She grinned, 'You do more for us than you know. Besides, when you do get up and about again, you can pay us back if you must.'

'Gladly,' I answered. 'I hope to avoid accidents and illnesses from now on.'

These proved to be bold words. An unkind fate was listening. Shortly after the birthday party a locum arrived from Dr Scott's practice with an anti-flu injection.

I said, 'I don't have anti-flu. I had a bad reaction in the hospital.'

'The hospital sent this for you, so it must be all right,' he answered. 'There is an epidemic on the way.'

I remembered that Prince Charles was down with flu at nearby Cheam School. If he could catch it, anybody could! I supposed it would be harmless and raised no more objections, but did being acquiescent hasten my downfall? I had never felt fitter but a few days after the anti-flu injection I was suffering a rip-roaring chest infection and was in danger of drowning in my own secretions which I could not cough up. The doctor was summoned and Dr Scott himself arrived. It was our first meeting. I begged him not to send me back to hospital. He could see that my anxiety was making my condition worse.

'I can't send you back to hospital lass,' he said. 'If you wish to stay home, knowing the dangers as you do, I'll do all I can to help you stay here.'

I told him that I would rather die at home than prolong my life in hospital.

'If you slip through our fingers, it won't be for the want of effort on our part.' He looked at my respirator and added, 'Frankly, I know nothing about this machinery but I promise you I will find out.'

He left me with the nurse while he zoomed off to the hospital to fetch an oxygen cylinder.

For the next few days, Dr Scott, Ken and the nurses took it in turns to stay with me constantly, winding my bed up and down, thumping my chest to compensate for my not being able to cough and keeping the little tubes from the oxygen cylinder in place in my nostrils.

In spite of Dr Scott's reassurances that I would not be returned to hospital against my will, I was terrified that my condition would worsen and I would be rushed off if I became unconscious. The fifteenth of October – my second polio anniversary – was looming and with it came the remembered shock and sense of loss that I had felt when first paralysed.

Pethidine helped enormously. In taking away the pain it took away associated ideas of the pain of polio. It also helped me to sleep. Gradually I grew to believe Dr Scott and to trust him through thick and thin. I also believed Ken, who promised never to let me return to hospital, no matter what any doctor said or thought.

I recovered sufficiently for discussions to begin about bringing Brian and Andrew home in time for the Christmas holidays but my illness had weakened me so much that next I went down with a bad dose of foreign flu. It looked as though Brian and Andrew would not be able to return until well into the New Year.

To complicate matters, the November fogs and freezing temperatures made my situation more hazardous. The atmosphere penetrated the house and made my condition worse. Then one morning my respirator began to fail. The hospital had allowed me no duplicate respirator in case of such emergencies. Now, in the freezing fog, we were faced with the problem of obtaining a replacement respirator from a hospital thirty miles away.

Dr Scott was not a man to be trifled with. He telephoned the hospital and made it plain that a replacement respirator must be supplied at once. Also a stand-by machine had to be despatched and both must be kept regularly serviced by our local hospital.

The attack of flu following the chest infection made me acutely ill and exhausted. I remained unable to be put into my wheelchair while my bed was made. My breathing became so laboured that Dr Scott called before eight o'clock each morning prior to setting off for his early surgery. Ken remained calm and reassuring. He dealt with the extra emergency tasks by clearing the decks. Every routine was reduced to the minimum. His time-and-motion studies were assessed and improved. When he made hot drinks no one was allowed to have a saucer and only one shared spoon was permitted for stirring. I protested weakly – a spoon and saucer seemed such little things to provide – but Ken told me firmly that so long as he coped with the washing-up it would be kept to necessities only. He was right of course. In paring all his jobs down to essentials he managed to stick to his routines as a good Virgo should.

He even made time to bake me a birthday cake. It was a gesture of consolation for the party he could see it was going to be impossible to arrange for me. Sadly, my weakened face-muscles lost their residual powers through the debilitation following the flu. I could not eat the cake. I would have given anything to be able to walk to the window and, unseen, drop the cake outside for the birds to devour. Being fed by Ken there was no escape. I could only say, 'I am sorry, but I cannot manage it. I don't have the strength.'

I could see Ken was disappointed although he put on a brave face. Our new way of life demanded a great deal of our acting abilities. It seemed that it was necessary to pretend that all would be well, in the hope that while we were going through the motions all *would* become well.

Our friends and neighbours played their part in the charade.

They talked to me as if I had not had polio but was just down with a dose of flu as they might be themselves. When going into town they would ask if there was anything they could bring me back for lunch so that I could build myself up again. If they dropped in for a few minutes they would tell me about normal everyday things, such as the latest make-up, clothes, furnishings and the many different man-made materials which were beginning to flood the shops. They described their evenings out with their husbands as though Ken and I would be going out together again soon. They told me stories of the shows they had been to see, what plants and bulbs they were ordering for their gardens to bloom the next year, where they were hoping to book their holidays, the pros and cons of holidays right away from it all and holidays at home with days out whenever the sunbeams beckoned.

Every day in every way I expected to feel better and better. It was the natural order of things. It was good of my neighbours to keep me in touch so that I could run my home with up-to-the-minute aids and materials. When I was completely recovered I would set off for the shops, theatre or a holiday without being disadvantaged by lack of information.

To build me up again, Dr Scott asked the Area Physical Medicine Consultant to visit me, with a view to starting physiotherapy sessions. This specialist, in all innocence, made the mistake of suggesting that I would soon be returned to hospital to be tidied up – whatever that meant. 'I have no intention of ever returning to hospital again,' I said firmly.

'Come, come, it isn't that bad is it? Why do you feel so strongly against it?'

I looked at him disbelievingly and wondered if he had any idea of the conditions at the Rehabilitation Hospital. 'You are left unattended, although totally dependent on a respirator,' I told him.

'I know that doesn't happen,' he objected.

'I have just come from there. You have not,' I answered. 'Who is most likely to know?'

Shortly after, he visited the hospital, found out that what I was saying was true and came back to tell me so, adding that many things would be changed from now on. I felt a great surge of respect for this man who had not only listened to me but had actually followed up my observations. But I made it plain that I still had no intention of returning to any hospital whatsoever.

Eventually I was allowed to have physiotherapy for half an hour on two mornings a week. After several months it was decided that as I had made no progress my treatment should be cut to once a week. This seemed to be the reverse of what was indicated to be necessary but I was too spent to raise any objection.

My inability to speak up for myself made me panic when I heard that the Rehabilitation Hospital specialist wanted to visit me. I dreaded being too weak to oppose the inevitable suggestion that I should return to hospital. I knew that I would be pressed to go back.

On the day of the visit, Dr Scott planted himself on one side of my bed and Ken on the other. This meant that the specialist was forced to stand at the foot of my bed facing the obviously determined battery of the three of us. When the inevitable suggestion came that I should go back, I found that my resolve to stay in my own home was as strong as ever. I heard myself asking, 'Why should I come back? What is available at your hospital now which wasn't there before?'

Fortunately for me there was no answer. I felt jubilant – I had managed to stand up for myself. The presence of Dr Scott and Ken had given me the courage to state my own case.

Against my deepest wishes, doctors were assuming far too great an influence on my life. Dr Scott was always welcome to the house; his presence was a great source of strength. I admired his choice of words and realised that he thought them out carefully as part of the psychological support at which he was so adept. He did not object when I said that I preferred to be visited only when I was ill but from time to time his Land Rover would draw up outside unexpectedly. He would jump down and hurry into the house with the cheerful greeting, 'I was just passing . . .' and then show me his latest piece of Guernsey knitting or tell me about the adventures of his children.

On one of these occasions I remarked to Dr Scott, 'You must be a very good doctor, you have already prolonged my life beyond the three months' expectation.'

He seemed embarrassed by such a direct compliment, put his fingers on my wrist to feel my pulse and said, 'With a good heart like yours you should last for some time yet.' Then, as though remembering something he had kept for such an occasion, he added: 'I have never known anyone with such tenacity as you.' The meaning of the word 'tenacity' flew into my mind. How kind of him to talk about my ability to hold on without the use of my hands.

If only I had eight tentacles it wouldn't matter if just two of them were out of action. I would still be able to attend to my family commitments, even when, as now, carol-singers were reminding us of holly and ivy and the little town of Bethlehem.

Although I remained very weak from the flu Ken decided that the children should come home as planned. It would be a tonic for all of us. My spirits rose as I looked forward to having our sons home again. I could think of little else but how we would sing the old songs, tell the old tales and giggle together as we shared private jokes. I remarked to Dr Scott: 'Christmas with the children will cure me.' He answered with one of his thought-provoking statements: 'Cure is a very big word.'

Chapter 22
Peace

December is a very busy time for everyone but it was especially so for me. I would have been hard-pressed preparing for Brian's and Andrew's homecoming had I had the use of my own hands and body. Making my arrangements through other people, as and when they were available, kept my mind in a state of feverish activity.

Ken's mother had agreed to make a Christmas pudding, cake and mince-pies and was storing them ready to bring with her at Christmas. June prepared Brian's and Andrew's bedrooms and cleaned out their little desks, disinfecting them just in case a polio bug was lurking anywhere. In Andrew's desk she found a tiny tin with bits of biscuit and apple stored in it against hard times.

We sorted out their clothes and gave them away to make room for bigger sizes. We emptied the toy-boxes and left them under their beds in readiness for the new things at Christmas. Our neighbours brought the presents from the shops on approval; Ken wrapped them meticulously.

Nellie and Margaret wrote my Christmas cards, including some to Prospect Park Hospital. I regarded the staff at Prospect Park as my friends but even those doors were closed to me now. I had discovered that once I entered a hospital I could be transferred to another one against my will.

Apart from the extra seasonal jobs having to be shared out among other people when their hands were free, Christmas, being the season of goodwill, brought extra visitors.

One day a local vicar came to see me. He parked his car outside our house and, unknown to me, left his two little boys on the back seat. Our privet hedge was very tall. I could see only the roof of the car. Suddenly it began to roll down the hill. 'Quick! Your car is moving!' I cried out as loudly as I could manage.

In two strides the vicar was across the room. He dashed out of the door, leapt up the steps to the street, ran round the car and flung himself against it to try to push it on to the pavement. Then car and vicar disappeared from view.

I rang my bell. June ran into my room. Anxiously we waited for news of what had happened. If the car reached the bottom of the hill it would hit a busy main road where vehicles were constantly roaring along.

We were relieved when the vicar returned to tell us that the boys were safe. He had chased the car down the hill, hurling it across the pavement with all his might so that it was brought to a halt by someone's front hedge. 'I didn't know the children could manage to take the brake off,' he said, and sped out to take his children home.

I thought that I must insist that Brian and Andrew were never left in a parked car. It began to dawn on me that many different people would be accompanying my children in my place on journeys on our increasingly busy roads. The onus was on me to protect my sons from the aberrations of others.

I was still certain that Brian and Andrew would be happier to be with me, incapacitated as I was, than in the care of the kindest of relatives.

The boys would take their example from Ken as always. Our suffering had drawn us all together so closely that nothing and no one – not even with the best of motives – could ever separate the bonds that bound us. Totally aware and dedicated, we were crossing the Rubicon.

A ripple of joy ran through us all when news in a letter from John reflected our mood of devotion. He, too, was taking an inexorable step. He had proposed to, and been acceptd by, Ses, 'the most beautiful nurse in the world'. After their marriage they were to set up home in a little bungalow in a village not far from the hospital. Remembering John's constant supply of red roses to me, we ordered some rosebushes for his front garden. We chose a strong, red variety appropriately named 'Tally-ho'.

Ken's parents brought Brian and Andrew home a few days before Christmas. The children ran in to kiss me, then disappeared upstairs into their rooms to find the few little presents I had secreted in their desks and under their pillows.

My mother-in-law had always asserted that it was impossible for two women to share a kitchen, so I mentally handed mine over to her for the holiday and concentrated on my children. This suited us both – my mother-in-law being an excellent cook.

We bought dozens of Peace rosebushes to give to our friends for Christmas and Ken, Brian and Andrew rushed around delivering them.

A lady from the Welfare Department arrived with a Christmas tree which had been standing in her last welfare clinic but when my nurse saw it, she arranged for it to be taken away again in case it was carrying some infection – so many babies seemed to be poorly that year. It was a relief as we had no room for it (my bed and respirator took up most of the living-room) but I would never have found the courage to do anything but accept the tree politely.

Of course we had to spoil the children that Christmas. It was so special. All our relatives were very generous and gave the children a sackful of games and books to amuse them. We also bought them new school clothes. Brian, being seven years old now, would be returning to the junior school where he had spent a few weeks as an infant before I had polio. The school population had bulged so much since then that a new and separate infant's school had been built. Andrew, at five years of age, was to go there. Both children had to go to school alone as I could not take them.

A neighbour, Edie, whose home was at the bottom of my garden, allowed the boys to climb our shared fence and take a short cut down her garden path on their way to school.

Edie often hopped over my fence and came visiting. She was lonely as her husband was away on atomic testing-sites. She said she remembered me from the first day I had moved in. I had bought my children an ice-cream from the van and, seeing her little boy hanging enviously over the fence, I had sent him in to ask his mother if he could have one too. A small enough gesture, I would have thought, but she was delighted to have been asked first. I was surprised to hear of children being given things to eat without their mothers' knowledge.

When Edie's husband, Bob, came home from the Pacific he brought boxes full of transparencies of the atomic testing-sites which he projected and commented on for us. So we were continually reminded of the terrible weapons that were developing parallel with our children.

All the children were at risk. Were mine more so? I had been certain that I could take good care of Brian and Andrew by proxy but I was horrified to admit that, far from being able to be a good mother, I needed *them* to mother *me*. This was brought home to me one Sunday when Ken was laid low with a bad migraine. Brian and Andrew rolled up their sleeves and looked after the pair of us, as well as themselves.

Brian wet a face-flannel and wrung it out, folded it and placed it on his father's forehead. Andrew climbed on my bed with another wet flannel and, reversing our old roles, washed my face. I was deeply touched by the care with which he removed the sleepy-dust from my eyes. He concentrated so hard that his tongue emerged from the corner of his mouth. I hoped that I had always been as careful when tending to him. They fetched cornflakes, milk and sugar and sat on my bed eating their breakfasts while we planned our campaign for the day.

Now and then I was useful to my children. On the morning that they started back to school Andrew came to me with his collar turned up and his tie hanging unknotted around his neck. I could just see him above my high bed. 'Can you tell me what to do, please, Mum?' He listened carefully to my step-by-step directions of the tie-tying process, then carried them through so quickly and surely that I was surprised and delighted. 'You have tied it better than I could have done it for you!' I exclaimed. 'Shall I help you with your shoelaces?'

'No thanks, I've done those already.'

I felt a glow of pride as the boys set off together on the twenty-minute walk to school in their royal-blue blazers, caps, grey shorts and socks. Their macs were over their arms in case it turned cold or wet. The did not look neglected or depressed and waved cheerily as they passed my window. Unable to wave back, I nodded and smiled in acknowledgement.

A strange kind of peace fell on the house and I began to plan what to do with my day. I listed the jobs for the week – shopping, cleaning, laundry. Now time had to be set aside for organising a life in which everything had to be done by other people's hands.

Brian and Andrew had asked if they could buy a pet with their Christmas money. Bill the budgie and Tish and Tosh the goldfish were regarded as household pets and had brought their names with them. The boys wanted to choose a hamster each and were prepared to do endless jobs to save their father's time so that he could make the hamster cages. I had to make a fair timetable for this.

I soon discovered that I was to become closely involved with the hamsters. They were easy to tell apart. Brian had bought a cream one with black eyes and called him Tommy. Andrew's hamster was white with pink eyes and answered to the name Snowy.

Tommy and Snowy would be placed under my candlewick bedspread where some hamster food was concealed. The hamsters soon made their way to the food, stuffed their pouches at the sides of their mouths and popped their heads out from under my coverlet.

I never minded watching the little shapes running up and down

PEACE

under my bedspread. There was always a good flannelette sheet, a thick cotton sheet and one or two blankets between me and the hamsters. My helpers were not always so amused. I noticed that when Brian and Andrew came towards my bed and slipped the hamsters under my bedspread, my helper would keep her distance.

One day as the nights began to draw out, a little girl came into our garden to play. Andrew let her hold Snowy and while they were all playing together she placed him on the ground, expecting him to stay put. In a flash the animal disappeared. Next-door's cat was coming down the garden path. Frantically the children ran hither and thither searching for the hamster.

'Snowy, Snowy, Snowy,' they called. Their voices sounded urgent and upset. Gradually it began to get dark. The children ran indoors and fetched their torches. They continued their search until it was obvious that Snowy was nowhere to be found. Ken said he had probably dug himself in for the night in a sheltered spot where he would be safe from predators. They would have to ask the children round about and at school if anyone had found a white hamster.

Snowy was never seen again. Andrew became sadder and sadder. So Ken bought another hamster, called Snowball, but only Andrew was ever allowed to hold him. Peace was once more restored – almost.

In my brain though, a little worm kept nibbling away about something Ken's mother had said at Christmas. She had described the lack of precautions taken when I had been whisked off to hospital after I had polio. She had contacted the Medical Officer of Health to ask when the house would be fumigated and was amazed to be told that all she could do was to open the windows and give the house a good airing. She was flabbergasted and asked, 'What about the children?' She was told to just keep them isolated for three weeks. Although it was now well over two years since I had polio, I kept all the windows open as much as possible and used gallons of disinfectant on the floors and drains.

I recalled the stories that Monica, the physiotherapist at the Rehabilitation Hospital, had brought back from South America about the anti-polio vaccine which had been produced shortly after I had polio. It was believed that children were killed and crippled by the very injections which were meant to protect them. I wondered if any of these batches of vaccine had been sent to this country. It seemed too dangerous to be given to Brian and Andrew. Why had I gone down with polio when my neighbours had not? Could it be that people picked up diseases not only because they were exposed to the causative virus but also because they lacked the necessary defences? Were my children like me, wide open to polio, or like their father who had escaped polio twice despite close contact, first as a child, then many years later with me and the small group of patients in the Isolation Hospital?

Every time Brian or Andrew came home from school with a cold they were isolated upstairs and kept in bed just as they and their friends had been two years earlier when I first had polio. Then the little worry-worm would bite. Was it really only a cold they had, or the beginnings of polio? I always asked Dr Scott to call to check their condition. As I could not go up to their bedrooms to see them, we missed one another very much. I sent Bill the budgie and the hamsters upstairs to keep them company but knew there was no substitute for an active mother.

Despite our precautions my own health went up and down hectically. This also meant that the children had to be excluded from my room frequently. At such times, they were not allowed to come in at all; not even to say good morning or good night. The boys did not dare to be naughty for fear that they would be sent away again. They became very anxious, especially when they could see preoccupied adults bustling in and out. Andrew particularly would stop outside the window as soon as he reached home and, unable to wait until he arrived at the door, would run down the steps and peep in at the window to make sure I was still there.

It seemed odd to all of us that we had waited so long to be together again and now that we were back under one roof we were sometimes forced apart. The only compensation, if anything, was the heightened pleasure we felt when we were together and the joy and peace of our rare days of family life based on my bed.

The boys spent their weekends helping Ken to look after me. They climbed on and off my high bed with consummate ease. They seemed to be aware of my needs and how to help me without being told. When my hands fell from their pillows, Brian or Andrew would rearrange them. Father-like, my children wiped my eyes when they saw me blinking or pushed my hair back from my forehead if they saw me frowning. Gradually a natural division of labour took place. Brian helped Ken fetch and carry in the garden. Andrew prepared simple meals at my bedside. He began by cooking potatoes in their jackets and rice pudding. He placed them safely in the cold oven and switched on the electricty afterwards. He always showed me how clean he had scrubbed the skins of the potatoes and where he had pricked them carefully with a fork. Later he increased his range and made us the best bread-and-butter pudding we had ever tasted.

Brian and Andrew could never play away from the house as it was impossible for Ken to leave me to go and look for them. On Sunday mornings we would watch the other families in the road piling into their cars and setting off for the seaside. When all the houses were empty and strangely quiet we felt like the last people left alive in the world.

At Whitsun my parents and my sister Pat came to stay. It was very satisfying to watch the boys running in and out of the house just like any other children now that there was someone around who could go to find them. As Ken was not the only adult available there was time to play games such as dominoes, rummy or sevens. There was always an escort on hand for trips into town.

At the end of June Andrew celebrated his sixth birthday by asking four friends to tea so that with himself and Brian they could have a little party for six. I ordered a cake with a white mouse on it from our bakery. Ken drew a donkey to hang on the wall so that the children could enjoy trying to pin a tail on to it while they were blindfolded. He arranged various games in the garden as well as doing magic tricks such as giving them brand-new pennies which he found in boys' pockets or produced from behind their ears.

Later we arranged a similar party for Brian's eighth birthday which he shared with Ken as their birthdays are only three days apart. The cake was decorated with an anchor but in fact this birthday was of enormous significance to all of us as it qualified Brian to join the Cubs of the local Sea Scouts. For an hour every week he would be able to slip his anchor while at the Cub meeting.

In the summer Inky wrote to ask if she could come to stay for a week in the school holidays. I was delighted. With Inky's company I could safely send the rest of the family to the grandparents' home in Bedfordshire. Ken had the job of packing for all three of them. I could no longer do it but I did make out some lists and tried to arrange for the necessary clothes to be clean in time, although I had a project of my own. There was much preparation and secrecy involved. My neighbours were helping me to prepare a plan of campaign to decorate my room and the hall. Somehow we managed to strip off the old wallpaper while I remained in the room. Bill the budgie and the hamsters Snowball and Tommy were transferred upstairs. We recruited an army of adults and children to help. The children were delighted to tear strips of wallpaper from the walls legitimately. I longed to have a go at it myself.

Margaret Richardson – one of the hospital nurses – and her husband Bob arrived from Southampton and gradually my surroundings were transformed. Cups of coffee and tea kept coming, simple meals were prepared and demolished. The worst part of the job was the paintwork on the skirting. Strictly speaking it was not paint at all: the wood had been dyed a dark brown treacle colour and layers of varnish made it immovable. After several attempts to remove it we gave up and decided to concentrate on the walls so that we could finish our project on schedule.

Nora and Cyril decorated the hall. They chose some white paint which was guaranteed to stand up to years of wear and tear. For my room we selected pale primrose paint for the three walls that suffered the most contact and a contrasting beige paper with tiny formalised pink rosebuds and green leaves for the fourth. A wine-red, gold-and-beige frieze was stuck along the tops of the walls to finish our scheme. Inky cleverly covered my fawn light- and lamp-shades with matching dark red edging. We were very pleased with ourselves. She brought some curtain samples from the shops with dark red-and-gold stripes with an alternating pattern which almost exactly matched the wallpaper.

The District Nurse offered to run the curtains up on my sewing-machine but when she saw it was driven by an electric motor she changed her mind. I offered to control the push-button with my toe and pointed out that she would then have both hands free to guide the material under the needle. I showed her how, at a flick of a switch, she could make the stiches run backwards or forwards. Also I would respond instantly to her commands. She had only to say, 'Stop. Go. Fast. Slow,' I would make the machine do exactly as she wished. At first she was not convinced but gradually her confidence grew. We finished the curtains in record time and were admiring our handiwork just as the *Newbury Weekly News* was delivered. I asked her to turn to the pages of advertisements where I was advertising for a Saturday-afternoon helper. She was very enthusiastic and giggled, 'You and your new helper could set up in business making curtains together.' Inky joined in the joke but I was deadly serious. By the time Ken, Brian and Andrew came home I had found our first regularly-employed scribe. This would mean that they could go swimming, shopping and do whatever other things father and sons do on a Saturday afternoon. I thought Ken would be very pleased.

Unfortunately, he was furious. 'Where do you think we are going to find the money? I can't pay the electricity and telephone bills now. We must reduce our costs, not add to them.' Although I was in the dog-house over this particular surprise I *had* pleased everyone with the transformation of my room. They admired the changed colour-scheme and their homecoming present of a large, deep red vase just happened to match the new decoration. It was – and still is – a lovely vase, and Ken stood it in the fireplace to hide the grate, filling it with beautiful tall flowers from his mother's garden.

I was desperate to keep my newly-found Saturday-afternoon hands. I tried hard to find the money to pay the wages. I entered dozens of competitions which offered huge cash prizes but I only ran up more bills for stamps. All I ever won was a leather book-mark from *Punch* and a couple of books from the magazine *John Bull*. At least competitions kept my mind exercised on something other than domestic problems.

Soon a year had passed since I had escaped from hospital yet I had not won back any movement at all. If anything I was weaker. My breathing was also more shallow even with my respirator going full-blast. Physically I tired rapidly but mentally my mind raced along. Words ran on in my head stringing themselves into stories. Brian and Andrew sometimes jotted down brief notes for me between chores. Now and then to speed the tasks we made up stories among ourselves. We tried to make them funny as we liked to laugh. Andrew always finished the stories by saying, 'And they all lived happily ever after'. We lived in a kind of frenzy. There was always far too much to do. My condition demanded a great deal of attention from helpers, nurses and family. The household jobs had to be fitted in as and when it became possible or not at all.

In the autumn two new helpers joined us; Nanette, a vivacious French brunette and Jean, a quiet reserved brown-haired girl who had always lived locally. Nanette loved shopping and cooking. Omelettes were her forte. She also baked her own bread and brought us a loaf each time she made a batch. Brian and Andrew had told Nanette about the times they had helped me to make things such as bread and Chelsea buns before I had polio. Nanette realised the massive frustration I experienced with my fingers no longer able to busy themselves with the cooking, sewing and other demands which a mother of school-age children takes for granted. She understood how deprived Brian and Andrew must feel through never being mothered in the usual way. She did her best to tease some smiles on to their increasingly serious faces. Some-how we all managed to show a brave front to the world but we knew that there should be far more to life than the kind of shut-in and restricted existence that was our lot.

Chapter 23
Blessings

Christmas Boxes took on a new meaning as my second Christmas at home grew nearer. Early one evening a group of excited neighbours were shown into my room. Their faces were flushed with exertion and a sense of occasion as they struggled through the doorway with a big box. They made a little speech saying how much they wanted me to have the happiest possible Christmas and that they had been planning it for a long time. Each one said a few words describing how they had collected salvage, old newspapers and money to raise enough to buy a television set which they hoped would give me hours of amusement. I felt shocked. I found I loathed the idea of being regarded as a charitable object. I felt appalled at the realisation that they had collected money for me without my knowledge or say so. I could not tell them how I felt but strove to hide the fact that I was saddened by their efforts. Instead I tried hard to find words to express what they wanted to hear. Eventually I said, quite truthfully and sincerely, how good it was of them to think of providing me with a television set and how moved I was that they should think of me as a recipient of their kindness but that I was sure there were other people who were in far greater need than myself and perhaps it should go elsewhere. Everybody looked crestfallen and protested: 'But we wanted you to have it'.

I gave up. I could not hurt them by saying what a blow to my pride their Christmas surprise had been, nor could I reveal my endless assertions to Ken that I would never give a television set house-room. I persevered in my frantic search for the right words. I heard myself saying that as they so particularly wanted me to have the television set I was pleased to accept it in the spirit in which it was given. Everybody brightened up at this – particularly Brian and Andrew! Cyril had been busy fixing up the television in the corner of the room. He switched it on and we all admired the clarity of the picture. No one wanted a cup of tea or coffee but said good-bye and left us to wonder at this act of neighbourly charity. The large cardboard box stood empty by my bed. It spoke volumes to me. When the children's television programme had finished Ken switched the set off and I suggested that Brian and Andrew should turn the container into a post-box. We could keep our Christmas presents for each other secure in its depths. No little fingers would be able to discern the contents of the packages. The box could stand high up on the sideboard where I could see it all the time. Such fun was had as they covered the box with red crêpe paper and decorated it with cotton-wool snow! They draped long fine strips of silver paper over the box to hang down like icicles. Ken printed a notice to fix below the mouth of the box. It read: NEXT COLLECTION CHRISTMAS DAY. CRACK OF DAWN.

As the days grew shorter the box filled with presents. Many protruded from its mouth. Others which were too big to go inside were heaped on top in an inviting pile. It made a very decorative addition to my room and set the atmosphere of Christmas even before Brian and Andrew had made their paperchains and hung them up. One unexpected present from the outside world had overwhelmed me but another was to come. Ken's colleagues, hearing of my efforts to write a book, bought the smallest available tape-recorder and sent it to me with their best wishes for my success. Experimenting with our recording was a great joy. We were amazed how different our voices sounded on the tape from what we had imagined. The next morning being a Saturday, Brian and Andrew waited with great impatience for Nanette to arrive so that we could tape the first thing she said and then surprise her by playing it back. Suddenly Nanette zoomed up, breathless as usual, on her red scooter, her black hair glistening with drops of moisture from the mist outside. We switched on the tape-recorder, tucking my counterpane around it so that it would not be noticed. Nanette burst in upon us with her usual cheery 'Good morning' and began describing to us how she had pushed her way through a herd of cows that had ambled along obstructing the road. I laughed, thinking what a lively first recording we were making, and said, 'That was a brave thing to do on that red scooter. What a good job the bull wasn't there.'

'Yes, wasn't it?'

We threw my cover back and rewound the tape-recorder. Nanette's eyebrows shot up in amazement. 'What is this? You haven't!'

'Yes, we have,' we giggled, as we wound back the tape and played her story to her.

'That is not ME,' she declared, but as she listened she admitted it was her story as she had just told it. She kept saying, 'Isn't it marvellous! Isn't it marvellous!'

This became one of our catch phrases and evermore we would comment on Nanette's stories by exclaiming, 'Isn't it marvellous' which always made us laugh uproariously.

By the time Ken's mother and father came for Christmas we were dab-hands with the recorder. Once more they steamed in with their cargo of turkey, ham, mince pies and so on. They admired the Christmas Box and Grandad drove into Newbury to buy little novelties to wrap up and put in it and around it. On top of the box he stacked two large packets which contained a big Boots diary each for Brian and Andrew.

Edie had given me her Christmas-pudding recipe and Andrew made his first Christmas pudding under my supervision. He washed the fruit thoroughly and showed me the blackness of the dirty water in the bowl. He had always done this when making bread-and-butter puddings but now that he was making the Christmas pudding which was almost solid fruit he was delighted at the amount of grime he had managed to wash out. He made our Christmas puddings every year after that.

Nellie Brown gave us a huge box of chocolates with a lovely picture of a rose on its lid. How we enjoyed selecting our favourites! I was glad to see the chocolates disappear as I desperately wanted the box to keep my manuscripts in to stop them from becoming dog-eared.

Someone had brought me a newspaper clipping announcing a children's book competition. I knew that no one had yet written about children trying to cope in our circumstances and I thought I should fill the gap. The competition seemed especially apt for me as it was a Nesbit Memorial and *The Railway Children* had always been one of my favourites. The formula of children falling on hard times because one of the parents was suddenly whipped away seemed heaven-sent.

I had amassed reams of notes for my book. They were stored in an empty cardboard grocery box under my bed where they were hidden from sight by my fawn counterpane. We enjoyed wonderful Christmas meals with the hamsters sitting on my bed while their presents were unwrapped for them to devour. They were given some special crispy biscuits of which they were particularly fond.

Nanette had given us a new grey-blue budgie called Trisha. She shared Bill's cage but he was out of it more often than not. They were given extra millet. The goldfish received more snails in their aquarium to help keep the water clear.

On Boxing Day Brian and Andrew counted up their Christmas money and found that they were each richer by fifteen shillings. They knew exactly what they wanted to do with their money. On their way into town with Grandad they had noticed some huge packing cases for sale at a local wood-yard. They had designs on these boxes. They wanted a shed like Ken's as a refuge from the comings and goings of the household and the noise of my machine. When I told them how much such a shed cost they had started to save up for some planks of wood in the hope that their father would help them build a small one each.

When the packing cases arrived Ken looked them over and measured them. He modified them to make the roofs slope and covered them with roofing-felt to make them waterproof. He also cut out two round window-holes in the sides and covered them with clear plastic. Next a front door was fitted complete with smart hinges and handles. Ken levelled off the best site at the bottom of the garden where the sheds could stand side by side, each separate in its own ground. He dug the plot over well and then left it to Brian and Andrew to tend so that they could grow their own things in their own gardens.

Then the boys creosoted their sheds. The children around hung over the fence, turning green with envy while Brian and Andrew's faces turned bright red with the effect of the creosote. Fortunately their skins were soon soothed with calamine lotion and they started on the less harmful decoration of the insides of their sheds. They papered their walls with pictures cut from magazines and made drawings with coloured chalks. They begged old pieces of carpet for their floors and an old saucepan to cook tins of beans on the little camp-fire they built with some bricks in the way that Ken had shown them. They each had a small box of enamelled mugs, plates, knives and cooking-spoons. They sat and sewed curtain hems with enormous darning needles which they stabbed through the material with such concentration that their brows furrowed with the effort.

Over the years the sheds gave the boys hours of enjoyment – little territories away from the house where the living space was commandeered by my bed and equipment. Gradually they added other refinements. An old piece of hosepipe made a talking-tube between them. Then they learnt how to fix up electric light-bulbs from batteries.

We still use the old Christmas Box instead of a tree each year. Every time we drag it down from the attic and the decorations are unpacked from its depths, we remember the year of the Christmas

Boxes when we began to establish new family traditions to fit our changed circumstances.

When the trees put out their leaf-buds in the spring Brian and Andrew sprouted spots on their faces, necks and backs. June regarded them with her professional eye.

'Chicken-pox. I know exactly what to do about that.'

She gave each of the children a bottle of oil-based calamine and some cotton-wool with which to dab the spots whenever the irritation became unbearable. She also gave them soothing baths at times when she could leave me, such as when the nurses came. Brian's chicken-pox spots spread far more than Andrew's, which seemed strange considering that he was older and should have had more time to develop his defences.

Ken had been over-working for so long that he was thoroughly run down. A large carbuncle glared at us from just above his collar like Chad peering over a wall. June poulticed it every morning before Ken set off for work. With the first patient taken care of, she tackled our spotty pair saying that working in our house was like running a small ops. clinic. This amused me. I thought how fortunate that I am only suffering from the consequences of respiratory polio; otherwise her casualty station would demand all her time. I would not have laughed so confidently had I known that I was to catch shingles from the children's chicken-pox. As the days and nights grew warmer I felt as though I had been stung by a wasp and blistered with a lighted cigarette-end along the nerve pathway down my back and across my ribs. The pain and irritation were intense but I could not remove my cuirass to cool the area down. This could only happen in the mornings when the nurses came. The shingle lines hurt mostly during the sleepless nights. I became very over-tired. My mother had been to visit us at Easter and I was very upset to learn that she had caught shingles too. What a family!

We all desperately needed a holiday. It was suggested that I return to hospital for a fortnight but we were all against this idea. I still loathed and feared hospital so much that going back would only do harm. My family appreciated this and could never enjoy a holiday without me if they knew that I was shut up again. What could we do? It was essential that Ken, Brian and Andrew should go away for a change somewhere.

We were delighted when another friendly physiotherapist – Pam – volunteered to look after me in their absence.

Pam had just returned from America. She described the

American obsession with deep shelters in case of atomic bomb attacks. She showed us the certificate which she had earned for riding on a mule to the bottom of the Grand Canyon and staying the night. I said she should qualify for a gold medal for surviving two weeks with me and my paraphernalia. We intended reading several books and writing letters to mutual friends. We managed some, but the opportunity to read and write through Pam's hands for a couple of weeks was a refreshing change.

While Ken was away I learned that our Saturday-afternoon helper was moving and that I would have to find someone else. This made me very sad but I cheered up when I realised that my new advertisement could be for someone to come one evening a week as well as Saturday afternoons. Ken had several evening meetings to attend every month. It would help to have one evening fixed permanently. It would not be such a hard job to recruit sitters to stay with me while he was absent. The more I thought about this idea the more I liked it. Ken was bound to be pleased. I had completely forgotten his response when I had first employed a Saturday helper. Afterwards he seemed to accept the situation quickly and enjoyed his new Saturday-afternoon freedom. But this time he was really angry with me. He wanted to know where I was going to find the money since he already had more bills than he could manage to pay.

I realised what a fool I had been but felt the situation was not entirely my fault. Ken kept me ignorant of his money worries and now gave me only the housekeeping money for food, etc. He juggled with the other bills himself; robbing Peter to pay Paul.

I pondered very hard on this question of where I could make some money. As I paid Mick my instalment for Ken's shed one week, she suggested that I should start a Mail Order Club and keep the commission instead of buying from her.

'Will that be enough to pay for Saturday afternoons?'

'Well, no,' admitted Mick, 'but it would help. I will buy some things from you and I am sure you can find a few other customers.'

Jean called through the hatch that she and her mother would buy some goods too. That is how I became a Grattan Agent. I was unable to find many customers, as I am too shy about asking for money from people who come to my house to help me and I never see anyone else. However I bought most of my household towels and sheets from Grattan and found buying the boys' clothes in this way had its advantages. They could parade up and down beside my bed in their new clothes and shoes so that I could see if they fitted properly. Heavens, how I missed my hands, but I learnt to watch very acutely. In the privacy of our own home we could have better discussions among ourselves about the things we were buying than we could have done in a shop.

Later I became an Avon representative. Brian and Andrew played shops on my bed, unpacking the soaps and cosmetics, checking them against the orders and putting them into little bags with the accounts pinned on to them in the approved way. My immobility meant I could not increase my number of customers very much, but I persevered for a while. I had no other way to make money. My book was taking a very long time to produce.

I exclaimed to June. 'Writing for children is harder than writing for adults. I don't know why I allowed myself to be persuaded to do this.' On Saturday afternoons and Tuesdays evenings my new amanuensis, Mrs Green, noted down the bits of the story I had been chewing over all week. Eventually we managed to finish our competition entry in first draft. My physiotherapist took a keen interest in what I was doing and during her weekly sessions with me I would tell her the next instalment of my story. As the closing date drew nearer it became obvious that we were never going to finish our fair copy in time. I was delighted when my physiotherapist offered to ask her friends to help type the manuscript. One of the typists she enlisted was also a writer who, possibly in self-defence, suggested that I tackled shorter pieces of work. She thought an article or two would be more manageable. I considered this advice but hoped that it would not be necessary to take it. I wanted to write books. I had far too much to say to fit it into articles.

Dr Scott expressed concern about my being shut up indoors during the long hot summer. He suggested that my window should be enlarged and french doors fitted in its place, with a verandah built up to the level of my room. I could be pushed out on to it in my bed.

Dr Scott contacted the Local Authority and we enjoyed the visits of the very considerate workmen. They made every effort to keep the noise and dust to a minimum and to work as quickly as they could to seal up the room before they left as I could not be moved out of it. Thoughtfully, I watched the workmen demolishing the wall. This gave me an idea for my book and I started taping a new slant to the first chapter. I had decided to call the book *The Builders*.

Escaping from my room was a wonderful tonic: the hot weather an added bonus. Although I spent only an hour or two in the sun, I was several shades browner each time Dr Scott called. It was exhilarating out in the open air, to look up at the vast blue sky instead of stubbing my eyes on the low ceiling. I revelled in the feel of the sun on my eyes and the wind in my hair. The fragrance of Norah's roses drifted across to me; I could see our own roses in their riot of reds, pinks, oranges, and yellows. My neighbours waved to me as they hung out the washing on their lines or terrified the weeds in their gardens. I admired Ken's shed which I had not been able to see before and his neat rows of vegetables.

I noticed that Brian and Andrew could do with some shrubs around their sheds for privacy. Their salad stuff was doing very well. I could see why Bill and Trisha enjoyed being carted down to the sheds in their cage. Fresh groundsel flourished there and could be bent at an angle to be poked through the bars to enable them to feed on the living plants.

I felt very fit and as I surveyed my surroundings found it difficult to believe that I could not leap from my bed to straighten the washing on my own line when a sudden wind tugged a sheet from the grip of one of its pegs so that it trailed on the ground. In many ways my outings emphasised my loss of ability and strength but I shut that out of my mind as the benefit was much greater than the disadvantages. When the weather broke we checked our procedure for power cuts. It was as well that we did.

One afternoon when Jean was preparing the tea and the boys had just climbed Edie's fence on their way home from school, the rain fell in torrents. Instantly gallons of water were rushing down our steps from the pavement like a mountain stream and swirling down our path. It was exciting to watch but we suddenly had more than we bargained for. My respirator stopped. Jean whipped off my cuirass and pressed my ribs in and out with her hands while Brian and Andrew changed the respirator motor over to hand-pump. We did not have to cope on our own for long. Ken's car swam into view. He rushed in and took over. He had leapt into his car and battled up the hill against the tide of water that was rushing down; he could see it running past him well over his mudguards but kept going, praying that the water would not get into the engine and make it stop.

As Ken hand-cranked my respirator the colour soon came back into my cheeks. We had all turned pale at the shock of the electricity being cut off.

In two years I had not managed to make any progress with my breathing or movements but remained totally dependent on family and friends. Ken had to keep himself fit and leave messages of his whereabouts even while at work so that he could rush home to deal with power failures whenever they occurred. Brian and Andrew continued to mother me or father me as it became necessary. More and more, Brian and Andrew withdrew to their sheds and inside themselves.

Our savings were disappearing rapidly through the cost of wear and tear on the house and the constant need to buy ready-made clothes and food which were less substantial than the things I would have sewn or cooked with my own home-making skills. Our summer bills for fuel were worse than most people ran up for the winter. Our inescapable winter bills were horrific.

The one bright hope to which I clung fiercely was that my book *The Builders* would win the competition. It had taken so much effort to finish my entry in time for the last posting date. It just had to win.

As the leaves on the trees turned to gold my outings became fewer. The spiders began to move indoors with me. I watched them weaving their webs in the window and began spinning another story so that I would have a second book ready by the time the competition results were announced.

Inky came for Ken and Brian's birthday weekend before boomeranging out to Australia, and Fiz was working her passage to Jamaica on a banana boat. Cheerfully I wished Inky and Fiz a happy time. I would miss them badly, especially as I could ill afford to lose such strong props.

The winter was approaching rapidly. I guessed we were in for another long endurance test with the children being banished upstairs each time they caught a cold. Among my post one day was the manuscript of my book – rejected.

Suddenly the view from my window was very bleak. The trees stood stark and bare against the skyline. Like Persephone I must wait until the spring before I could feel the sun on my skin once again.

Chapter 24
Joyfulness

One night in December I woke up feeling bitterly cold. A wind had got up and was moaning around the house evoking a *Wuthering Heights* kind of haunting and calling. I wondered what had disturbed me. A figure appeared at the foot of my bed. I thought it must be Brian or Andrew alarmed by the swish of the wind shaking the trees and rattling the window-panes.

'What do you want?' I whispered.

There was no reply. Slightly louder I asked, 'What are you looking for?'

Still there was no answer. The figure just stood there. Shining.

A voice in my head cautioned: *it's a ghost*; another voice sighed: *there are no such things*. I wanted to pull the blankets over my head but as I could not move I must shut my eyes. Tight. When I opened them again the apparition had vanished.

The room temperature had dropped far below zero. I knew I could not get warm unaided as polio had destroyed my ability to shiver and recover my normal body temperature.

Feeling the need of human reassurance I gave a tiny ping on my bell to wake Ken without disturbing the children.

Ken's sleepy voice asked, 'What do you want?'

'I'm perished. My sheets are like ice.'

Ken climbed out of bed. He shivered and agreed. 'It's like the Arctic in here.'

He felt around the foot of my bed to find my dead, cold hot-water bottle. He rubbed my frozen ankles and walked away to refill the bottle. I did not want him to leave me.

'No wonder it's freezing in here. The door's open.'

'Who opened it?'

'The wind, I expect. It's blowing a gale outside.'

When he returned with my warm hot-water bottle he said: 'How strange! The fire has gone out. I'll have to light it again. I may as well make a cup of tea – do you want one?'

The hot-water bottle, the flickering fire and the reviving tea worked their soporific magic. I did not tell Ken that I had seen my first and only ghost. It would sound silly.

The next morning we heard that a typhoon had hit the town, ripping the tiles from neighbouring roofs. Our roof had not lost so much as a single slate.

A few days later a sad letter arrived to say that John had caught a cold and not woken from his sleep one morning. His widow, Ses, wanted us to know that he had always been very proud of his Tally-ho roses and had boasted that his garden grew the best roses for miles around. How paradoxical that Ses's letter should remind us of roses in December, and tell us of John's passing, when Christmas is about birth.

Christmas 1959 – our third Christmas at home – was more of a challenge than the first two had been. Ken's mother had been unwell and could not come to us. Nan's illness was a source of worry; it also meant I had a great deal of detailed reorganising to do if the workload was to be managed by the few pairs of hands available.

One of the consequences of Christmas is the mountain of washing-up. Anxiously I sought the best way to scale the formidable pile on my horizon. My interest flared when Mrs Green told me about the washing-up machines which were used at the local hotel where she worked on a Saturday evening. With her help I made inquiries about a domestic dishwasher. We discovered that I could buy one on very reasonable terms over a period of years. I could no longer insist that we should save for what we wanted. I already bought on credit from Grattans; all around me people did the same – even laughing openly about their debts and overdrafts. I persuaded myself I was adapting in order to survive, that this was the intelligent view.

Organising delivery of the dishwasher as a surprise for Ken was a problem but somehow I managed to arrange for it to be plumbed in on the day before Christmas Eve.

Ken found the machine insufferable. Not only was the purchase madly extravagant, he said, but also that the gallons of hot water it needed would run up constant bills for electricity. I was not to be put off. I remained cheerful about my commitment to the dishwasher and even began to call it 'mum'.

On Christmas Day I pooh-poohed the idea that washing-up should be done at the end of each meal. I insisted we should pack it all into the machine so that 'mum' could do it later.

Washing-up was, after all, only one of the chores. Ken and the boys still had all the preparations and cooking to do. They had to dish up and feed me first before sitting down together to eat their own meals. We all started to feel that perhaps the dishwasher was not such a bad idea after all.

At lunch-time Ken gave me the chicken wishbone. Andrew helped me to break it. He expressed all our feelings when he said, 'If I had one wish, Mum, I would wish for lots of wishes and then I would wish them all to make you better.'

We needed more than wishes on Christmas night. Ken staggered into the kitchen carrying the final trayful of used cups, saucers, plates of all sizes. He filled the dishwasher to the top and switched it on. Nothing happened. Muttering to himself but aware that we were all listening to him intently, he checked the fuse, the plug, the switches – everything seemed to be in order. He switched the machine on and off several times but still nothing happened.

Sighing, he rolled up his sleeves. Wearily he began to unpack the dirty dishes and stack them on the draining-board. We had not stinted ourselves but had used every item of crockery we possessed. Grease and bits of food had by now congealed on the plates. The gunge was going to be far more difficult to remove than if the dishes had been washed up immediately after use. I could have cried as I listened to Ken and the children washing-up by hand. It seemed to be taking hours. Suddenly all the joy had drained out of Christmas. My gift had turned into another burden. I hated the great white elephant of a machine that was standing uncooperatively in my kitchen while I desperately needed its help. If I could have struggled out of bed I would have kicked it . . . *hard*.

It took weeks to find someone to come and mend the machine. I refused to pay the instalments until it was repaired and became very unpopular with the shop from which we had bought it. When it was mended everyone refused to use it in case it should break down again. However, I did manage to persuade Ken to use it just on Sundays. It seemed only sensible to run it once a week to keep it in order.

Ken had made a much wiser choice of present for me. He had bought a bird-table which was to provide endless amusement during the winter when bluetits, robins, sparrows and starlings swooped on our crumbs. Ken fixed the bird-table outside my window on a metal stand which was impervious to Tibby's claws.

The dishwasher was not the only problem that Christmas. On Boxing Night we had a power cut and experienced a frantic time hand-pumping my respirator by candlelight. After the shock of our very first power cut, Ken organised a routine in which torches, candles and matches were assembled, lighting established and my breathing-machine changed over to its hand-cranking position. Ken began hand-pumping immediately. Brian and Andrew, young as they were, placed their hands beside Ken's and learnt to 'help'. This early training was very valuable as, although one small boy could not possibly operate the machine by himself, two small boys together could establish emergency breathing arrangements at once, while waiting for an adult to take over. Neighbours soon hurried along to our house to lend their hands at working my respirator as well as manning the telephone to find out why the cut had occurred and how soon power would be restored. The Boxing Night power failure was caused by a youth who had been given a new airgun for Christmas. He had shot out the insulators on the overhead power-lines into town and plunged the whole area into darkness. How vulnerable we were to the casual thoughtlessness of others!

Before the New Year, our vicar brought his little daughter to see us. Jenny had been born a blue baby and was now handicapped. She arrived clutching an enormous toy lion. When she left she insisted on leaving it on my bed to keep me company. The vicar urged me to do as Jenny said but when they left I sent her a note to thank her for the wonderful company of her lion. I explained that I would dearly love to keep him but unfortunately he was pining. The only way to make him happy again was to return him to his mistress. I have never forgotten Jenny's self-denial nor the sensitivity which prompted her to make me a present of her treasured lion.

We telephoned my in-laws to tell them about our Christmas doings, making the escapade with the washing-up machine sound hilarious. We would never have admitted that it was no joke really. It made my parents-in-law realise how indispensable they were. My father-in-law had tracked down an astonishing electric blanket to keep the cold at bay. It was the first time I had come across a blanket designed to be used on top of the bed instead of on the bottom as usual. This meant it was as safe as it was possible to make it.

As 1960 turned not only a new year, but also a fresh decade, we began our new diaries. In mine I stated boldly that I would make a tremendous effort to escape from the house.

I had been inquiring about a new portable respirator. We were determined to experiment with it. When it arrived we tried it out indoors. The pumping part resembled a cylindrical vacuum-cleaner. It made a great deal of noise – considering the little help it gave – but so long as it remained in one place it ran for about half an hour. Its breathing rhythm was strange and fierce and totally different from the evenly-maintained breathing provided by my usual big machine.

When we tried to take the portable machine out for a run it turned nasty. We spent several hair-raising Sunday mornings driving anxiously down the road, up the hill and around the block.

We would start off in the car with me settled into the front seat. Ken had specially built this up at an angle and with a neck support. I would be wedged in on either side with tall cardboard boxes topped with cushions to support my arms, the vacuum-cleaner respirator would puff away behind me; Brian and Andrew would clamber into the back seat. As we set off, our hopes would rise. Perhaps this time it would behave beautifully. We would drive off – but before we had gone far the machine would stop. Ken would have to drive home fast with Brian and Andrew pushing my chest in and out to keep me breathing. Obviously we could not take these chances. The responsibility on all of us – especially the children – was far too great.

It looked as though I was condemned to another year of being shut up. The farthest journeys I could expect to make were the excursions on to the verandah on fine days. It seemed hard. Could I really travel only a few yards in my bed? Could it be true that not so many years ago I had trudged through the sands of Egypt to the Pyramids, flown in an old Dakota around the Acropolis, knelt by Keats's grave just outside Rome?

Being pinned down in one spot by my breathing limitations intensified my search for machines to extend my usefulness where I was. Help arrived surprisingly when I developed a chest infection. Dr Scott was on holiday; his partner, Dr Peters, called to see me instead. He commented on my new made-to-order telephone. He watched my demonstration of how I could bring the hand-set to the side of my face so that I could make and take my own calls merely by pushing on a pedal with my toe. He said goodbye but reappeared about five minutes later. I thought he had come back for something he had forgotten. Instead I heard him say, 'Your telephone has given me an idea. If you tell me the half-dozen or so things that would be of most use to you to operate with pedals like your telephone, I could arrange them on a foot-board that could be fixed permanently to your bed.'

My tape-recorder and bell were already at my feet so these two headed the list.

'What about the television and the lamp?' asked Dr Peters.

'Yes, please,' I answered. 'Would it be possible to include my radio and electric blanket?'

He thought for a moment. 'The radio would be simple but the electric blanket is more complicated. Can I see what type it is?'

We showed him the transformer and the switch that controlled the heat.

'I will see what I can do,' he smiled.

He enlisted the help of an inventor, John Taylor, and soon my remote-control was taking shape at the foot of my bed. Pedals controlled my lamp, television, radio, tape-recorder, record player and a selection of bells. These last, upstairs and downstairs, gave a tiny ping or a Morse code message depending upon what was required. Ken also fitted a ship's bell to be clanged mightily to make everyone who heard it come running. My electric blanket took a little while to perfect and was eventually controlled by the wheel from a toy elephant. I can't forget that somewhere in the world there is an elephant running on three wheels so that I can be kept warm.

With my control panel I identified strongly with astronauts. Like them I lived a restricted life in a tiny space and depended totally on machinery for my communications and air supply. How liberating to have my whole world at my feet!

I was too joyful. One Saturday Ken went upstairs to be quiet with a blinding migraine. On her way in, Peggy, the nurse, picked up our letters and brought them for me to read. To my horror, one of the letters was a threat to cut off our electricity because we had not paid the bill. I felt the colour drain from my face.

'Can they do this, Peggy?'

'Not while I am about,' she asserted.

She marched out of the house in a very determined way, returning later to say that not only had she warned the Electricity Board that on no account must my supply be cut off but also that she had bumped into a friend who was associated with the British Legion. She asked his advice. He was shocked that we were having to pay for me to breathe, especially as our bills were so huge. He came to see us to verify the situation, established a temporary pension for me of a pound a month, and, after a long-drawn-out battle, managed to persuade the Health Authority to take responsibility for a proportion of the bills. The Wrens' Association were also notified of our predicament and for some time they sent us a pound a week.

Other charities were approached. They responded in their various ways.

I was chastened by my realisation of just how difficult it was for

Ken to pay our way. Very reluctantly I had to abandon my dreams for equipping the kitchen with labour-saving machinery such as the disastrous dishwasher. I drew my horns in and kept them in. It was the only contribution I could make and it cost me a lot.

At last, at last, at last the whole family could go away on holiday together – me included.

This promising event was made possible by the British Polio Fellowship whose caravan at Portsmouth was supervised by a doctor from a nearby hospital. Several people on respirators had stayed there. When we were invited to take up a vacant week in the spring we were encouraged by the doctor's promise to transport me in his specially-adapted car.

To our delight Ses said that she would come with us to look after me. She could do with a holiday by the sea. Ses brought a huge fruit cake to last us all the week and helped me to make a list of the best sorts of foods to take with us.

As it happened Ses proved invaluable, not only for her culinary experiences but also because we almost did not make it to the coast. We started out in good time with me tucked safely beside the doctor on a specially-designed and shaped shell of foam rubber. His portable respirator pump puffed away in the back of the car to keep my cuirass breathing me. Ses sat in the back beside the respirator keeping an eye on it and me.

Ken followed in our car tightly packed with Brian, Andrew, and our luggage.

In high spirits we zoomed up the hill and out of the valley but before we could clear the outskirts of the town the respirator stopped.

None of us could believe that the machine had failed during the first few seconds. When I began to feel the pressure of suffocation in my desperate lungs I could have cried with gratitude as I heard Ses instruct the doctor to return home – at speed. He turned his car rapidly and flew down the hill with Ken in close pursuit.

I do not remember being rushed from the car to my bed and reconnected to our domestic power. I just had to concentrate every ounce of strength I could muster on my fight for breath. Ses, Ken and the boys were all experts and acted immediately and efficiently together.

The disappointed doctor examined the broken respirator but could not make it go. Even if it had shown signs of life we would not have trusted it again. Had the beastly thing stopped any further from home, my chances of survival would have been nil.

Unfortunately the doctor had been given the wrong information. He thought I wore a cuirass only to assist my breathing. He did not know that I depended totally on my equipment. We all tried to be cheerful for his sake but he must have guessed that we were putting on an act. He gave Brian and Andrew a half-crown each. They tried to refuse but he insisted that they took it. Through the window we watched him drive away with the lost promise of our long-awaited holiday.

We turned away and sized up our situation. We had cancelled the butcher, the baker and the milkman. We had completely emptied the fridge – and the larder too – and given all our helpers a week off. Brian and Andrew had farmed out the goldfish, hamsters and budgerigars. Our warm and supportive home had turned into an inhospitable house.

Ses decided to make us laugh by asking who would like a piece of current cake. She sorted through our mountain of luggage trying to find the right tin.

'We can have a holiday at home,' she said.

I felt I had endured too many holidays at home already. My longing for the sight, smell and sound of the sea had grown into the kind of sea-fever that John Masefield described in his poem of that name. Not the nausea that is suffered on board ship on a rolling ocean, but an acute and distressing sense of loss caused by my unrelenting separation from the sea.

Ses found the cake-tin and began stripping the sellotape from its side. 'Oh Ses! Please don't unpack,' I cried, feeling high on accumulated carbon dioxide and the surge of adrenalin that had been released during our flight in fright.

She clapped her hand to the side of her head. 'I have an idea! I could ask my old boss if he could lend us his Dormobile and help hand-pump your machine to the coast.'

'He will need to be fit if he is to help hand-pump so many miles.'

Ses held up her hand to indicate an end to any argument. 'He's a great chap. I know he'd want to be asked.'

'How far is it to Portsmouth?' I asked Ken.

'About fifty miles.'

'Could one person manage to hand-pump all that way? If not, who else could we ask?'

'I wonder whether Cyril . . .'

Ses hurried to the door: 'Shall I go next door to ask him?'

'Yes please.'

And so it was arranged.

Beverley – Ses's boss – brought his van and a strong friend to make a team of three hand-pumpers with our neighbour Cyril. I was to travel in the Bodyline chair which John had bequeathed me. Ses would stay by me all the way. Ken would follow in his car as before.

By the time we were assembled and the vehicles packed, much of the light had gone. With great merriment I was hoisted aboard the Dormobile with my two respirators, having just learned the hard way never to depend on one machine only. Last of all before we left the house, we telephoned the doctor to tell him that we were coming to the coast after all. He was delighted and promised to have the caravan unlocked and made ready for us again.

As we drove into the night I felt that I was in fairyland. I was still very high on carbon dioxide, adrenalin and excitement. It began to rain but even the wet weather could not put a damper on our mood. If anything the raindrops made the lights shine brighter through the wet windows and increased the sounds of vehicles swishing by and splashing through the puddles. I had not been out at night since I had had polio. The sight of the lights twinkling in the main road shopfronts acted as a tonic.

The hilarity of our arrival on the caravan site, our greetings to the people there and goodbyes to our enterprising escorts before they drove back to Newbury and Oxford, had to be suppressed. Our surroundings were bible-black. It was obvious that everyone else was fast asleep. I whispered to Ses, 'Under Milk Wood on Wheels.'

We all slept very well that night but shot into action early next morning when the power failed. 'We should have expected this,' Ken commented, as he set up the hand-pumping handle on the machine and started to push the bellows up and down manually.

Ses ran off to find the Site Manager. She returned to report that there was no power cut. We should have been told that the electricity depended on a supply of shillings. We were horrified. We had no idea how long a shillings-worth of electricity would last with my heavy-duty respirator working full blast – and daren't experiment to find out. Ses set out once more with several pound notes to exchange for shillings to feed the meter. When the power began to flow again and took over the job of breathing me, Ken stretched his back thankfully.

Outside the rain persisted. We did not mind the little tears of rain running down the window but we hated our conversations being drowned by the sound of the rain on the roof. A vicious wind was biffing away at our caravan and making it bounce. It seemed inevitable that the van would be blown over. My bed and two heavy respirators occupied one end of the caravan and I was not sure how much all this unbalanced its weight. I hoped that if the van tipped up it would not roll me out of bed. I could do nothing to save myself.

To divert my mind from these depressing thoughts I looked around at the rest of the caravan. It was beautifully equipped with a little sink and fridge. Ses slept in the kitchen area on a narrow bed. Ken's bed was nearer to me on a couch which doubled as seats when the collapsible table made the centre section into a dining area. A television set was moved about to whichever place was available as we changed things around according to whether it was bed-time, meal-time, play-time and so on.

There was no room for Brian and Andrew in our caravan – they had to occupy a little one opposite ours. I hated this idea as I could not see whether they were in or out but everything mechanical seemed to conspire against us and keep our minds fully occupied.

We turned our attention to the newspapers that Ses had brought back with her from her hunt for shillings. In the evening paper two advertisements caught her eye, the first because we had been watching plane after plane flipping courageously across the bay in the teeth of the gale.

'There is an airfield near here. Those kamikaze pilots must fly from there. Shall I ring up and say we would like a trip?'

'How would we keep me breathing?'

'Hand-pumping, of course.'

'Won't my machine be too heavy? I wouldn't want to see it disappear through the floor of the plane.'

We laughed helplessly at the thought of my respirator and me, like Icarus, plunging into the sea. We turned to the other advertisement which was a *son et lumière* show on HMS *Victory*.

'How can we reach the *Victory*?'

'We can stuff you in Ken's front seat and fix you upright with cushions and so on. I can hand-pump your machine from the back seat.'

'Will it fit in?'

'I don't know but we can try. I'll ring up first to see whether we can park near the front of the audience so that we can rush away if needs be.'

Fortunately, before we had to experience trundling my heavy respirator around, we heard that a portable respirator was available in Oxford. The Ward Sister who intended to visit the caravan was going to bring it down. Also Night Sister was coming to see us from Winchester.

We were thrilled at the chance to borrow a lightweight portable respirator. I refused to think about what we would do if it stopped while we were up in the air and we booked the flight.

Once in possession of the new breathing-machine we agreed we must try it out straightaway. First we went along to the nearby shops on an experimental trip to see from where Ses was fetching the papers and shillings. Ses sat in the back with my heavy-duty respirator at the ready in case the new machine should fail. It did not. It behaved beautifully.

Each day we became more daring. We spent an hour one afternoon sitting in the closed car on the deserted sea front. The immense waves crashed on to the shore and splashed high in the air to meet the falling rain. Even inside the car we could hear the roar of the wild sea and the rattle of the pebbles as they were sucked down the beach by the immense force of the returning water.

We were lucky with the weather on our air trip. This was just as well as we had to leave my big respirator in the car and put me in the centre of the plane where the weight of the portable machine would not unbalance it. We expected a smooth flight. The pilot had strict instructions to return to the airfield at once should my machinery fail. As I listened to the precautions being explained I felt suddenly terrified. What had I done? Why was I risking taking my whole family up in the air with a machine that might plunge through the floor of the aircraft and cause chaos or a crash?

'Are you sure it's safe?' I asked.

'Of course it is,' said Ses. 'Can't turn back now.'

Quickly, I overcame my fear, prayed hard and covered my anxiety by talking to the children about the view. They had never flown before and were very impressed by the cleanliness and clarity of the scene beneath them. Ken pointed out the traffic moving along the roads like Dinky toys and HMS *Victory* looking like a scale model in Portsmouth dockyard.

We enjoyed our flight immensely and our thanks to the crew and the organisers were deeply felt. We dashed back to the caravan while our luck with the new machine held and found the doctor on one of his visits. I remarked how lovely it was to fly around Portsmouth Harbour but he misunderstood me and said, 'Yes, but you couldn't go.'

We all fell guiltily silent.

He continued, 'The air would be too rare for you up there.'

None of us said a word. There did not seem any suitable ones to say. We waved him goodbye cheerily as he set off for the hospital.

Our arrival at the dockyard for the *son et lumière* show was arranged with typical naval concern for detail. We were counted in and berthed alongside the gate so that we could slip away easily if necessary.

Seeing the *Victory* from the air had reawakened old memories of walking its decks and marvelling at the cramped quarters endured by Nelson and his crew. Having enjoyed an inside view and an overview, I revelled in the show.

We were enthralled by the re-creation in sound and light of Nelson's famous battles of the Nile, Copenhagen and Trafalgar. We wiped our eyes as he whispered 'Kismet' to Captain Hardy. The image of Nelson was strongly evoked. I remembered following in his footsteps to Caserta and Naples where his presence and that of Sir William and Lady Emma Hamilton had been almost tangible. Although the spirit of Nelson remained hauntingly, like an afterglow, about the *Victory*, our visit had to end. Our departure from the dockyard was arranged as carefully as our entry had been. Even in the car it was easy to imagine that we were still transported to the Mediterranean. I was very high on carbon dioxide but our arrival back at the caravan site brought me back to reality. Tired but intensely happy, we slept deeply and woke up ready to leave.

After breakfast it stopped raining. I was parked outside the caravan in John's chair. My machine, which had been purring opposite me, suddenly stopped. Fortunately Brian had been posted to keep an eye on me. He quickly called his father and Ses who were on their knees washing the floors of the caravans. Ken came to my rescue instantly. Ses took on the job of finishing both floors. At first we hoped that we had burnt up the shillings in the meter but when we inserted a few more coins nothing happened. We realised we had indeed a genuine power cut on our hands. When Cyril, Beverley and his friend arrived they were astonished to find us hand-pumping even before the journey began. We consequently had no time to write our comments in the visitors' book. We did not remember it until we were speeding home.

That was our only break in routine. Ken's mother was still unwell, so it was not possible for her to have Ken and the children to stay. We all lived on the memory of our wet week in Portsmouth for the rest of the year.

Chapter 25
A Start of Sorts

The first time I saw my words in print was in the old Post Office magazine. I had written a letter of praise and thanks to the engineers who had designed and built my new telephone and put the world within my reach once more. It was the first time, the engineers said, that a telephone had been made to measure for a disabled person. I felt their achievement should be acknowledged by the person who appreciated it most. *Me.* This printed item was to be followed quickly by another when an unexpected birthday present was thrust through my letter-box. It was the acceptance of my article by the editor of *The Rose* and a cheque for £3 16s 0d. I longed for the day when I would see my words in print. I had expected a rejection slip and had prepared myself to be cheerful about it. This immediate success of my first attempt was unnerving. I gave the children half-a-crown each to help swell their Christmas savings. The evidence that you could earn real ready money for writing words on paper fired their imaginations. The next time they were banished upstairs with colds they asked if they could borrow my typewriter. They had learned to type little notes for me when I had wanted to remember ideas for my book. Now, to our surprise, they typed letters to our local newspaper. Andrew wrote about cooking and Brian about his hamster. Both received five shillings from the publication.

Dr Scott heard of our successes through the medical bush-telegraph and called in to congratulate us all. 'You could write a book,' he commented.

'I would rather read one,' I exclaimed.

'What is your favourite book?' he asked.

'Huckleberry Finn,' I replied. 'I loved it so much that I chose it for a school prize from a tormenting list of totally desirable books.'

I went on to explain that, in order to read in peace and quiet, I escaped from my younger sisters by hiding in the thickly-leaved branches of my favourite sycamore tree.

Huckleberry Finn now lit Brian's and Andrew's imaginations in their need to take refuge in their dens from our bustling household. I nodded towards the bookcase by my bed where Huckleberry Finn was rubbing shoulders with several other books which were also prizes. Most of them were concerned with animals, as one might expect. My special favourites were also Brian's and Andrew's favourite books and words such as platypus, okapi and caribou were part of their earliest vocabularies.

I talked of the way Brian and Andrew spun stories for our mutual amusement and how Brian had already put together his own first book about a school trip along the River Kennet. He had spent much time and trouble illustrating it with drawings and picture postcards and had received a special prize. 'I expect my books influence my children,' I said. 'My father's prize, Black Beauty, left a lasting impression on me.'

Fortunately my fondness for animals enabled me to cope with the processions of pets deposited on my bed by surrounding children.

A rabbit had wet my counterpane, evidently more frightened of me than I was of him and no doubt alarmed by the noise of my respirator, which would sound very loud in his long, sensitive ears. A grass snake had curled himself comfortably at the foot of my bed, immediately above the place where my hot-water bottle was providing an oasis of warmth. Various frogs, lizards and beetles had hopped, lounged and scurried from side to side, making it difficult to catch them before they leapt to the floor or on to my person. We always shut the budgies in their cage when other pets came visiting. Eventually we did not need to take this precaution, as one by one the budgies and hamsters died and sad services were arranged for their funerals.

The sense of loss was depressing and we decided not to acquire any more small animals with their short expectations of life. Instead, we adopted a dog whose master could not keep him. His name was Jackie. He had barked too loudly and grown too big to be tied up all day. He needed children to run with him and a garden in which to bury his bones. When Jackie arrived I was surprised to see how large he was. As he stood up on his back legs he could rest his front paws on my bed. He was advertised as a mongrel terrier but turned out to be a cross between a black Labrador and a Welsh sheep-dog. His fur was unbroken-black except for his sharp white shirt and socks. His eloquent eyes spoke volumes, telling us of his gentle nature and total honesty. He would sit beside the tea-trolley looking longingly at his favourite sponge-cake but he never tried to steal any.

Now that there was a dog to consider in the family we wondered whether we should buy any fireworks for Bonfire Night but we felt we had something to celebrate with our literary successes. We selected an assortment of especially beautiful coloured sprays of stars, golden rain, Catherine wheels and sparklers, avoiding the noisy ones so as not to frighten any animals.

On the fifth of November we arranged a rota with Brian and Andrew taking turns to look after me and my respirator indoors or helping Ken feed the bonfire and set off the fireworks in the garden. From the kitchen we could smell the aroma of the jacket potatoes that Andrew had popped into the oven to cook. Every time the back door was open the air indoors was pervaded by the unmistakably acrid scent of garden bonfires and spent fireworks. Our display started after everyone else's. Before we could light our bonfire, a lighted stick from somebody's rocket fell down our chimney and ignited the soot. The chimney roared. Clouds of smoke billowed from our roof and swirled about the window. A fire-engine raced to our house and the firemen ran down our steps and into my room at great speed. There was nowhere I could go. Outside it was bitterly cold. I stayed in my corner and tried to keep calm. Ken covered my nose with several thicknesses of sheet to stop me from inhaling the smoke. I insisted he did not mask my eyes as I was fascinated by the skill of the firemen. They poured water gently and carefully on the flames so that the steam hissed up the chimney and extinguished our blaze. When they were sure that the danger was over they amazed us by sweeping up the pieces of burnt soot which had fallen into the fireplace. They took the rug outside and shook the bits of debris from it. Incredibly, they left everywhere looking neater and tidier than when they had arrived. We were very impressed.

After the firemen had driven away, we turned out the lights so that we could watch through the window the spectacular patterns made by our bonfire and fireworks. They threw into sharp relief the slim silhouettes of skeleton birch trees.

Only Jackie and I stayed indoors all the time. He did not know what to make of the whizzes and bangs and looked from face to face intently as if trying to understand our obvious enjoyment of such a peculiar pastime. The only part of the evening which gave him pleasure was his jacket potato, which we had to cool and cut up first for him as we knew he would wolf it down in a few gulps.

Jackie barked loudly at anyone approaching the house, but when Norah came his tail wagged so violently we knew who he was expecting to come to the door. This devotion was in sharp contrast with his feelings towards Norah's cat. One day Jackie was surprised to find Tibby sitting in the sun on one of our gateposts just a few feet from the ground. Enraged at this trespass on his territory, Jackie rushed up to the post and told the cat to go away in his unmistakable assertive barks. Unfortunately, his bark soon turned to a yelp and he ran indoors with his nose scratched and bleeding. We bathed it and sympathised with him but from then on we noticed that he was very careful to keep a respectful distance from the cat.

Jackie was injured again one day when he ran into the road. A car just missed killing him but it bruised his paw. Some children carried him home and told us what had happened. We made a special day-place for him on a blanket on the sofa. Jackie became so used to the idea that people coming into the house would sympathise with him and look at his paw that, in time, as soon as anyone appeared he would raise his paw and wait for the sympathetic words to flow. Eventually we told him he was an old fraud and that his paw couldn't still be painful after such a long time but he kept the habit up and made us smile. We liked to think he was intelligent enough to act the clown to amuse us.

Too many people boast of their dogs' intelligence for us to want to claim that Jackie was particularly gifted but he seemed to have a sixth sense about the dangers of power cuts. As soon as the sound of my machine stopped and the house became eerily silent, he would rush into my room, lie on guard under my bed and not relinquish his duty until my respirator took up its whoosh-shoosh breathing powers once more. It may have been that he did this because he was usually with Brian and Andrew and as soon as they heard my machine stop they would make their way to my bed to see what they could do to help, then stay as long as necessary. They usually left with smiles of relief when the power was restored, heading for the kitchen for a hot drink and biscuits, with the dog at their heels.

After Christmas, some of our helpers left for family reasons and were gradually replaced by others. We were always very sad to say goodbye but gradually – without realising it – we were building up a network of people who were to stay for many years, to give stability when other helpers disappeared. One day I heard myself saying to my children: 'Helpers come and helpers go but I go on for ever.' We all looked at one another and smiled with relief. I realised that far from living only three months at home, I had survived more than three years. It was a wonderful moment and, although I was not foolish enough to forget the doctor's warning, I felt a fresh surge of confidence in my hold on the future and the increasingly strong family bonds which were strengthening all of us.

Some weeks later, when Dr Peters bustled in with inventor John Taylor to put the last touches to my remote-control panel, I felt a sense of command over myself and my circumstances. That in itself was a kind of therapy. Dr Peters had been treating Prince Charles for measles. He must have been very very busy as a large number of boys were in isolation. For once we were all healthy. I revelled in the thought but should have known the Fates must be about to pounce on us.

Soon after the panel was completed. Ken collapsed with a severe attack of flu. With my new independence I was able to watch over Brian and Andrew sleeping on the floor between my bed and the put-you-up where their father usually slept. I kept watch throughout the night, in case Ken needed anything. From time to time I switched on my lamp with the help of my new control panel and looked towards my slumbering sons and husband – a rare and much-prized event – and knew a great sense of satisfaction of being useful at last.

As another Christmas approached, our family routine seemed firmly established but we could still be caught by surprise. A thick manilla envelope arrived through the post containing a complimentary copy of *The Rose*. The unique thrill of seeing my first article published with my own by-line could never be repeated. The Editor, Leonard Hollis, had kindly enclosed a big Christmas card with three perfect roses on the front.

I was exultant. My spirits leapt. I would treasure this card always as a reminder of the occasion. I knew that my feelings were quite different from those I had experienced on seeing my letter in the Post Office magazine. I had been pleased and satisfied to be able to give public praise where praise was due, to the telephone engineers. My article also acknowledged praise where it was due – this time to roses – but it was not only satisfaction that stirred my blood. A professional editor had considered my article worthy of payment; he had also validated my words by giving them the dignity of print. I had again written sincerely and from the heart, but I had also tried to consider the pattern of the piece and how I should arrange the various items to give the most pleasure to the imagined readers. I felt what I hoped would be a forgivable glow of justifiable pride in something which I had desired to do well – just as in my pre-polio days I might feel pride when I made a special birthday cake which turned out better than I had anticipated. To celebrate the publication of my first article, Ken presented me with *The Oxford Dictionary of Quotations*.

One emotion surprised me. It was fear. What had I done? I had set down, for everyone to see, my innermost feelings about myself and those I loved. I remembered some lines from Edward Fitzgerald's Rubáiyát of Omar Khayyám:

> The moving finger writes; and, having writ, Moves on:
> nor all thy Piety nor wit Shall lure it back to cancel half
> a Line, Nor all thy Tears wash out a Word of it.

Ken, Brian and Andrew were all delighted to see my name in print. They knew the piece by heart as they had typed frequent notes for it. I showed my article to everyone who came to the house. All who read it liked it. Anxious to improve my style, I kept asking for criticism – but none was given.

Then another emotion assailed me. This time I was *under*whelmed by a failure of confidence. I thought to myself, it is all very well to manage to write *one* piece for publication but how do you follow that? Perhaps it was a fluke. Did I have any talent? Where could I find out? Who would be the best person to advise me? I had seen advertisements for the London School of Journalism. Perhaps they would counsel me. I tried out several inquiries in my head. Ken or one of the children typed them out for me as the mood took me. Eventually, I thought I had produced an inquiry that was good enough to send. My long-suffering family could give their fingers a rest.

The only member of the family who had not typed anything was the quick, black-and-white dog who sat watching the proceedings, looking completely foxed, holding his head first to one side and then the other, with one ear cocked inquiringly.

'What a pity you can't type, Jackie,' I commented. He looked at me and yawned. He knew of better pastimes.

I could not think of anything in the world I would rather do than write something else that would be published. I wanted to write more than I wanted to cook, or sew, or garden, or even swim, cycle or dance. I needed to put my whole heart and soul into writing. So long as I could write for publication I could manage my patient hold on my frustration and wait and work philosophically towards the return of my pre-polio abilities. I did not want to become known as 'that disabled girl who writes'. I wanted to be a writer first, second and last.

To my great and lasting joy, the London School of Journalism

accepted me for their free-lance journalism course. I reread my
first article to see what there was in it that had made them think I
could develop my talents. I read until I knew by heart my initial
article. It ran as follows:

A BED OF ROSES
by Ann Armstrong

I have discovered there is a therapeutic quality about roses
and the things I remember about roses.

I was in my iron-lung in a very famous orthopaedic
hospital when I realised this for the first time. One of the
young men in a small ward further along the corridor had
sent me a red rose. Neither of us could write in those days
and no one could spare the time for taking long messages so
the only means of communication was by flower language.
We did not always have roses but usually we managed to find
or scrounge a red flower of some sort and send it with the
message: *Think of this as a red rose.*

The sight of my latest bloom from John, which always stood
alone in its own vase on my locker, stimulated many memories
and so helped make the very long and rather monotonous
hospital days pass that much more quickly. My wedding
bouquet had been made entirely of red rosebuds. It had been
very difficult to get them in June 1947 but now in June 1957 I was
very glad that I had insisted on them and nothing else and that
they had been magically produced on the day.

The wishy-washy walls of dirty cream would melt away as
I relived that wonderful time when I was so young, so agile,
and so active. From my wedding, my mind would wander on
to the other happy occasions – the usual anniversary tribute
from my husband was one long-stemmed perfect red rose;
my children sent me cards and handkerchiefs on Mother's
Day with roses on them and we had all enjoyed walking on
my beautiful new green carpet, on which the main motif was
pink and red roses. One of my best-loved dresses was of a
rose-patterned fabric. The children referred to it as my
pretty dress. So many rose memories, so many precious
souvenirs. . . .

Since I had had polio all my friends sent me roses and
pictures of roses and so John and I were able to keep up this
wonderful flirtation.

'Does he know you are married?' one of the young nurses
asked me.

'Oh yes,' I answered, trying to look as wicked as I possibly could, 'but you won't tell my husband, will you?'

'But you have children too,' she scolded and went away thinking what a dreadful person I was.

But for John and me this flirtation, which started off as a joke, something for a laugh, in a place where it was customary to do almost anything for a laugh, ended in a very true and very deep and lasting affection for each other.

When I arrived home it was with one of the most beautiful red roses that I have ever seen, tied with blue ribbon – from John, of course. Six months later, when John himself went home after winning the heart of a very lovely staff nurse and marrying her, I sent rosebushes – red rosebushes called Tally-ho – for his wedding present. I heard afterwards that they were the best roses for miles around. I was very grateful that they had bloomed so well, especially as John was not to have very long with us on this earth.

Since I have returned home I have experienced such kindness that I have come to realise, if nothing else, that my disability has enabled a force for good to work very hard in this world.

All my neighbours bring me their first roses. Last year when I ordered roses for Christmas presents – as I think there is no lovelier present – I ordered some lavender ones called Prelude. I have had many roses brought to me from the bushes that I gave and at a local show an arrangement of lavender and pink flowers built around lavender roses from one of these bushes won first prize. It was then borne in to me in triumph and has graced my room ever since.

Physically I am rather a useless creature but spiritually I am able to do so much still for my family and friends. The giving of roses has helped me create something lovely from what was a very horrible experience. Perhaps in time I shall learn more about roses and – who knows – even how to grow them! Perhaps in time I shall even produce a lovelier rose – if that is possible – than any rose now grown.

If ever I do, I shall call it Phoenix – and you will know why.

Postscript

At the time of going to press in the summer of 1985 Ann is at home, breathing through her respirator. Ken is 'on duty' for fourteen hours out of every twenty-four, a job undertaken in addition to his full-time professional commitments. Brian and Andrew have left home and follow their own careers.

It is twenty-eight years since Ann left hospital, yet there are still a mere handful of people allowed home while wholly dependent on a respirator. She is the only person in the world in this situation who also writes. The book was dictated, transcribed by a succession of helpers, each typed page then being pinned above the bed for Ann to check and correct.

Since the publication of her first article, Ann has written for *The Times*, the *Guardian* and many magazines. In 1963 she founded *Responaut*, a magazine for and about respirator-aided and other gadget-aided people. She was awarded an MBE for her work in journalism and for editing *Responaut* in 1968.